THE BEST OF
DOGFRIENDLY STAYS

DEB BRIDGES

ACKNOWLEDGEMENTS

We thank all the reviewers who have been involved in the DogFriendly Magazine over the last 20 years, taking the time to travel the country with their dogs and share their adventures. This book is dedicated to them and their pets.

Published 2022

DogFriendly Ltd
Unit 4 Bramley Road
St Ives, Cambridgeshire
PE27 3WS

Go to www.dogfriendly.co.uk to discover the best places to visit, stay and play with your dog in the UK

ISBN - 978-1-3999-4101-3

All photographs by authors of the reviews, except where indicated.
Front cover photo: Jenni Eley.
Page 1 photo: Vicky Kaderbhai

Concept and management of publication by James Waters

Design by William Dawes

Printed by Cambrian Press Ltd, Pontllanfraith

"Places that real dog lovers like yourself have visited..."

Lin and I are extremely proud of the work our wonderful reviewers do in providing us with their experiences of dog friendly places they have visited, for publication in our DogFriendly Magazine and across our website. This colourful book rediscovers some of the best dog friendly accommodation they have enjoyed over the last five years.

Of course it's not just about the accommodation, but also where your dogs may be welcome in the surrounding areas.

In each review, you will see we have included local places to visit, as well as pubs and cafés that may welcome your dogs. Over the last twenty years, the acceptance of dogs and what they are offered has changed greatly, but we understand not all dog owners are looking for the same type of vacation. This book includes details of dog-welcoming hotels, B&Bs, cottages, lodges, glamping and camping! We hope that, through this book, you will find some of your favourite destinations - and do share your own experiences by recommending places via our website dogfriendly.co.uk.

All the very best in your journeys, to you and your dogs from Lin and myself.

Steve Bennett

Deb Bridges

Who better to curate this *best of* selection of dog friendly places than Deb Bridges, author of two walking books and regular writer for dog magazines. She has sifted through the last ten years of DogFriendly excursions and selected the most interesting and welcoming places to visit with your dogs, presenting them in the words of the original authors.

NOTE:
The reviews in this book are based on previous visits that were featured in the DogFriendly Magazine. For ease of use, we have separated them into sections, by destination. At the time of printing, all the places shown were dog friendly, but things can change - so please do double-check before making long journeys. You can also

find the most up-to-date dog friendly places to visit, stay and play on our website, dogfriendly.co.uk.

CONTENTS

KEY FOR MAPS

Cottages and Self-Catering

Hotels/B&Bs

Lodge

Camping/ Caravan Park

Boat House

South West - Farthing Cottage Pg.37

Scotland - TirlagganStudio Pg.187

North West - Crag Cottage Pg.108

South East - Egerton Hotel Pg.23

East - Herring House Pg.169

North East - Paddock Cottage Pg.152

Wales - Dogs Love Holidays Pg.69

Midlands - The Pointer Pg.89

ADVICE FOR TRAVELLING WITH DOGS

These days, more and more of us are taking our dogs away on holiday. Whether it's a short city break in a plush hotel or a minimalist camping experience in the middle of nowhere, we're packing a bag (okay, several bags) for our dogs, so they can come, too.

In meeting the demand for dog friendly accommodation, many establishments are now going way above and beyond in providing for their doggy guests and it's possible to find all sorts of little extras on offer which make travelling with dogs that bit easier.

While many are seasoned travellers with dogs, here are a few tips which might come in useful for any new kids on that particular block.

Getting there...
Once you've pinpointed the area of the country you wish to visit, the first thing to consider, of course, is the journey.

If a long car journey is in the offing, you will need to factor in sufficient stops for watering, toileting and stretching the legs. It's recommended this should be approximately every 2 hours and a bit of forward planning to earmark the best spots for the purpose can certainly pay off. Some motorway service stations cater for canine travellers better than others and there are plenty where thought has gone into their comfort, with designated areas for a little stroll, away from the car park, and fresh water on offer. Some even allow dogs into the main buildings.

You might be undertaking a train journey and, if your dog is unfamiliar with this mode of transport, a gradual introduction will be necessary. This could involve starting with a few sessions of just sitting and watching the comings and goings on the platform of your local station, before trying a short, one-stop journey and increasing the journey length as confidence grows. You might even consider a day out, with a trip on a heritage railway thrown into the mix, as part of the training programme.

Questions, questions, questions...

Having arrived at your destination, it's nice to know you'll have everything on hand to manage your dog's needs and, here again, forward planning is key.

The trick is to work out what is important for you and your dog and, in choosing your accommodation, pick the ones which meet your specific needs. For example, some dogs will happily settle in an unfamiliar room, possibly in a crate, while their people enjoy a meal (it's worth checking this is allowed) but, if being left alone would cause distress, it would be better to select accommodation where dogs can stay with their people at mealtimes. Or you might be looking for somewhere with warm water dog-washing facilities, in order to avoid the nightmarish mud-magnet-meets-cream-carpet scenario.

It's useful to have a checklist, so you can make sure all necessary boxes are ticked. Also, if items are provided at the accommodation, such as a dog bed, it may save you vital packing space. Everyone's requirements are different but here are a few questions you might like to ask before you book.

All accommodation:

- If your dog normally sleeps on your bed, is this allowed and, if so, is a throw provided for the purpose?

- Are food/water bowls and/or a dog bed provided?

- Is there somewhere you can clean your dog and are towels provided?

Hotels and B&Bs:

- Is the room large enough to allow space for a dog bed?

- Can you easily get outside for early morning/late night toilet time?

consider important.

Getting out and about...
Time is precious when you're on holiday so it's a good idea to check out the dog friendliness of anywhere you want to visit in advance, i.e. beaches, gardens, tourist attractions, etc, as well as any dog friendly pubs and restaurants in the vicinity. You're likely to find a welcome pack in many holiday homes and hotels, which includes a list of these details, but the really good ones will send you this information well before your stay, enabling you to work out a game plan before you even leave home.

Whilst walking in the countryside, always keep dogs on a lead around livestock and follow the Countryside Code. For more information, go to www.outwiththedog.co.uk/useful-info/the-countryside-code/.

Packing List
It's a well-established fact that dogs do not travel light. Again, a checklist is a good idea and here are a few suggestions for your dog's suitcase:

- Bed (even if one is provided, your dog may prefer their own, or at least a blanket that smells of home)

- Crate, if your dog normally uses one

- Towels

- Food - bear in mind a little extra may be needed, if it's a high mileage holiday

- Bowls

- Toys

- Any medication

- Simple First Aid kit, including tweezers

- If you're taking dog food or medication that needs to be kept cool, do you have access to a fridge?

- Can your dog stay with you when you eat or are they allowed to remain in the room (if you're confident he/she will settle)? Note - some establishments expect dogs to be left in cars when their owners are eating and, if the weather is too hot or cold, this might not be appropriate.

Self-catering cottages:

- Are dogs allowed upstairs/in bedrooms?

- Is the garden securely fenced?

Do bear in mind that things can change, so it's worth double-checking any details you

(useful for thorns in paws) and a tick hook

- Cooling vest/mat, if your dog suffers in the heat

- Waterproof or warm coat if travelling in the winter

- Brush/comb

- Make sure your dog's collar tag is up to date and legible - some places provide a temporary tag, which includes the phone number of your holiday home, to be worn in addition to your own

- Poo bags and receptacle (i.e. a Dicky Bag or similar - see dickybag.com)

- If no dog-washing facilities are available, you might consider taking a portable shower, i.e. a Petacarium (petacarium.co.uk) or Mud Daddy (muddaddy.co.uk)

SOUTH EAST

THE STABLES - P.22

Cambridge

CLOPHILL ECO LODGES - P.29

THE LODGE - P.16

THE BEAR - P.25

BETHNAL & BEC - P.20

Oxford

THE HEDGEROW - P.13

THE EGERTON HOTEL - P.23

HOLIDAY INN - P.14

THE WELLINGTON ARMS - P.26

CHILTERN HILLS

London

Southend-on-Sea

GREEN HILL FARM - P.17

WARBROOK HOUSE HOTEL - P.12

ST PANCRAS RENAISSANCE LONDON HOTEL - P.27

HIGH WEALD

WOODLANDS LODGE HOTEL - P.17

THE LODGE AT SOLENT - P.19

LE BOAT - P.32

NEW FOREST NATIONAL PARK

SOUTH DOWNS NATIONAL PARK

Isle of Wight

HAVILAND COTTAGE - P.11

SENTRY MEAD - P.15

POMONE - P.28

HAVILAND COTTAGE, ISLE OF WIGHT

By James Waters

Ideally situated only a mile from the town of Ventnor, Haviland Cottage offers luxury accommodation in a highly-awarded period property, a short walk from the beach.

A 1-mile gentle stroll downhill from Haviland Cottage takes you to the small, quaint seaside town of Ventnor which was quiet when we visited out of season. There is also an alternative route of around 600 yards to the beach, which can be reached via a secret garden door.

There is a hot tub on the front patio with a gate that takes you to a well-maintained, walled garden, which was a delight. Stanley and our kids were excited to be presented with such a large space to run around and explore.

The bedrooms are beautifully decorated but the real doggy delight is the snug room downstairs, which is specially made for dogs and backs onto a second garden - very convenient for them to easily get out for a run and a sniff.

Overall, the accommodation was a pleasure to stay in. The owners had thought of everything to make your and your dog's visit something special.

Normally, we try to venture a bit further afield but the cottage was so nice and Ventnor such a lovely town that we spent a lot of time just relaxing.

FACT FILE

Location: 66 Madeira Road, Ventnor, Isle of Wight, PO38 1QY
Website: havilandcottage.com
Contact: 01983 632432
Type of accommodation: Cottage
Number of bedrooms: 4 (sleeps up to 7)
Number of dogs accepted: 2
Enclosed garden: Yes
Local interest: Charles Dickens literary walks from the cottage, Ventnor Park Gardens, Castle Cove
Best eats: Toni's Tea Room and The Spyglass Inn at Ventnor, Bonchurch Inn at Bonchurch

WARBROOK HOUSE HOTEL, HOOK, HAMPSHIRE

By Anna Bernard

Set in 121 acres of formal gardens and woodland, Warbrook House Hotel is an impressive Grade 1 listed mansion, conveniently located close to the M3.

You can tell that most, if not all, of the staff at Warbrook House own a dog. It was the epitome of the phrase dog friendly. Everyone was so accommodating and genuinely lovely to my dog, Ken. Even the other guests were very happy to see him.

Our room was on the ground floor, as all their pooch-friendly rooms are, to give easy toilet access, and the best part of the room was an enormous, comfortable bed.

Dogs are welcome in every area of the hotel except the restaurant but they will happily set up a dining table in the bar for pooches and their humans to dine. They set up breakfast for me in the bar, as an alternative to the restaurant and they actually cooked Ken fresh sausages!

The grounds at the hotel are lovely, complete with their own Versailles-style canal and Waterloo bridge. It's not a big walk around but enough for an early morning or evening toilet stroll.

As it was Pancake Day on our last day, we finished off our little adventure with 3 crêpes from Jackson's, the café at California Country Park, which Ken and I shared before heading home after spending a really lovely few days.

FACT FILE

Location: The Street, Eversley, Hook, RG27 0PL
Website: warbrookhouse.com
Contact: 0118 973 2174
Type of accommodation: Hotel
Number of bedrooms: 68
Number of dogs accepted: 2
Enclosed garden: No
Local interest: Basingstoke Canal Walk, Yateley Common, Swinley Forest, California Country Park
Best eats: Warbrook House, The Barley Mow at Oakley, The Tally Ho at Eversley, Jackson's at California Country Park

THE HEDGEROW, WAINHILL, OXFORDSHIRE

By Vicky Kaderbhai

Overlooking The Ridgeway, in the heart of The Chilterns, The Hedgerow offers comfortable, self-catering accommodation in dog-walking heaven.

There is only one word that can sufficiently describe The Hedgerow at Wainhill and that's cosy. It is a gorgeous timber lodge with its own driveway, private parking and secure garden. We were able to get settled in nice and quickly, while allowing our dogs, Buddy and Rory, a chance to explore without worrying about them.

The view of the hills from the cottage is spectacular, especially in the early autumn light. With horses, chickens and family dogs, this definitely feels like a truly rural getaway. Fantastic really, when you consider it's only an hour outside London.

Visiting in the autumn, with the early dark nights and lower temperatures, it was such a cosy experience, shutting the blinds and cuddling on the sofa. But I think it would be great to go back in the spring or summer, to explore the hills much later into the evening and sit out on the decking with a glass of something chilled in hand, while the dogs run in and out.

The Hedgerow is the kind of place you go when you want a proper break. The peaceful atmosphere and beautiful surroundings make for a real break from reality.

All four of us thoroughly enjoyed our stay at The Hedgerow and it was great to finally find a place that was able to exhaust even our most energetic dog. We only had two nights and we both agreed that, if we had more time, we would spend it exploring the local villages.

FACT FILE

Location: Thatched Cottage, Wainhill, Chinnor, Oxfordshire, OX39 4AB

Website: wainhill.co.uk

Contact: 01844 352864

Type of accommodation: Timber lodge

Number of bedrooms: 1

Number of dogs accepted: 1 medium or 2 small

Enclosed garden: Yes

Local interest: Walks from the door, Waddesdon Manor, Hughendon Manor, Blenheim Palace, Stonor Park

Best eats: The Red Lion at Chinnor, The Lions of Bledlow, Duo Chef's fusion Indian restaurant at Chinnor

THE HOLIDAY INN, SOUTHEND-ON-SEA, ESSEX

By Helen Price

Dogs are made incredibly welcome at this 4-star hotel, which is ideally-placed for visiting the equally dog friendly local towns.

So, when you hear Southend-on-Sea for a weekend break, I'm sure you are thinking about arcades and amusement parks, and wondering what the area offers us dog friendly fans. The answer to this would be - lots of hidden gems.

On arrival with our two terriers, Tilly the Jack Russell, aged 14, and Orla the Norfolk Terrier (1), we visited Hadleigh Castle, where a gate leads onto a footpath towards Leigh-on-Sea. This walk is so pretty and follows a hilltop path all the way to the town, where we headed straight for one of the ice cream parlours.

The Holiday Inn, Southend, is next to Southend Airport. We had the most fabulous welcome with the girls from the staff. Tilly and Orla were lapping up the attention, as we were shown to our room and treats were waiting for team terrier in our spacious bedroom. The hotel is soundproofed, so there is no noise from the planes.

There aren't a lot of rules for your canine companion. The dogs aren't allowed in the main restaurant or bar, but you can take them to eat with you in the lounge.

Southend and Leigh-on-Sea gave us a wonderful weekend, exploring so many locations and we came away saying how friendly the people were in this lovely Essex seaside town.

FACT FILE

Location: 77 Eastwoodbury Cres, Southend-on-Sea, SS2 6XG

Website: ihg.com/holidayinn

Contact: 01702 543001

Type of accommodation: Hotel

Number of bedrooms: 129

Number of dogs accepted: 2

Enclosed garden: No

Local interest: Southend-on-Sea, Hadleigh Castle, Thorney Bay Beach, Canvey Island, Belfairs Nature Discovery Centre

Best eats: Cookies & Cones and Sara's Tea Garden at Leigh-on-Sea, 1935 Rooftop Restaurant and Bar at the Holiday Inn (no dogs but they can be left in room if you inform Reception), The Angel Inn at Shoeburyness, Roberto's, Rossi Ice Cream Parlour and Dog & Co at Southend-on-Sea

SENTRY MEAD, TOTLAND BAY, ISLE OF WIGHT

By James Waters

Sentry Mead invites guests to relax in comfortable surroundings and is well-placed both for ferries and for visiting the many places of interest on the island.

With the kids packed off to their grandparents, we had a rare chance to take our dog, Stanley, away for a few days. Our destination was Sentry Mead at Totland Bay on the Isle of Wight.

At the hotel, we were given a warm welcome by managers Gayle and Mark. The downstairs is quite spacious and has a dining room for breakfast and a lounge/snug room. It also has a lovely patio area which leads into the garden - perfect for pooches who need a goodnight wee. Sentry Mead also operates an honesty bar, which we enjoyed using while sitting out on the patio with Stanley.

It's a short walk from Sentry Mead to Totland Bay promenade which has a small, shingle beach and is used largely for yacht mooring and some water sports. There are also two bars/cafés.

We took a planned to visit Carisbrooke Castle, where Charles I was imprisoned during the Civil War. The castle is very dog friendly, apart from inside the café (there is sheltered outdoor seating) and the museum building, which is only small, so it's easy to take turns.

We enjoyed our time on the Isle of Wight. As for dog friendly points, it definitely ranks quite high and offered a very relaxed atmosphere all round. Totland Bay is good for evening walks and you could spend a day visiting each corner of the island if you were there for a week.

FACT FILE

Location: Madeira Road, Totland Bay, Isle of Wight, PO39 0BJ
Website: sentrymead.co.uk
Contact: 01983 753212
Type of accommodation: Hotel
Number of bedrooms: 9
Number of dogs accepted: 1 per room, maximum 2 in hotel
Enclosed garden: No
Local interest: Carisbrooke Castle, Godshill Model Village, Yaverhill Beach, Fort Victoria Country Park
Best eats: The Waterfront and The Bay Café at Totland Bay, The Hut Restaurant at Colwell Bay, The Cow Restaurant at Tapnell Farm

THE LODGE, DUXFORD, CAMBRIDGESHIRE

By Jenny Green

Conveniently situated just off the M11 and billed as a great place to work, eat and sleep, boutique hotel, The Lodge, is surprisingly welcoming to doggy guests.

We arrived at The Lodge on a foggy day in December and its twinkling lights immediately drew us to the beautiful, old building, which was fully renovated in 2019.

Once we had been given a warm welcome at reception and admired the cool wallpaper and pop art prints, our Westie, Ernie, led us straight to where we were staying - in one of the hotel's 4 dog friendly Stable Rooms.

The Stable Rooms vary in size and some have their own kitchen facilities - perfect for longer breaks, or if you prefer to luxuriate in your room of an evening. They also open straight out onto the garden, which is convenient. Ours was No1 and, although it was a little on the cosy side, it was more than big enough for a night's stay. The large bed was wonderfully comfy and we had a Smart TV and a retro radio. The room had a mini-fridge - great when travelling with dogs - and a Nespresso coffee machine. There was also a small decanter of a boozy liqueur, which was a nice touch and made for a perfect post-dinner tipple.

Dogs are welcome throughout the grand main building, including the bar, the basement Graze Café and even in the main Scoff restaurant which, at the time of our visit, had been lovingly decorated for Christmas.

After a fantastic meal, we retired to our room and slept like babies. And after a delicious breakfast the next day, we felt genuinely sad to leave. It would have been nice to round off the evening with a drink at the bar, but I guess that just gives us the perfect reason to go back.

FACT FILE

Location: Ickleton Rd, Duxford, CB22 4RT
Website: thelodgeduxford.com
Contact: 01223 755677
Type of accommodation: Boutique hotel
Number of bedrooms: 4 dog friendly Stable Rooms
Number of dogs accepted: Negotiable (depending on size)
Enclosed garden: No
Local interest: Wandlebury Country Park, Saffron Walden market town, Audley End (grounds only), Cambridge
Best eats: Scoff restaurant at The Lodge

WOODLANDS LODGE HOTEL, NEW FOREST, HAMPSHIRE

By Helen Price

Fine dining and a warm welcome for 4-legged guests make Woodlands Lodge a great place to stay and enjoy the many attractions of the New Forest.

Entering the New Forest on a sunny afternoon, on lanes surrounded by beautiful towering trees, we were extremely excited to explore a place which was new to me and my husband, Ben (and to our Jack Russell cross, Tilly, of course).

We arrived at Woodlands Lodge Hotel in the late afternoon. The staff were so helpful, supplying us with maps and information, and were happy to chat to us about places to go and enjoy during our stay.

Tilly ran the perimeter of our room, full of excitement and finished by jumping up to have a look out of the bay window at the people sitting in the gardens, enjoying an afternoon drink. But her attention was quickly diverted when she realised I had found her welcome pack, which included a gluten-free bone.

The information sheet for dog visitors is kind to dog owners and didn't contain a long, scary list of rules to follow, which was refreshing. It listed the areas of the hotel where your dog is welcome, which is most places except the main restaurant. The hotel also asks that dogs are kept on-lead in the grounds, as it is shared with other guests.

For dinner on our first night we ate at the hotel. We had heard that the food was amazing and we were not disappointed. *(continued...)*

FACT FILE

Location: Bartley Road, Southampton, Hampshire, SO40 7GN

Website: woodlands-lodge.co.uk

Contact: 02380 292257

Type of accommodation: Hotel

Number of bedrooms: 17

Number of dogs accepted: 3 (with prior approval)

Enclosed garden: No

Local interest: The Woodlands Hotel walk, New Forest Heritage Centre, Buckler's Hard, Bolton's Bench at Lyndhurst, Exbury Gardens & Steam Railway, Hurst Castle, Moors Valley Country Park & Forest

Best eats: Woodlands Lodge Hotel, The Rockingham Arms at West Wellow

The hotel staff went above and beyond the call of duty, giving us the choice of lounge or conservatory to have our meal in, both by the windows with lovely views over the grounds. We opted for the lounge, where they then set Tilly up her very own little dog space, with a cosy bed for her to relax on while we ate.

Tilly's favourite part of the trip was the river cruise from Buckler's Hard and she loved the wind that the speed of the boat whipped up. Other visitors were smiling and enjoying watching her have a great time.

Woodlands Lodge provides a map for a walk from the hotel and this was my favourite walk of the weekend. It was a quieter area and we saw endless New Forest ponies, which really makes staying there wonderful.

New Forest, we loved you and everything about you. We will be back soon, as there are still so many more places to see and walks to explore.

THE LODGE AT SOLENT, FAREHAM, HAMPSHIRE

By Hilary Keens

Handily placed for visiting Southampton or Portsmouth and only 2 minutes from the M27, The Lodge at Solent has dog friendly rooms, where everything doggy guests may need is provided.

Arriving on a dank November evening, with Tess, my much-loved and well-travelled American Cocker Spaniel, I received a very warm welcome at The Lodge at Solent. Guests check in at the bar, The Parson's Cellar, which was already buzzing with Friday's after-work drinkers.

I had a double, dog friendly room upstairs, with a balcony. In warmer months, it would be lovely to have the doors open and be able to sit outside with your dog, who would be free to wander between the cool, laminate floor and the securely-enclosed balcony. A supplement for dogs is expected but, here, represents good value because of the attention to detail for doggy guests.

Tess and I returned to the Parson's Cellar, where the all-day menu offered urban pub fare - nachos, pizzas, burgers and grills. There were a few other dogs in our part of the bar and all had been provided with fresh water bowls.

Fareham is on the 'Solent corridor' between Southampton and Portsmouth and there are a number of shopping areas and business parks nearby. The Lodge at Solent is a couple of sound-proofed minutes from the M27 and I would recommend it as a dog friendly base for anyone visiting the south's universities. In less than an hour, you can be in the heart of the New Forest, too.

There is lots of variety to be found in what is ostensibly an urban area.

FACT FILE

Location: Rookery Avenue, Whiteley, Fareham, Hampshire, PO15 7AJ

Website: lodgeatsolent.co.uk

Contact: 01489 880035

Type of accommodation: Hotel

Number of bedrooms: 54

Number of dogs accepted: 1

Enclosed garden: No

Local interest: Holly Hill Woodland Park, River Hamble, Portchester Castle (outer bailey only), Forest of Bere, Manor Farm Country Park, canal walk at Titchfield, Titchfield Haven

Best eats: The Lodge at Solent, The Cormorant at Portchester, The Titchfield Mill

BETHNAL & BEC, COTTERED, HERTFORDSHIRE

By Steve Lamb

With its eclectic mix of high tech and vintage chic, Bethnal & Bec's adult-only accommodation offers a truly rejuvenating stay, overlooking a beautiful wildflower meadow and uninterrupted countryside views.

Living in the Cambridge Fens, for us, the neighbouring county of Hertfordshire had been a 'passing through' kind of county, with its new towns giving the impression that this was modern and a little too close to London for a relaxing weekend. It was therefore with some trepidation that we

set off for a couple of days at Bethnal & Bec in Cottered, near Buntingford.

We found the accommodation easily, with ample signage and excellent directions included in the info pack. Entry to our room was swift and easy, whereupon our perceived modernity of Hertfordshire was certainly reaffirmed.

Chris and Vicky have clearly gone to great lengths to ensure that the 2 rooms, Bethnal and Bec, provide every luxury and facility anyone could ever want on a stay away from home. From iPad controlled lighting (iPad provided in room) and a Bluetooth record player, to a drop-down home cinema screen and projector for Netflix nights in, every tech-lover would feel at home here.

The bathroom was equally well equipped, with a bath big enough for 2 and a wet room-style rainfall shower.

The kitchen areas in both rooms are equipped with an induction hob and combination microwave/oven. Although the accommodation is offered on a self-catering basis, this does not mean food isn't available. In addition to some staples,

FACT FILE

Location: Cottered, Hertfordshire, SG9 9PU
Website: bethnalandbec.com
Contact: 07790 901051
Type of accommodation: Room
Number of bedrooms: 1
Number of dogs accepted: 3
Enclosed garden: Yes
Local interest: St Bartholomew's Church, Buntingford, Therfield, Cromer Windmill
Best eats: The Cricketers at Weston, The Fox at Aspenden

included in the price, the fridge/freezer is packed with all kinds of easy to prepare meals and snacks, along with a very well-stocked drinks supply and, of course, doggy treats galore. Everything is clearly priced and run on an honesty basis.

Outside, in the private garden area, accessible directly from the room, was a steaming hot tub, along with bistro table and chairs, a fire pit and sun loungers.

The gardens of both rooms also have direct access to a paddock to the rear of the property, which was more than big enough to provide even the most energetic of pets with ample space to go crazy.

We planned some local walks, with the aid of several guides and maps provided in the room. On the final morning of our stay, we followed a curtailed version of a suggested walk in the info pack, starting from the paddock and finishing at Cromer Windmill, Hertfordshire's sole surviving windmill.

As we joined the A10 back to Cambridgeshire, we realised both Bethnal & Bec and Hertfordshire had the same impact on us. At first sight, they appear thoroughly modern but, once you take a few deep breaths, relax and slow down, the underlying history and relaxing rural village, combined with the easygoing luxury and seclusion of Bethnal & Bec, reveal themselves and leave such a deep impression that you'll being planning your return before you leave.

THE STABLES, FULLER'S HILL COTTAGES, CAMBRIDGE

By Kiri Nowak-Smith

Less than 30 minutes by car to Cambridge, Fuller's Hill Cottages offer a variety of apartments and cottages in a countryside setting, with walks straight from the door.

Although the cottages are situated just a few miles from Cambridge, they feel quite isolated, with gently undulating countryside all around, sheltering them from the outside world. All have been converted sympathetically from original outbuildings.

We stayed in The Stables. The living space is open-plan, with a spacious kitchen at one end and a lounge, with dining area, at the other. The kitchen has all mod cons, including a trendy coffee machine. And if you're worried about being entertained in wet weather, there's a flat screen TV, free Wi-Fi and a DVD player. In the master bedroom, there's a super-king-size bed and a large corner sofa in the lounge, so we could unwind in style.

One of the best things was the hot tub in the communal garden. It was the height of luxury, with soothing mood lighting, powerful water jets and a socket, so you could play music as you relaxed. We used it every day.

A network of pathways makes exploring the countryside a pleasure. John and Jenny were extremely helpful when we booked, advising us about local attractions and John has made things easier by describing a number of suitable walking routes on the website.

Fuller's Hill Cottages make an ideal countryside retreat, as you can walk miles straight from the door. Dogs are very welcome and, although there are a few rules, these didn't cause any problems. I'd also recommend them if you fancy a romantic getaway or an activity-based holiday.

FACT FILE

Location: Fuller's Hill Cottages, Sandy, SG19 3PG
Website: cambridgeholidaycottages.com
Contact: 07544 208959
Type of accommodation: Cottage
Number of bedrooms: 2 (sleeps up to 6)
Number of dogs accepted: 3
Enclosed garden: No
Local interest: Warsley and Gransden Woods, Hayley Wood, Little Gransden Airfield, Cambridge
Best eats: The Coach House at Potton

22

THE EGERTON HOUSE HOTEL, KNIGHTSBRIDGE, LONDON

By Emma Bearman

Anyone looking for a truly opulent, dog friendly experience in the centre of London, need look no further than The Egerton House Hotel in Knightsbridge.

Many people think visiting London with a dog would be stressful, but I travel a great deal with my Springer Spaniel, Alfie, and am now relatively relaxed. I just give myself plenty of time and avoid commuters, whenever I can. Alfie's quite the professional and takes it all in his stride - especially the extra cuddles from passers-by!

The Egerton House Hotel is an impressive building, with gorgeous brickwork and elegant gold detailing. We were welcomed warmly by the team when we arrived and shown our suite.

It was an amazing room, with spectacular views right over the gardens and decorated stylishly throughout. Overall, the standard was extremely high - the bed linen was out of this world and the furniture, refined, and I could have spent hours soaking my cares away in the bath. Marble may be cold but it screams luxury. If you're a bit of a tech addict, it has all the latest technology, including a Bose portable speaker, super-fast broadband and Nespresso machine.

Alfie was also treated like royalty. We found everything he could possibly need - smart food and water bowls, a tasty selection of treats, a leather bed, a blanket and a personal welcome message. The hotel also has a pet concierge - ideal if your dog requires grooming or walking, or if you have a night out planned and require a sitter. *(continued...)*

FACT FILE

Location: 17-19 Egerton Terrace, Knightsbridge, London, SW3 2BX

Website: egertonhousehotel.com

Contact: 020 7589 2412

Type of accommodation: Boutique hotel

Number of bedrooms: 23, plus 5 suites

Number of dogs accepted: Varies, depending on size of room

Enclosed garden: No

Local interest: Hyde Park

Best eats: The Egerton House Hotel

We headed downstairs to take afternoon tea. And it wasn't just an ordinary afternoon tea. It was Doggy Afternoon Tea. We found a stylishly dressed table by the window and, taking our seats, were each given a glass of chilled champagne. A tantalising selection of delicate finger sandwiches, scones with cream and jam, and a wide variety of scrumptious homemade cakes appeared and then vanished!

Alfie wasn't neglected either as his 'tea' included meat loaf with parsley garnish, a selection of handmade biscuits and a bowl of Billy & Margot ice cream. The atmosphere was so friendly that I didn't worry about him at all and, at one point during the proceedings, Alfie even played fetch with the hotel manager, Michelle.

The Egerton House Hotel is within walking distance of Hyde Park and we enjoyed a peaceful stroll whilst the sun set.

Although there isn't an official restaurant at the Egerton House Hotel, you can dine in the bar or lounge area, or order room service. Since we'd loved eating in the lounge earlier, we headed down again with Alfie.

I loved every minute of our stay but, without any doubt, breakfast was my favourite experience, where Alfie was also given a menu. It was a tricky decision but, after much procrastination, he had a sausage patty with scrambled eggs and baked beans. I think he liked it because it certainly didn't last long!

THE BEAR, WOODSTOCK, OXFORDSHIRE

By Hilary Keens

Steeped in history and tradition, The Bear is a 4-star hotel, conveniently situated in the centre of the charming market town of Woodstock, with lovely walks on the Blenheim Palace estate right on the doorstep.

Overlooking the square, The Bear dates from the 13th century, which makes it one of the oldest establishments in the country and some consider it one of the prettiest. It was also recently named one of the most haunted. However, with its ivy-clad façade, original oak beams and roaring fires, it exudes warmth and didn't feel at all spooky.

I was pleased we'd been given a room in the courtyard, rather than the main building. Much as I loved the inn's period features, I thought Tess might bark at every creak during the night. My room was surprisingly spacious, with a king-size bed, a seating area, a small desk, a Freeview TV and a modern coffee machine. The ensuite bathroom was wonderful - clean and bright, with a luxury bathrobe. Breakfast was available between 7 and 10 am and the late finish was much appreciated. I also found a sign with the words *Dog in room*, which I thought a great idea.

Woodstock is a charming town, with buildings of warm, honey-coloured stone and many royal associations. The main reason I chose Woodstock was Blenheim Palace and the pedestrian entrance is about 3 minutes' walk from The Bear. The view across the lake was amazing, particularly of the Palladian bridge, with the water reflecting the blue sky and the orange and crimson autumn tints.

We spent several hours rambling through the parkland and were completely alone. There are a number of circular walks and leaflets describing these are readily available. I recommend The Bear, although I think it's best out of season because Woodstock can get rather crowded during the summer.

FACT FILE

Location: Park Street, Woodstock, OX20 1SZ
Website: macdonaldhotels.co.uk
Contact: 03448 799 143
Type of accommodation: Hotel
Number of bedrooms: 54
Number of dogs accepted: 2
Enclosed garden: No
Local interest: Blenheim Palace Estate, Stowe, the Oxford Canal
Best eats: The Chef Imperial, The Kings Head at Woodstock

THE WELLINGTON ARMS, BAUGHURST, HAMPSHIRE

By Gareth Salter

Conveniently situated a short distance from Basingstoke, The Wellington Arms is more than an extremely dog friendly pub - it's also a highly praised establishment which has won rave reviews from many of the country's best critics.

The Wellington Arms is an award-winning pub that was once a hunting lodge. It lies on a quiet country lane and enjoys a picturesque location. First impressions count and the pub is a charming sight, especially with the warm glow of firelight flickering through the windows. The entrance is further enhanced by solid lead planters, bursting with plants.

The Wellington Arms may have earned its reputation as a restaurant but its bed & breakfast accommodation is also highly regarded. I stayed in the Hayloft, where the exposed brickwork, green oak timbers and slate tiles (with underfloor heating) make the most of its rusticity.

I couldn't resist a meal in the restaurant, where the menu makes maximum use of local, seasonal and home-grown produce. I've never licked a plate clean in my life and wouldn't, obviously, but I was sorely tempted.

I slept peacefully that night - the only sound was an owl hooting in the distance. I woke early and headed along a track through the grounds until I reached a field, where Pixelo could have a run. I then enjoyed a wonderful breakfast and Pixelo's home-reared pork sausage disappeared in a flash!

There are plenty of walking opportunities, including the North Hampshire Downs. I drove to The Vyne, a 16th-century country house near Sherborne St John, where dogs are welcome in the grounds.

There can be no doubt The Wellington is the best place I've ever stayed.

FACT FILE

Location: Baughurst Rd, Baughurst, Hampshire, RG26 5LP

Website: thewellingtonarms.com

Contact: 01189 820110

Type of accommodation: Bed and breakfast

Number of bedrooms: 4 (2 dog friendly)

Number of dogs accepted: 2

Enclosed garden: No

Local interest: North Hampshire Downs, grounds of The Vyne

Best eats: The Wellington Arms

ST PANCRAS RENAISSANCE LONDON HOTEL, KINGS CROSS, LONDON

By October Willis

Dogs are made surprisingly welcome in the grandeur of the iconic St Pancras Renaissance Hotel.

The St Pancras Renaissance London Hotel has been hailed as the capital's most romantic building - its glorious Gothic Revival metalwork, gold leaf ceilings and amazing wall designs are as dazzling today as they were when the original opened in 1873.

We stayed in a Chambers Grand Junior Suite and our room, with its high ceiling and ornate mouldings, was amazing. Light and spacious, it was a vast improvement on others I've experienced in London and the bathroom wasn't lacking, with an enormous bath, a power shower and a tempting range of toiletries. We met several members of staff and, naturally, Watson was the centre of attention. He doesn't play the 'I only have 3 legs' sympathy card but has clearly realised he's irresistible.

We relaxed over afternoon tea in The Chambers Club, which is a private area where residents can enjoy breakfast, drinks and snacks during the day. Dogs aren't allowed in the self-service area, near the bar, but this wasn't a problem as the waiters kindly served us at our table.

Thinking Watson might need a walk, we asked the concierge for ideas. He suggested several places nearby and we chose a small park around the corner. We ate at The Lighterman on Granary Square that evening, which is a complete contrast in style. A modern building with enormous windows overlooking Regents Canal, it has a vibrant atmosphere.

The next morning we caught the Underground and went shopping in Covent Garden. A wonderful end to our canine adventures in London.

FACT FILE

Location: Euston Rd, Kings Cross London, NW1 2AR
Website: stpancraslondon.com
Contact: 02078 413540
Type of accommodation: Hotel
Number of bedrooms: 207 rooms, 38 suites
Number of dogs accepted: 2 (maximum weight 22lbs)
Enclosed garden: No
Local interest: London green spaces
Best eats: The Lighterman on Granary Square

POMONE, TOTLAND BAY, ISLE OF WIGHT

By Carolyn Williamson

In a peaceful spot, at the end of a single track road, 3 former coastguard cottages offer cosy accommodation with fine views all the way to the mainland.

January's quite an unusual time, but I like getting away out of season, especially after the Christmas festivities and I thought Pomone would be ideal.

I stayed in the third of 3 red-brick cottages overlooking the sea - it's where the coastguards who manned the lighthouse once lived. Now owned by the National Trust, the holiday rental properties stand within 370 acres of downland, also owned by the National Trust.

A single-storey building dating from the 19th century, it felt remarkably solid. Inside, there's a large kitchen-diner, a lounge (with open fire), a bathroom and a couple of bedrooms - a double and a twin. We found a doggy welcome pack when we arrived, with bowls, poo bags and a towel.

A washing machine and tumble dryer are available but these are shared with the other properties. Although there isn't a garden, there's a grassy area at the front and some rough land behind. There's quite a sharp drop so I'd be cautious if you have an excitable dog, but Shanty was fine.

Walking from Pomone was a real joy, with Tennyson Down immediately outside and, if you're feeling energetic (which I wasn't!), you can walk to Freshwater Bay or continue around the island on the coastal path.

There is an advantage to taking a holiday during the winter and that's the complete lack of restrictions on the beaches (except Whitecliff Bay) so Shanty could have a proper run.

FACT FILE

Location: Totland Bay, Isle of Wight
Website: nationaltrustholidays.org.uk
Contact: 03448 002070
Type of accommodation: Cottage
Number of bedrooms: 2 (sleeps 4)
Number of dogs accepted: 2
Enclosed garden: No
Local interest: Tennyson Down, Freshwater Bay, Parkhurst Forest, Ventnor Botanic Gardens, The Garlic Farm, Isle of Wight Pearl
Best eats: Sails at Cowes, cafés at The Garlic Farm and Isle of Wight Pearl (outside only)

CLOPHILL ECO LODGES, CLOPHILL, BEDFORDSHIRE

By Rhian White

Close to the A1 and the M1, and only an hour from London, Clophill Eco Lodges are nestled in a tranquil, woodland copse, with fantastic walking right from the door - and no television!

I'm passionate about the environment and believe we should live sustainably, if we can, so I was interested in the eco lodges created by The Clophill Heritage Trust.

Enjoying a picturesque woodland setting, the lodges lie near St. Mary's Church, a scheduled ancient monument that's just a short walk from Clophill.

Four of the five lodges provide family-friendly accommodation (including one with disabled facilities) and the fifth contains an activity room, breakfast area and kitchen. They are laid out cleverly in a horseshoe, which gives privacy to the balconies at the rear, whilst creating a communal living space in the centre, where people can socialise.

One of the sleeping areas has a double bed and the other has twin beds. The latter can be converted into a lounge if you want more space, and there's an adjoining shower room and WC. The lodges are bright, airy and clean with full-height windows overlooking the balconies that ensure you can enjoy the views. Guests can use the kitchen and eat meals in The Nest, a communal lodge, or you can request breakfast or a packed lunch from one of the wardens. It's worth noting that there aren't any televisions and there's a small charge if you use the WiFi.

Although the trust doesn't limit the number of dogs, the lodges aren't large and could feel cramped if you take more *(continued...)*

FACT FILE

Location: Old Church Path, Clophill, Beds, MK45 4BP

Website: clophillecolodges.co.uk

Contact: 07935 911207

Type of accommodation: Eco lodges

Number of bedrooms: 2

Number of dogs accepted: No restrictions but space limited

Enclosed garden: No

Local interest: On-site themed walks, Woburn Abbey parkland, Barton Hill, Greensand Ridge Walk, Old St Mary's Church

Best eats: The Flying Horse at Clophill and The French Horn at Steppingley

than one. I found the attitude towards dogs refreshingly relaxed. The managers trust you'll act responsibly and don't impose hundreds of restrictions about where you can go. I've never stayed anywhere like it and Boo spent most of the time off-lead, sniffing around the grounds on her own. She was always within eyesight but had much more freedom than normal.

The highlights of our holiday were the walks. You can head straight out from the lodges without using the car. We particularly enjoyed strolling through the woods, which were so peaceful that we even spotted deer sauntering past.

One of the best things about the lodges was the complete lack of noise. It was wonderfully quiet whilst we were there, so relaxation came easily. I found it quite different to staying in a B&B or cottage and loved every minute we spent there, as did Boo.

A number of walking routes have been created around the site, many designed around special interest themes such as birds, architecture or geology. If you fancy exploring the area, you can research these in depth at www.greensandridgetrails.org. uk. I think it's a wonderful place, so please visit if you can.

GREEN HILL FARM, SALISBURY, WILTSHIRE

By Naomi Mackay

Activities for children, lovely walks and popular tourist attractions - a camping holiday at Green Hill Farm has something for everyone.

The New Forest is a special place - where else in the country can you encounter ponies, pigs and cattle, wandering freely around the woods, and yet be just a short drive from the seaside? The New Forest boasts so many attractions that it's become one of our favourite holiday destinations.

We particularly like Green Hill Farm Caravan & Camping Site. It can get busy but we usually get a pitch at late notice. We've also found it enjoys better, less temperamental weather than sites nearer the sea. It welcomes dogs and there are some lovely walks nearby.

The campsite suits a wide variety of holidaymakers. Adults without children often choose a picturesque area under the trees, around small lakes. Those with children usually prefer one of the fields instead, which are more spacious. There's a football pitch and a playground with a zip wire and you can pay extra and try more on-site activities. The bar has an outside seating area and those who enjoy group entertainment can try musical bingo, karaoke and video game contests.

We visited Hurst Castle on a sunny day, parking near the ferry at Milford on Sea. You can walk along the spit but the shingle makes it hard work and we always love a boat trip, so caught the little ferry instead. Friendly dogs are welcome and travel free of charge.

The beauty of the New Forest is that much of it is 'wild', unfenced and feels completely natural.

FACT FILE

Location: Green Hill Farm Camping & Caravan Park, New Rd, Salisbury, SP5 2AZ
Website: lovatparks.com/locations/new-forest
Contact: 0333 2001010
Type of accommodation: Camping and caravans
Number of dogs accepted: 2
Enclosed garden: No
Local interest: Hurst Castle, New Forest Reptile Centre, Lymington, Buckler's Hard, Exbury Gardens
Best eats: Café at Hurst Castle and The Captain's Table Tea Rooms at Buckler's Hard (outside only)

LE BOAT, CHERTSEY, SURREY

By Liz Morphew

No boating experience is required to explore the River Thames aboard a luxury boat.

If you're always on the lookout for an exciting getaway that's 100% dog friendly and 100% adventurous, we highly recommend a weekend break with Le Boat. Despite my lack of seafaring experience, all it took was a short debrief and a quick test drive, and we were headed off down the Thames.

An impressive 13.5 x 4.3m, the Horizon 3 is no joke of a boat. Comprising 3 bedrooms (each with its own bathroom) and a large kitchen/entertaining area, there's plenty of space. And for sun-worshippers, the sun deck has 2 sun loungers, a large central dining table and a barbecue.

We were met on board by the friendly (patient) Le Boat staff, who took us through the basics of boating etiquette, as well as how to navigate a massive floating holiday home. It's amazing how quickly you pick up the controls and feel at ease. And to top it all, the Le Boat team gave Simon, our 2-year-old cavapoo, his very own captain's hat and doggy life jacket.

We downloaded the River Thames Guide Lite app, which shows the locations of pubs, attractions and locks along your chosen route. As relative novices to boat life, it was surprising how relaxing we found cruising along the water. Before we set off, we were worried that Simon might end up jumping in but, in reality, that was never a problem. Simon spent the entire trip settled and with the wind in his face.

Usually a weekend away is either an 'adventure' or 'relaxing'. This weekend was both, and then some.

FACT FILE

Location: Gate 5, Penton Hook Marina, Staines Rd, Chertsey, Surrey, KT16 8PY

Website: leboat.co.uk

Contact: 023 9222 2177

Type of accommodation: Boat

Number of bedrooms: 3 (sleeps 7)

Number of dogs accepted: 2

Enclosed garden: No

Local interest: Various - see River Thames Guide Lite app

Best eats: The Bridge Hotel at Chertsey, The Swan Hotel at Staines (more on River Thames Guide Lite app)

THE MANOR HOUSE HOTEL - P.60

CHARINGWORTH MANOR - P.49

BOUNTY COTTAGE - P.64

COTSWOLDS

WALES

RAVENDERE RETREATS - P.53

PRIMROSE HOLIDAYS - P.36

THE RED LION - P.65

BURLEIGH COURT - P.46

Bristol

Bath

WOODLAND COTTAGES - P.40

QUANTOCK COTTAGES - P.38

SOMERSET GARDEN YURT - P.44

CLOCK HOUSE B&B - P.48

BUTTERMILK COTTAGE - P.45

Barnstaple

EXMOOR NATIONAL PARK

Yeovil

BLUE HILLS TOURING PARK - P.59

YEOMADON FARM - P.68

WNI - P.43

TREVELLA CARAVAN & CAMPING - P.52

Exeter

THE ARUNDELL ARMS HOTEL - P.57

DARTMOOR NATIONAL PARK

SPANIEL COTTAGE - P.41

EAST CLIFF HOTEL - P.61

HARRIS COTTAGE - P.66

Newquay

Plymouth

BEDFORD HOTEL - P.67

SHELTER SHED - P.55

PENVENTON PARK HOTEL - P.50

FARTHING COTTAGE - P.37

SOUTH SANDS HOTEL - P.56

THE WOODLAND COLLECTION - P.34

HELL BAY HOTEL - P.62

Isles of Scilly

WOODLAND COLLECTION HOLIDAYS, TOWNSHEND, CORNWALL

By Deb Bridges

In an ideal location for visiting Cornwall's famous beaches and a variety of attractions, accommodation in the 4 dog friendly holiday cottages which make up the Woodland Collection is both practical and comfortable.

Sycamore Cottage is one of 4 identical, purpose-built, eco friendly cottages, set in a neat row on Sunrise Farm, where wildflowers are grown on a grand scale, making it a particularly beautiful spot for a late spring or summer break.

We missed the wildflowers on our 2-night, early autumn stay but having the 30 acres of meadows just a few yards from our gate was wonderful. We'd barely chucked our bags through the cottage door before we were strolling the mown paths in the sunshine, down to a woodland garden.

Each cottage is accessed via a back gate into a paved, fully-enclosed garden. There's outdoor furniture, a barbecue and, even better, a warm shower - so no worries about returning with a muddy or sandy dog.

French windows lead straight into the open-plan kitchen/dining/lounge area, which is fresh, bright and pleasingly uncluttered. The furniture is leather, the floor is laminate and the work surfaces are marble. The downstairs toilet also houses a washing machine and is roomy enough to provide useful storage for shoes, rucksacks, etc.

The dining table seats 6 and the lounge features three 2-seater settees, grouped around a Smart TV and an uber-modern letterbox fireplace set into the wall, which creates an instant cosy feel at the touch

FACT FILE

Location: Sunrise Farm, 68 Bosence Road, Townshend, Hayle, TR27 6AL

Website: woodland-collection.co.uk

Contact: 07786 268828

Type of accommodation: Cottage

Number of bedrooms: 3 (sleeps 6)

Number of dogs accepted: 4

Enclosed garden: Yes, plus large fully-fenced field

Local interest: St Michael's Mount, Cornish Seal Sanctuary, Tremenheere Sculpture Gardens, beaches, Minack Theatre, St Ives, Lands End

Best eats: The Big Green Shed (on site), The Packet Inn at Rosudgeon, Crown Inn at Goldsithney, The Rockpool beach café at Gwithian

of a remote control button. The overall impression is one of good quality furniture and fittings which are as stylish as they are solid.

The kitchen is fully equipped, with a built-in electric cooker, ceramic hob and dishwasher but, having only 2 nights away, we weren't planning on using anything more adventurous than the kettle.

The bedrooms are inviting and restful, and all 3 have their own ensuite shower rooms, with rain showers. The rooms aren't particularly large but the space is well used - they all have plenty of shelving and hanging space, plus a wall-mounted Smart TV. The beds are comfy, with lovely, puffy duvets and crisp white bed linen.

I chose the room at the front, not for its king-size bed but because it had the best space for Ula's bed (dogs are allowed upstairs on their own beds but there is a stair gate, if you prefer to sleep alone). It was close to the road but, after 11 pm, vehicles were few and far between. The other standard double bedroom is at the back and has fully-glazed French windows which look out onto the gardens, across the wildflower meadow to a far-reaching view of the countryside beyond. The third bedroom has bunk beds.

Opening the curtains the next morning, we were faced with a damp, dreary day and headed over to The Big Green Shed, which is an on-site bistro. Mike tucked into a full Full English and my smashed avo and poached eggs - so often delivered in Lilliputian proportions - was definitely enough to keep me going all day.

There were dogs in all 4 of the properties. The gardens between each pair of cottages can be opened up, if more than one family is holidaying together - which is what the occupants of the other pair of cottages had done. It's a sociable arrangement and we were all soon on cheery waving terms.

Helen and Richard make their guests, both human and canine, very welcome and, outside the busiest months of July and August, they're more flexible than some holiday property owners with regard to the duration of bookings. My advice - stay as long as you can!

SYCAMORE

PRIMROSE HILL HOLIDAYS, MINEHEAD, SOMERSET

By Jo Southway

Set in a peaceful and secluded location between Exmoor National Park and the Quantock Hills, Blue Anchor Bay is the perfect holiday destination for exploring all that West Somerset has to offer.

Primrose Hill is a superb countryside retreat. There are 4 self-catering bungalows on site, along with a games room, barbecue area, laundry room and boules pitch.

Inside the bungalow we had everything we needed, with all of the kitchen appliances covered. The rooms were all spacious with very comfy beds, but the icing on the cake was the beautiful view. Primrose Hill is the perfect choice if you are looking for somewhere that is dog friendly and you have extra mobility needs. With wide doorways, level access and disabled friendly bathrooms, they tick all the boxes.

Another great positive is that you can get frozen meals to cook in your bungalow. For those of us travelling with our dogs, they have a lovely little woodland walk next to the cottages.

Less than 3 miles from Primrose Hill is the picturesque medieval village of Dunster. Famous for its castle and watermill, dogs are welcomed here in all of the grounds but not inside the castle.

If you are wanting great views, then look no further than Dunkery Beacon. It is the highest point not only on Exmoor but in the whole of Somerset. The views are exceptional and you may also get to see some of the local wildlife or Exmoor Ponies that roam the land.

We thoroughly enjoyed our stay at Primrose Hill.

FACT FILE

Location: Wood Lane, Blue Anchor, Minehead, Somerset, TA24 6LA

Website: primrosehillholidays.co.uk

Contact: 01643 821200

Type of accommodation: Bungalow

Number of bedrooms: 2 (3 bedroom bungalow also available)

Number of dogs accepted: 2 (negotiable)

Enclosed garden: Yes

Local interest: Dunster, Blue Anchor Beach, Blue Anchor Railway Station, Tarr Steps on Exmoor, Dunkery Beacon, Minehead

Best eats: The Dunster Watermill Tea Room, Locks Victorian Tea Rooms at Dunster, Driftwood Café at Blue Anchor Bay, The Blue Anchor at Minehead, Tarr Farm Inn at Tarr Steps

FARTHING COTTAGE, POLPERRO, CORNWALL

By Jenna Shippey

An old fisherman's cottage in the centre of the picturesque fishing village of Polperro, Farthing Cottage enjoys fantastic views of the harbour and is ideally placed for a dog friendly break.

It was a long drive down to Polperro from the north of England. However, the journey proved to be worth it, when we saw the lovely view of Polperro, with the tram parked in the car park at the top. We had our own private parking bay and had arranged for our luggage to be dropped off at our cottage. It went ahead and we walked down with Alfie, a good 10 minutes' walk, through lovely little narrow streets. There were loads of doggies on holiday and we noticed the village was very dog friendly - lots of water bowls outside shops.

We opened the door to a lovely, sweet, old-world fisherman's cottage, right in the centre of the village. The first floor windows look over the harbour, with all the fishermen's boats bobbing about in the water and the seagulls not far behind. The top floor has a view to die for, and Alfie certainly liked the window seats.

We found early evening was best to take Alfie for his last walk over to the small beach, where dogs are allowed off-lead after 6pm. Boat trips to Fowey and Looe also come and go from this point and dogs are allowed on board.

For our last night, we booked a meal at Michelle's restaurant. The food was amazing and they do really make a fuss of your dog. The waitress gives them water and treats, on arrival. We were told that, if you have Sunday lunch, they bring a little roast meal out for doggies, too.

It was just a perfect ending to an amazing little trip to Cornwall. Polperro was so lovely and very dog friendly.

FACT FILE

Location: Talland St, Polperro, Looe, PL13 2RE
Website: toadhallcottages.co.uk
Contact: 01548 202020
Type of accommodation: Cottage
Number of bedrooms: 1
Number of dogs accepted: 1 small
Enclosed garden: No
Local interest: Smugglers' Museum, coastal walks, Talland Bay
Best eats: The Three Pilchards at Polperro, Talland Bay Beach Café, The Museum Tea Room and Michelle's Restaurant at Polperro

QUANTOCK HIDE, QUANTOCK COTTAGES, SOMERSET

By Steve Bennett

Luxury combined with dog friendliness are taken to the highest level in 3 uniquely-styled cottages, set in the glorious Quantock Hills, with the sea only a short drive away.

Our drive to the Quantock Hills brought back memories from my childhood, when I lived on the outskirts of Bristol and used to cycle to the coastal towns of Clevedon, Portishead and Weston-super -Mare. These were the names that were appearing on the motorway exit signs, as we got closer to our destination. The directions we had been given were clear. The road is very narrow, with a couple of blind bends and Quantock Cottages are literally at the very end of the road, right up in the Quantock Hills. I had a really good feeling about what we were about to see and, goodness me, we were not disappointed.

The walk from our car to the cottage was like a journey into Narnia which, at night, was emphasised by the little white lights on the side of the path. We walked down steps into an opening which reminded me of a luxury spa - outside seating and towels beautifully presented with flowers on them (yes, real flowers) and the hot tub on another level of the garden.

Just outside the front door was a bath for the dogs with a shower - just one of the clear signs that the owners really do understand what being dog friendly means - and the garden is split into 3 dog-secure areas. We were already amazed at what we had seen and we hadn't even opened the front door yet!

The cottages are the ultimate in 'luxury'

FACT FILE

Location: Pardlestone Lane, Kilve, Somerset, TA5 1SQ

Website: quantockcottages.co.uk

Contact: 01278 741643

Type of accommodation: Cottage

Number of bedrooms: 2 (sleeps 4)

Number of dogs accepted: 3 (more possible, on request)

Enclosed garden: Yes

Local interest: Weston-super-Mare, Great Wood at Adscombe, Sandy Bay Beach, Kilve Beach, West Somerset Steam Railway, Dunster Castle

Best eats: The Foxy Bean at Great Wood, Sandy Bay Tea Rooms, The Hood Arms at Kilve, The Castle Coffee Shop at Dunster Castle, The Purplespoon Café at Bridgwater, Chantry Tea Rooms at Kilve Beach

accommodation. Quantock Hide has a large, beautifully-furnished living room, with big throws provided for the dogs. The kitchen, perfectly situated in the corner of the ground floor, has a massive American fridge.

A small flight of stairs takes you to the first floor. There's a bathroom on the left, with a huge shower, and a double bedroom on the right, where our son fell onto the sumptuous bed. Our room was, quite simply, magnificent, with ensuite facilities, a huge bed, a bath under the main window and drinks to make us feel even more welcome, if that was at all possible.

Both Lin and I were dumbfounded by the quality of the cottage and the fittings, as well as the thought that had gone into making the cottages dog friendly - truly dog friendly!

Quantock Cottages are the epitome of luxury - and if you don't have a dog with you when you visit, you will be the odd one out!

WOODLAND COTTAGES, NEWTON TRACEY, NORTH DEVON

By Mark Wall

In a rural setting, with dog friendly beaches and excellent walking opportunities nearby, Woodland Cottages offer comfortable and award-winning dog friendly accommodation.

There are many holiday homes, cottages and hotels which allow dogs. And then there are some that welcome dogs. But there are few that positively encourage you to bring your dogs - and Woodland Cottages in North Devon is one of these!

The owners have dogs themselves and their vision for the holiday homes is totally focused around dogs. The floors are stone and the sofas are leather, for ease of cleaning. Each of the 3 cottages has a small, enclosed, paved courtyard, where you can sit and enjoy the view, while your dog is safe to wander around. There is also a securely-fenced, 1-acre field, where your dog can run around. This is shared with the other 2 cottages which, for us, was a bonus. There are also dog washing facilities and additional freezer space for dog food, if you need it.

We were in Badger Cottage, which has 3 bedrooms and is extremely well equipped and maintained. The double ensuite bedroom is upstairs and, being accessed by a spiral staircase, may not be suitable for some dogs. However, there is a twin and a single bedroom on the ground floor.

Woodland Cottages are an excellent place to stay with your dogs - extremely welcoming, very well equipped and wonderfully situated. It's no surprise that they were Gold Award winners in the dog friendly category of both the Devon and South West Tourism awards, 2019–20. Recommended.

FACT FILE

Location: West Woodlands, Newton Tracey, North Devon, EX31 3PP

Website: woodlandcottages.org.uk

Contact: 07759 210607

Type of accommodation: Cottage

Number of bedrooms: 3 (sleeps 5)

Number of dogs accepted: Multiple

Enclosed garden: Enclosed courtyard garden

Local interest: Westward Ho!, Great Torrington, enclosed 8-acre woodland walk from the door, dog friendly beaches, coastal walks, Tarka Trail

Best eats: The Waterfront Inn at Westward Ho!

SPANIEL COTTAGE, STOKE-SUB-HAMDON, SOMERSET

By Vicky Kaderbhai

Situated in a pretty village with dog friendly eateries and a country park on the doorstep, car trips are optional during a stay at the beautiful Spaniel Cottage.

Spaniel Cottage, in the picture-perfect village of Stoke-sub-Hamdon in Somerset, has got to be one of the most charming holiday homes I have ever been lucky enough to visit. Situated at the foot of Ham Hill, a 360-acre country park, the cottage has an unobstructed view of the war memorial on the spur of the hill.

The cottage itself has the loveliest home-away-from-home feel and we all immediately felt relaxed. While we humans busied ourselves checking out the cosy kitchen and impressive bathroom, with its walk-in shower and roll-top bath, the dogs had fun exploring the enclosed back garden.

We were eager to explore our beautiful new surroundings, so we walked up to the war memorial, where we were treated to views of the South Somerset Moors, Exmoor and the Mendip Hills. We then walked to a series of stones that had been erected as part of a special project for the millennium. The dogs loved exploring these and giving each stone a sniff!

The hosts had left a lovely welcome pack, full of information about the cottage, the local area and day trips. Lyme Regis caught my eye, as it is somewhere I visited a lot as a child, and I was excited to discover it was only a 45-minute drive away. *(continued...)*

FACT FILE

Location: 27 Castle Street, Stoke-sub-Hamdon, Somerset, TA14 6RF

Website: spanielcottage.com

Contact: 07384 467567

Type of accommodation: Cottage

Number of bedrooms: 2 (sleeps 3)

Number of dogs accepted: 2, more by prearrangement

Enclosed garden: Yes

Local interest: Ham Hill Country Park, Lyme Regis, The Donkey Sanctuary at Sidmouth, Wayford Woods near Crewkerne, the gardens at Montacute House, St Michael's Hill at Montacute

Best eats: The Prince of Wales and Priory Coffee at Stoke-sub-Hamdon, The Lord Nelson at Norton-Sub-Hamdon, The Pilot Boat at Lyme Regis, The Kitchen at The Donkey Sanctuary, The Kings Arms at Montacute

We visited Lyme Regis on one of the sunniest days of the year, so it was packed. During the summer months, there are restrictions on the main Cobb Beach and Church Beach, but Monmouth Beach is open to dogs all year round. Before heading back to the cottage, we decided to make the 20-minute journey from Lyme Regis to The Sidmouth Donkey Sanctuary, which is really dog friendly.

After a year in lockdown, we opted for quite an active holiday but if you wanted a more relaxed break, then Spaniel Cottage can work for you. With its cosy feel, log fires, decadent bathroom and welcoming lounge, you can put your feet up and unwind. With Ham Hill on your doorstep and the beautiful village to explore, you could easily park the car up and not bother with it again, until you leave.

Both my husband and I were totally taken with the cottage and the area. It was lovely to feel so welcome with our dogs, wherever we went. There's no doubt we'll be back, as Spaniel Cottage has earned a special place in our hearts.

KEWNI YURT, WOONSMITH FARM, CORNWALL

By Anna Ward Murphy

Although only 20 minutes in the car from both Penzance and St Ives, the setting of Woonsmith Farm feels very rural and their cosy yurts are much more than big tents!

"That's a lot of money for a big tent." Steve, my other half, was less than enthusiastic when I excitedly showed him the yurt I had found on airbnb. However, after a bit of gentle persuasion, I got my own way. We booked 4 nights at Kewni Yurt and there was no extra charge for our dog, Pepper.

As we arrived at the farm, we spotted our yurt nestled in its own little garden area, complete with decking, table and chairs and a small barbecue. The garden is unsecured and, as there are cows nearby at times, dogs need to be kept under control, but they are very welcome.

The yurt was stunning - spacious and beautifully decorated, with an artistic, wooden bed, a wood burning stove, twinkling lights, a large, swivelling cuddle chair and a table, complete with a tasty Cornish cream tea to welcome us after our journey.

There was also a kitchenette and - a real bonus for a comfortable glamping experience - a well-equipped ensuite bathroom. Result! We had everything we needed and were set for a comfortable and relaxing stay. Pepper quickly settled in and, within minutes, had found a little window to gaze out of, at perfect dog-eye height.

Our stay was full of weather, adventures, explorations and memories. As we packed up our belongings to leave, I asked Steve what he thought of my 'big tent' idea now. His response? "Brilliant. I'd definitely come back here! What quirky place can we go to next?"

FACT FILE

Location: Nancledra, Penzance, TR20 8LP

Website: woonsmith.co.uk

Contact: woonsmith@outlook.com

Type of accommodation: Yurt (summer months only)

Number of bedrooms: 1

Number of dogs accepted: 2

Enclosed garden: No

Local interest: St Ives, Baker's Pit Nature Reserve, St Michael's Mount, Land's End

Best eats: The White Hart at Ludgvan, The Tinners Arms at Zennor, Porthcurno Beach Café, The Logan Rock Inn at Treen

SOMERSET GARDEN YURT, TAUNTON, SOMERSET

By Jo Southway

A cosy yurt on a safely-fenced site beside the canal makes a great base for families to enjoy all the local area has to offer.

As you arrive at the Somerset Yurt, you feel like you are stepping into a story book. Walking across a little bridge and down the path lined with toadstools and woodland animals, it's just like a fairy tale and children will take delight in the magic of the place.

There are various different parts to the holiday setting, including the kitchen, toilet and shower block, a wood-fired pizza oven hut and a sitting room type set-up, where you will find a wood burner, dining table, games and more, all hidden under the natural vines and undergrowth.

On the lawn is a picnic bench for eating outside and a firepit, with natural seating. The firepit makes for a spectacular centrepiece and a great place to bring everyone together in the evening. We spent each night sat around a fire, feeling cosy and warm, toasting marshmallows.

The yurt itself is a wonderful, wooden hideaway, brightly decorated with sparkles and lights. It is a huge space, with two double beds and a bunk bed - room to sleep a whole family, with plenty more space for the dogs.

Being right next to the canal is a huge bonus. With access straight onto the towpath, you can walk for miles, taking in the tranquility water and countryside brings.

We thoroughly enjoyed our stay at the Somerset Garden Yurt. For both dogs and children it really is just perfect, with everything you could need for a delightful holiday.

FACT FILE

Location: Cobweb Cottage, 4 Outwood Cottages, Outwood, West Lyng, Taunton, TA3 5AL

Website: gardenyurt.co.uk

Contact: 01823 491622

Type of accommodation: Yurt

Number of bedrooms: 1 (sleeps 6)

Number of dogs accepted: Multiple

Enclosed garden: Yes

Local interest: Bridgwater & Taunton Canal, Cliff Woods, Thurlbear Wood, beaches at Burnham-on-Sea, Brean, Kilve and Minehead

Best eats: Maunsel Lock Tea Rooms, The Farmer's Arms at West Hatch

BUTTERMILK COTTAGE, COOKBURY, DEVON

By Jo Southway

A former goat shed, Buttermilk Cottage is set in the quiet Devon countryside, with walks straight from the door.

We loved the fact that Buttermilk Cottage used to house the owners' goats and, although renovated to the highest standards with modern features, it still retains the original charm. On first impression, the finishing touches of this delightful cottage make it feel luxurious, while having all the essentials you could need.

The indoor set-up is comfy and compact, with the loft area being a great bedroom-like den for children. The bathroom is well laid out for the size of the room and, although the bath is a little smaller than normal, the owners were installing a hot tub in the garden. The main bedroom is a great size and we haven't even mentioned the massive bed yet.

Outdoors there are 2 areas just for your use and there is an outside dog bath with a warm shower.

The location of the cottage could not have been more perfect - set in the quiet Devon countryside, with walks straight out of the door and surrounded by woodland, rivers, ponds and fields.

If you are looking to take small people, then there are endless activities to keep them busy, from helping with the animals to making clay creations or playing on the many swings. You can even take the boat out for a spin around the pond.

When going out for a walk, you are spoilt for choice, or a quick car ride or longer walk takes you to Cookworthy Forest, where you will find acres of Forestry Commission land with easy-to-walk paths.

We wouldn't hesitate to go back.

FACT FILE

Location: Cookbury Court, Cookbury, Devon, EX22 7YG
Website: pillowsandpawscottages.co.uk
Contact: 01409 281311
Type of accommodation: Cottage
Number of bedrooms: 2 (sleeps 4)
Number of dogs accepted: 2
Enclosed garden: Yes
Local interest: Dunsland (National Trust), Cookworthy Forest, Ferworthy Reservoir
Best eats: The Bickford Arms at Holsworthy

BURLEIGH COURT, STROUD, GLOUCESTERSHIRE

By Steve Bridgewater

Nestled in 4 acres of gardens, with views over the golden valley, Burleigh Court is a boutique manor house hotel, where the team are committed to their motto - 'Eat well, sleep well and feel well".

With its golden stone buildings, quintessentially English villages and rolling hills, the Cotswolds are justifiably a tourist 'hotspot'.

Arriving at Minchinhampton Common,

FACT FILE

Location: The Roundabouts, Brimscombe, Stroud, Gloucestershire, GL5 2PF

Website: burleighcourtcotswolds.co.uk

Contact: 01453 883804

Type of accommodation: Boutique hotel

Number of bedrooms: 18 (2 dog friendly)

Number of dogs accepted: 1 or 2, depending on size

Enclosed garden: No

Local interest: Minchinhampton Common, Rodborough Common, Woodchester Mansion, Painswick Rococo Garden

Best eats: Winstone's artisan ice-cream shop at Rodborough Common, The Falcon Inn at Painswick, The Painswick Pooch Coffee House, Jolly Nice Farmshop & Kitchen at Frampton Mansell

you are instantly struck by the beauty of the area. Burleigh Court is located just off the Common and - as the directions on the website point out - it's a case of 'keeping the faith', as the narrow (but well-maintained) country lane drops down a hill, over cattle grids and through gates. Then, just as you're about to give up and turn back, you are greeted by a beautiful, ivy-clad country house.

At the hotel, we were met by the ever-smiling Emma, who checked us in, made a big fuss of our Miniature Poodles, Howie and Franklin, and showed us to our room, in the adjacent coach house. Seven of Burleigh Court's 18 rooms are pet-friendly and are decorated to a very high standard.

Burleigh Court was purchased by James and Corinna Rae in March 2019. Leaving their careers in London, they followed their dream to create a place where people can retreat and relax under the motto *Eat well, sleep well, feel well.*

Howie and Franklin were itching to explore the area, so we set off for a walk across the Commons. The views across the Stroud Valley are nothing short of idyllic and a hearty stroll from Minchinhampton Common to nearby Rodborough Common reveals yet more breathtaking scenery across the Severn Estuary.

We could easily have spent a couple of days relaxing on the Commons but risk-averse Franklin was unconvinced that being so close to cows was a good idea. As such, we decided to explore a little further afield.

There are a multitude of places to go and things to see in the Cotswolds - from arty festivals to scenery, shopping and fine dining.

As dog owners, you are often distanced from the main restaurant when eating in hotels, but at Burleigh Court this doesn't feel the case. There are 2 oak-panelled dining rooms - one of which is dog friendly and the staff could not have been friendlier towards Howie and Franklin.

Well, we certainly ate well and the combination of a comfortable room and plenty of walking ensured we slept our best sleep in a long time. We left feeling infinitely better than when we arrived. Mission accomplished!

CLOCK HOUSE, MARNHULL, DORSET

By Mark Wall

Clock House, situated in the large village of Marnhull in Dorset's Blackmore Vale, has undergone extensive renovations to create comfortable B&B accommodation, where dogs are made very welcome.

After foolishly ignoring the sat nav and driving straight past my destination, we arrived at Clock House a little late, to a warm welcome from Christine and her 2 spaniels, Tizzie and Ben.

FACT FILE

Location: Burton Street, Marnhull, Sturminster Newton, Dorset, DT10 1PH

Website: clockhouse-marnhull.com

Contact: 01258 820645

Type of accommodation: Bed & breakfast

Number of bedrooms: 4

Number of dogs accepted: 2 small to medium size

Enclosed garden: No

Local interest: Duncliffe Wood, river walks at Sturminster Newton, Sturminster Newton Water Mill

Best eats: The Crown Inn and The Blackmore Vale Inn at Marnhull, The Kings Arms Inn at East Stour

Clock House has 2 double and 2 twin ensuite rooms, one with easy access for anyone with restricted mobility. There is also a large lounge with sofas, dining table, radio and fridge - all purely for the use of guests. All rooms benefit from French doors leading to the garden and have tea and coffee making facilities.

After tea and cake, Daisy demanded a run, so we took advantage of the excellent paddock at the back of the property, which is big enough to chase a ball without getting lost.

Our room, no 3, was neat, clean, spacious, well designed and well equipped, with a lovely bathroom and huge shower. There was a dog welcome pack, which made us both feel as if we were in a place that understands us.

Breakfast at the Clock House is continental and certainly extensive. A choice of cereal, yoghurt and lots of fruit is followed by eggs done whichever way you like, as much toast as you want and some croissants.

There is also a 3 bedroom cottage available for rent, where dogs are welcomed.

CHARINGWORTH MANOR, CHIPPING CAMDEN, GLOUCESTERSHIRE

By Evika Kienne

With its quaint villages and sweeping views, there's much to admire in the Cotswolds and it's all right on the doorstep of the luxurious Charingworth Manor.

It is incredibly hard to make a list of the best places to visit in the Cotswolds, as there are so many to choose from. In fact, the entire area is stunning - full of quaint little villages and a variety of walking trails with sweeping views.

If you need to reboot your energy and spirit, you have to stay at the luxurious Charingworth Manor, with its exceptional location and calming views over the surrounding Cotswold hills. You will be treated as royalty from start to finish.

Our room was spacious and distinctive, with a comfy bed and lots of amenities like a kettle, ample drawer and closet space, a safe, bottled water and robes and slippers for that extra bit of comfort. It is all about the little finishing touches that make a stay memorable and I can certainly give 5 stars to the Charingworth. We were made so welcome, with personalised letters and carefully-selected welcome baskets for the hounds.

As we were a bit tired from exploring the surroundings of the hotel, we ordered dinner in our room and around 20 minutes later, we were fine dining in our PJs.

Any hotel's goal is to create an unforgettable experience that guests will want to repeat and tell their friends, family and colleagues about. Charingworth Manor certainly succeeds - exceptional hospitality, luxury setting and one of the most dog friendly places we have ever stayed at.

FACT FILE

Location: Charingworth, Chipping Campden, The Cotswolds, GL55 6NS

Website: classiclodges.co.uk/charingworth-manor

Contact: 01386 593555

Type of accommodation: Hotel

Number of bedrooms: 26

Number of dogs accepted: 2

Enclosed garden: No

Local interest: Chipping Camden, Birdland Park & Gardens at Bourton-on-the-Water, Bibury, Broadway Tower, Lower and Upper Slaughter

Best eats: Charingworth Manor

PENVENTON PARK HOTEL, REDRUTH, CORNWALL

By Charlotte Clark

After a day exploring Cornwall's famous beaches, dogs and people can relax and enjoy being pampered in the opulent Georgian splendour of The Penventon Park Hotel.

Arriving at The Penventon Park Hotel, we were welcomed by a lovely lady who showed us to our room - the dog friendly Garden Suite. The room had a classic, country interior, intertwined with grand, elegant features. I particularly loved the fact that, like all the garden suites, it has patio doors opening directly onto partially-enclosed private gardens, which is ideal for early morning and late night doggy toilet trips.

The beds are spacious and very cosy. You're guaranteed a great night's sleep and all dog friendly rooms include a sitting area. The room also has an impressive minibar and the kettle is kept here too, alongside beautiful, delicate cups for your morning tea.

After we had unpacked our bags, we headed out to investigate nearby Porthtowan Beach. This beautiful stretch of beach sits snugly between two cliffs, one of which offers a stunning cliff walk. Unfortunately, we never got round to going on this walk, but it looked amazing. Like many beaches, there is a stream that flows down the beach to meet the sea, so you can guess where Spaniel, Max, spent most of his time ...

Returning to the hotel wet and sandy, we cleaned the dogs off before getting ready for dinner. Once we'd made ourselves look more presentable, we went for dinner which was very kindly set up for us in the secluded, quiet lounge, so the dogs could join us. The staff absolutely love dogs and are so friendly. We felt very welcomed. The

FACT FILE

Location: West End, Redruth, Cornwall, TR15 1TE
Website: penventon.co.uk
Contact: 01209 203000
Type of accommodation: Hotel
Number of bedrooms: 63
Number of dogs accepted: 2
Enclosed garden: Partially enclosed
Local interest: Dog friendly beaches and local walks
Best eats: Penventon Park Hotel

next morning, after letting the dogs out in the little garden, we headed for breakfast. Once again, the staff were absolutely lovely to us and set up a table in the grand lounge, so the dogs could join us. The dogs were also treated to a plate of scrumptious sausages, lucky boys.

After a fun day on some gorgeous beaches, we decided to indulge ourselves with the hotel's afternoon tea and we sat with the dogs in the grand lounge, in front of a beautiful open window. I'm not lying when I say the scones were the best I've ever had, and I can be quite fussy with scones. We spent our days making the most of being by the coast. Dogs are always very happy at the beach and it's so heartwarming to see.

After packing our bags and checking out of the hotel, we gave the dogs a run on Perranporth Beach, a beautiful stretch of golden sand. With the dogs worn out, we began our long journey home.

Overall, we had a wonderful stay and were treated exceptionally well. I was very impressed with the hotel and the dogs had a great time!

TREVELLA CARAVAN & CAMPING PARK, NEWQUAY, CORNWALL

By James Waters

Just 2 miles from the huge expanse of sand at Crantock Beach and with a variety of dog friendly attractions nearby, Trevella makes a great base for a family holiday.

We arrived at Trevella Caravan Park at dusk and were delighted with our accommodation.

Our caravan was very smart, tidy and quite spacious, with good facilities, including a doggy bed and throws, awaiting Stanley's arrival. There was also a gated decking area, which was perfect for Stanley to hang out and he was happiest lounging on the decking, particularly in the sun.

The accommodation provides a really good welcome book, giving you great dog friendly places to eat and drink, as well as dog friendly days out to try. The campsite also has a dedicated dog-walking area.

The park is generally quiet, with plenty of space between the static caravans. It has a good atmosphere and, as well as being dog friendly, it has a few things for the kids to do, with an outdoor swimming pool and a small games room, which is next to their takeaway food bar - great when you can't be bothered to cook!

Once the kids were tired out with a swim and some games, we'd take Stanley for an evening walk around the campsite, making a stop at the on-site Piskie Inn. Apparently, it's the smallest bar in Cornwall with just 8 seats and, of course, dog friendly. Being so small, the bar is perfect for chatting to other dog friendly holidaymakers.

We enjoyed our weekend break at Trevella and can't wait to plan another trip to the south west with Stanley.

FACT FILE

Location: Crantock, Newquay, TR8 5EW
Website: parkholidays.com
Contact: 03431 787070
Type of accommodation: Static caravan
Number of bedrooms: Sleeps 6
Number of dogs accepted: 2
Enclosed garden: Gated decking area
Local interest: Crantock Beach and village, St Michael's Mount (grounds and café only), Healey's Cornish Cyder Farm at Truro, Tanglewood Wild Garden at Penzance, Pencarrow House & Garden at Bodmin, Cornish Seal Sanctuary at Gweek
Best eats: The Bowgie Inn and The Old Albion Inn at Crantock, on-site takeaway food bar

RAVENDERE RETREATS, ILFRACOMBE, DEVON

By Rhian White

Set in 12 acres of private woodland on the beautiful North Devon Coast, award-winning Ravendere Retreats offers a luxurious woodland escape, with walks from the treehouse door and a quiet beach within strolling distance.

With stunning valley views, this secluded adults-only retreat offers rest and relaxation and is the perfect escape from busy life. Surrounded by nature, you can experience the beauty of the ancient woodland in all seasons and you may be lucky enough to catch a glimpse of a deer family, as they make their daily commute through the woodland.

Set in the picturesque village of Lee, with the beach within strolling distance and Ilfracombe and Woolacombe close by, there are plenty of sights to see and places to explore. There is also an abundance of dog friendly beaches and scenic walks.

Nestled in the canopy of mature beech trees, you can enjoy the views and complete seclusion in the bespoke, handcrafted treehouse. The furnishings and decor are stunning and the interior was designed by a team of stylists.

Staying in the warm and cosy treehouse was the perfect relaxing break. There is a giant bathroom, with a walk-in shower and a large, open-plan living space, with a wood burner and a comfy sofa and chair, where you can relax with the many inspiring books around the place.

There is a lovely, homely kitchen area, with everything you could need. It's extremely well thought-out and brilliantly stylish. The dogs especially loved sleeping by the wood burner, after a walk at the local beach. *(continued...)*

FACT FILE

Location: Crowness, Lee, Ilfracombe, Devon EX34 8LN

Website: ravendere.co.uk

Contact: 07769 186953

Type of accommodation: Treehouse

Number of bedrooms: 1

Number of dogs accepted: 2 medium size

Enclosed garden: No

Local interest: Woodland walks from the door, beach, Ilfracombe, Woolacombe

Best eats: The Grampus Inn at Lee Bay

Upstairs, there is the bedroom, where the luxurious king-size bed is fitted with Egyptian cotton bed linen. It's very impressive, with a beautiful interior and wallpaper, plus lovely views out to the surrounding beech trees from all sides. It was very soothing to hear only the sound of the wind in the trees and the occasional hoot of a nearby owl.

Outside, there is a wood-fired pizza oven, a gas barbecue and outdoor leather lounge chairs, in a seating and eating area. Although it was a bit cold and rainy when we went, I can imagine lovely, long summer evenings on the terrace. Still, we very much enjoyed the views and the sounds of nature that surrounded us.

You could spend all day here and not go anywhere else. There are plenty of walks to enjoy, straight from the treehouse and it's surrounded by paths around the local woods. It's also about a 5-minute drive to the local beach which, I would imagine, never really gets that busy.

When you were younger, you may have built your own treehouse in your back garden. This is above and beyond what you could ever have imagined that to be. I could live here - I should be so lucky!

SHELTER SHED, LULWORTH COVE, DORSET

By Jude Stephenson

Perched high on the hill above the iconic rock arch of Durdle Door, a holiday cottage on the Lulworth Estate is perfectly placed for enjoying everything this inspirational location has to offer.

Six architect-designed and ecologically built cottages occupy what was once a group of working period farm buildings and each has its own character. All guests can enjoy exclusive use of the fitness and recreation barn, the heated outdoor swimming pool (open in the summer) and the miles of stunning Dorset countryside on the doorstep.

We stayed in the Shelter Shed, a beautifully-styled cottage which is ideal for 2. With its spacious open-plan living area and full-length glazed windows and doors onto the courtyard, it is light and welcoming. The bedroom shares the same fully-glazed aspect over the courtyard. Outdoors, there is a sitting area, which captures the late afternoon and early evening sunshine.

The minute we stepped into the Shelter Shed, we felt at home. Molly absolutely loved her early morning walks, either through the woods to Durdle Door or just across fields, all straight from the door.

The Lulworth Estate incorporates 5 miles of World Heritage Jurassic Coast, including the world-famous Durdle Door and Lulworth Cove. The estate is also home to Lulworth Castle and Park and an outdoor adventure centre. Amazing pubs, walks, sites and places to visit - it's impossible to list all the opportunities that await.

I highly recommend this fabulous part of the world and Lulworth Cove Holiday Cottages. We will be back!

FACT FILE

Location: The Lulworth Estate, East Lulworth, Wareham, Dorset, BH20 5QS
Website: lulworth.com
Contact: 01929 400888
Type of accommodation: Cottage
Number of bedrooms: 1
Number of dogs accepted: 2
Enclosed garden: Enclosed communal courtyard
Local interest: Walks from the door, The Jurassic Coast, Durdle Door, Lulworth Cove, Lulworth Castle (grounds only), Thorncombe Woods at Hardy's Cottage
Best eats: The Lulworth Cove Inn

SOUTH SANDS HOTEL, SALCOMBE, DEVON

By David Edwards

Ideally located on the stunning south Devon coast, within easy reach of many local attractions, South Sands Hotel offers stylish accommodation, fine dining and great hospitality.

Where South Sands Hotel excels is in the friendly and helpful nature of its staff and the superb quality of its meals. We could have eaten out more but found that, having enjoyed every one of our meals at South Sands, we couldn't justify eating anywhere else. Dogs are welcome in the bar, so we could have eaten there with Orinoco, but left him asleep in his crate in the room during breakfast and dinner.

Salcombe, which is just over a mile away, can be easily reached by walking along the coast road but we used the South Sands Sea Tractor, which was great fun - like something out of a Famous Five adventure. It doesn't operate all year round and is weather dependent.

We found most of the shops welcomed dogs and a large percentage tempted them with treats. The Lifeboat Museum admits small dogs on leads, if it isn't crowded. A ferry ride takes you to the beaches of East Portlemouth.

Devon makes a wonderful holiday destination, with attractions that suit those of all tastes - romantic sandy coves, windswept moorland paths, picturesque English villages, bracing seafront promenades and quaint old harbours.

We really enjoyed our holiday in Salcombe and, thanking Antoine wholeheartedly as we left reception, said how sad we were to be leaving because the hospitality had been amazing.

FACT FILE

Location: Bolt Head, Salcombe, Devon, TQ8 8LL
Website: southsands.com
Contact: 01548 845900
Type of accommodation: Hotel
Number of bedrooms: 22, plus 5 beach suites
Number of dogs accepted: 2 in smaller rooms, 3 in larger rooms
Enclosed garden: No
Local interest: Lifeboat Museum, South Sands Sea Tractor, Slapton Sands, Blackpool Sands, Dartmouth, Burgh Island, Greenway, Torquay, Brixham
Best eats: South Sands Hotel, The Venus Café at Blackpool Sands, Leaf & Bean at Dartmouth

THE ARUNDELL ARMS HOTEL, LIFTON, DEVON

By Helen Millbank

A stone's throw from the Dartmoor National Park and a short drive from the Cornish coast, the upmarket Arundell Arms Hotel takes a relaxed approach to its canine guests.

The Arundell Arms Hotel in the sleepy Devon village of Lifton is so smart, it feels strange to be wandering around, dog in tow. Well behaved she may be but our Labrador, Millie, has a loud, boisterous air about her that belies her 11 years. Would she really be welcome in the sumptuous rooms at The Arundell Arms, we wondered? We soon found the answer to be yes, as we were ushered inside our plush hotel room, complete with dog bed, bowl and a treat for Millie.

My husband, John, and I had arrived, along with our daughter, Georgie, to be met with a refreshing lack of 'don't let your dog on the bed/chairs/carpet' style notices, although you are, of course, urged to use your common sense. And, despite her raucous entrance, Millie was soon lounging on her new bed, probably wondering what had prompted the sudden upgrade in her sleeping arrangements.

The Arundell Arms is a family-run hotel, situated on the Devon/Cornwall border, where it is well placed for exploring both dog-walk-rich counties. The village is a stone's throw away from the Dartmoor National Park, and a half-hour drive away from either the north or south Cornish coast.

Millie can personally recommend Bude - a dog friendly oasis for beach-loving canines, as the majority of its beaches allow dogs all year round. She spent our first full day there, slipping on rocks, trying to drink the *(continued...)*

FACT FILE

Location: Lifton, Devon, PL16 0AA

Website: thearundell.com

Contact: 01566 784666

Type of accommodation: Hotel

Number of bedrooms: 21 (8 dog-friendly)

Number of dogs accepted: 2 in rooms, indoor kennel space also available for 4 dogs

Enclosed garden: No

Local interest: Dartmoor National Park, dog friendly beaches, coast walks, Bude, River Lyd

Best eats: The Arundell Arms Hotel

sea water, rocketing around the beach with a pack of spaniels and generally having the time of her life, while Georgie hunted around in rock pools for crabs. It's a dog and child friendly spot that has all the amenities of a small town on its doorstep. What more could a young child and a pasty-loving Labrador want?

Back at the hotel, we left Millie to sleep off her excesses, while we sampled the bar food (cheaper than the main restaurant, although still top quality). The hotel has a 2 AA Rosette restaurant, and you only have to taste the poached eggs at breakfast to see why.

On day two, we decided to leave the car and explore locally. Footpaths that follow the River Lyd allowed us to explore as far as energy levels permitted. Breakfast in the hotel is so ample, you'll be fuelled for miles, and it's great to abandon the car for a few hours.

Sadly, our stay was too short (just 2 nights) and our dog walks curtailed slightly by the fact we had a young child to entertain (which meant beach days rather than epic hikes), but it left us wanting more. More of the hotel, and more of the local countryside.

Come if you want to holiday in style, dog by your side, in a spot that's brimming with potential dog walks. Cheap it isn't, but luxury's worth paying for. That's Millie's new motto, anyway!

BLUE HILLS TOURING PARK, ST AGNES, CORNWALL

By Michelle Holden

Enjoying picturesque views along Cornwall's rugged coast, Blue Hills is a peaceful campsite which has won an award for its dog friendliness.

We've always wanted a camper van and, after saving up, we finally bought one and thought we'd head south in it from our home in Lancashire. Since camping was a completely new experience, it was important the site was just right, with somewhere our Lancashire Heeler, Bailiie, could run and, even more importantly, decent facilities. After learning Blue Hills was voted the UK's most dog friendly caravanning and campsite in the annual DogFriendly awards, we made our decision and it's one we've never regretted. The campsite is at Trevellas, which is within easy walking distance of St Agnes and lies on a route we'd explored several times already.

We arrived on a lovely Sunday afternoon and chose a quiet pitch in the corner of the field, adjacent to the dog-walking field. Bailiie quickly made friends with Harley, the campsite dog.

The state of the campsite's facilities is incredibly important and we couldn't fault those, in any way. Ginny and Martin are the friendliest of hosts and extremely knowledgeable about this part of the country.

It was great meeting holidaymakers with similar interests and, although the site was increasingly busy, we never felt cramped because the pitches are so generous in size. There are loads of dog friendly pubs nearby and we visited a number of attractions locally, but didn't use our van, walking everywhere instead.

We had such a lovely time that we immediately planned our next visit.

FACT FILE

Location: Cross Coombe, Trevellas, St Agnes, Cornwall, TR5 0XP
Website: bluehillscamping.co.uk
Contact: 01872 552 999
Type of accommodation: Campsite
Number of dogs accepted: 2 per pitch
Enclosed garden: Dog-walking field
Local interest: Coast walks, beaches, St Agnes, Cornish Mining World Heritage Site
Best eats: The Driftwood Spars at Trevaunance Cove, The Watering Hole on Perranporth Beach

THE MANOR HOUSE HOTEL, MORETON-IN-MARSH, GLOUCESTERSHIRE

By Duncan Whitney Groom

Perfectly placed for exploring the Cotswolds, there are 35 individually-designed rooms in this magnificent 16th century manor house, offering superb hospitality and fine dining.

The Manor House Hotel holds a very special place in our hearts, as it was where we were married. We return whenever we can and, with our wedding anniversary fast-approaching, we couldn't think of anywhere we'd rather celebrate.

Set in a picturesque Cotswold valley, the countryside around it is wonderful and we've always had superb service from the staff, who've become friends over the years.

We most often stay in Room 11, which overlooks the High Street. There's a king-size bed and a spacious ensuite bathroom. If you enjoy more privacy, you can also stay in Apple Tree Cottage, which is located in a secluded corner of the grounds. We walked Delphine in the walled gardens, then relaxed beside a roaring fire - lovely!

The hotel, like all those in the Cotswold Inns group, is extremely dog friendly and we've found that Delphine is welcome in our bedroom, the library and the lounge. She has never suffered from separation anxiety, so we leave her in the bedroom, with the television on in the background, when we eat.

A traditional market town, Moreton-in-Marsh is popular with shoppers. The High Street is lined with elegant buildings, many dating from the 17th century.

There are so many walking routes you can enjoy that I would heartily recommend the Cotswolds, if you fancy a treat.

FACT FILE

Location: High Street, Moreton-in-Marsh, Gloucs, GL56 0LJ

Website: cotswold-inns-hotels.co.uk/the-manor-house-hotel/

Contact: 01608 605501

Type of accommodation: Hotel

Number of bedrooms: 35 (29 dog friendly)

Number of dogs accepted: 2

Enclosed garden: No

Local interest: Batsford Arboretum, Chastleton House (dogs in fields only)

Best eats: The Manor House Hotel, The Sheep at Stow-on-the-Wold, The Black Bear, The Inn on the Marsh, The Swan Inn, The Bell Inn, The Redesdale Arms Hotel and Tilly's Tea House at Moreton-in-Marsh

EAST CLIFF HOTEL, BOURNEMOUTH, DORSET

By Jonelle Salter

Overlooking the beach, the distinctive East Cliff Hotel is close to many tourist attractions and is only a 10-minute walk from Bournemouth town centre.

Situated right on the seafront, The East Cliff Hotel enjoys a spectacular location. The beach could hardly be any closer, as there's only a road between them.

Our room overlooked the English Channel and we could clearly see the beautiful beach. Our dog, Gaia, was extremely excited as her welcome pack included a bouncy ball, a packet of doggy chocolate, a mat, a bowl, some mineral water and a towel.

Nestling beneath a magnificent line of cliffs, the beach boasts miles of golden sand and enjoys panoramic views of the English Channel, the Isle of Wight and the Purbecks.

There's a wide range of restaurants in Bournemouth but we had already been tempted by the hotel's brasserie, which was stylish, with modern art and a flickering fire. We could have eaten in the bar, where Gaia could join us but, as she was tired after playing on the beach, we thought we'd let

her sleep, and did the same in the morning, whilst we had our breakfast.

There's a novel transport system in Bournemouth. Land trains run along the beach between Alum Chine, Bournemouth Pier and Boscombe Pier and another route links with Boscombe Precinct and Boscombe Chine Gardens. It was very enjoyable and Gaia travelled free of charge. There are stops along the route, with one just a short distance from the hotel itself.

Although we only stayed one night, we had a lovely time and would definitely visit again.

FACT FILE

Location: East Overcliff Drive, Bournemouth, BH1 3AN
Website: bestwestern.co.uk
Contact: 03330 035441
Type of accommodation: Hotel
Number of bedrooms: 67
Number of dogs accepted: 2
Enclosed garden: No
Local interest: Restriction-free beaches at Alum Chine, Middle Chine and Fisherman's Chine, Hengistbury Head, the Aviary on Pine Walk in Lower Gardens
Best eats: The Brasserie at East Cliff Hotel

HELL BAY HOTEL, BRYHER, ISLES OF SCILLY

By Sarah Selway

On the tiny island of Bryher, Hell Bay Hotel is the highest rated hotel and restaurant on the Isles of Scilly, offering luxurious accommodation, overlooking the ocean or gardens.

The Isles of Scilly have long been on my bucket list. They've been described as the Caribbean of the British Isles and it's easy to see why, with pictures of crystal clear water, pure white sand and lush planting.

Bryher, the smallest of the inhabited islands, has a population of about 100 people. You can hop between the islands

FACT FILE

Location: Hell Bay, Bryher, Isles of Scilly, TR23 0PR
Website: hellbay.co.uk
Contact: 01720 422947
Type of accommodation: Hotel
Number of bedrooms: 25 Suites
Number of dogs accepted: 2
Enclosed garden: No
Local interest: Sandy beaches, virtually traffic-free island walks, island-hopping
Best eats: Hell Bay Hotel

quite easily, using one of the tripper boat services. These run regularly but the times change, depending on the tides.

After landing, we were collected by the hotel car, one of only 5 I saw on the island. There's a saying that location is everything and that's where Hell Bay Hotel wins hands down. Facing due west, with the Atlantic throwing everything it can at you, it's unbelievably dramatic and you can understand how Hell Bay got its name.

We stayed in a studio suite with views across the lawn and, through the subtropical planting, of the garden, to the sea. It was spacious, airy and decorated in light seaside colours. Our king-size bed was wonderful and Timmy hadn't been neglected either, as we found one in the corner for him, with blankets and bowls. I wouldn't say our room was luxurious, rather that it was charming and homely, which is just what you want on a dog friendly holiday. The highlight of our visit was the private terrace where, on day 3, we finally basked in the sunshine, using the loungers provided.

Although the Isles of Scilly are one of the warmest places in the UK during the

62

winter, and also one of the sunniest, with an average of 7 hours per day in summer, April proved as changeable as ever. Despite the weather, we had the most amazing time exploring the island. Timmy was in his element, especially with so many wonderful beaches within easy reach. The landscape resembles that of Cape Cornwall - quite wild in places, with swathes of colourful heath and dramatic rocky outcrops.

The pace of life is slow, with travel dictated by the weather and tides. The community is friendly and its isolated position and lack of traffic are liberating, making it perfect if you have children or dogs. There aren't any of the organised activities, theme park attractions or seaside amusement arcades you get elsewhere - not the kind of thing I would ever miss anyway.

The sun shone on our last day but, even though it left its appearance rather late, I felt completely invigorated after our stay. I realise our holiday cost the same as a package deal in the Canaries but there really is no comparison, especially as Timmy was with us the whole time, and I would visit regularly if I could - the food alone made it worth the journey.

BOUNTY COTTAGE, LONGBOROUGH, GLOUCESTERSHIRE

By Jane Travis

Midway between Moreton-in-Marsh and Stow-on-the-Wold, Bounty Cottage makes an excellent base for exploring the Cotswolds.

Bounty Cottage is surprisingly spacious inside. There's a large glass extension at the rear and light floods in through the roof, windows and French doors, creating a wonderfully bright, open-plan kitchen which, with a stylish central island, sofa and chairs, was where we relaxed in the evening. And it isn't lacking in mod cons because there are wall-mounted flat screen TVs in the kitchen and the lounge. The wood burner creates a cosy atmosphere

and having a dining area and playroom made it extra special. The icing on the cake was (literally) the incredibly generous hamper that we found when we arrived.

There are 4 bedrooms, all with king-size beds. There are 3 bathrooms upstairs and a downstairs WC. It was so peaceful that we heard little but the sound of the church bells chiming.

Longborough is surrounded by wonderful walking country but there are plenty of other attractions nearby. The picturesque village of Stow-on-the-Wold is just a few miles away, as is Moreton-in-Marsh. The landscape isn't particularly challenging, so it suits walkers of all abilities and Nelson, my 10-year-old working Collie x Labrador, loved every minute.

We may have spent several days in the Cotswolds but we barely scratched the surface. However, what I enjoyed most was walking through the countryside with my family, and Nelson ambling happily at my side. That's the best way of seeing the Cotswolds. I realise it isn't the cheapest holiday destination but it's so picturesque and dog friendly that I don't regret a thing.

FACT FILE

Location: Church Street, Longborough, Moreton-in-Marsh, Gloucestershire

Website: lastminute-cottages.co.uk

Contact: 02036 370812

Type of accommodation: Cottage

Number of bedrooms: 4 (sleeps 7)

Number of dogs accepted: 2

Enclosed garden: Yes

Local interest: Batsford Arboretum, Stow-on-the-Wold, Moreton-in-Marsh, Heart of England Way, Evenlode Valley

Best eats: The Coach & Horses Inn at Longborough

THE RED LION, OAKFORD, DEVON

By Deb Bridges

Nestled in a quiet agricultural area, close to the border with Somerset, the small village of Oakford is perfectly placed for visiting the many attractions to be found in this part of Devon.

My first visit to the family-owned and run Red Lion was of the passing through variety. I'd been walking in the area and arrived at the pub with a muddy dog and a desperate need of caffeine. Despite being within a whisker of lunchtime closing, I was warmly welcomed and suitably revived!

Refurbishment hasn't spoiled the cosy, traditional pub ambience and it's clearly popular with locals. There are log-burning stoves in both the bar and the dining area and the floor is laminate throughout, so Ula's mud quota was of no consequence.

There are 4 bedrooms and a family suite on the first floor and all have well-equipped, ensuite bathrooms. With a window overlooking the lane, Beech is a bright, airy room with a king-size bed and everything you might need for a comfortable stay, including tea and coffee-making facilities and a TV. Dogs are welcome in all the rooms and can accompany their owners in the bar or the dining area for all meals.

Sheets detailing local walks can be borrowed from a folder in the bar. For the adventurous-spirited, a 10-minute drive will take you to the Exmoor National Park and anyone walking The Two Moors Way can take advantage of the pub's pick-up and drop-off service for backpackers. The historic town of Bampton is only a few miles away and Tiverton, where there are lovely walks beside the canal, is also nearby. There are 2 National Trust properties within easy reach, Knightshayes and Killerton, both of which offer fine walking opportunities in their extensive parkland and woods.

FACT FILE

Location: Rookery Hill, Oakford, Tiverton, EX16 9ES

Website: redlionoakford.co.uk

Contact: 01398 351569

Type of accommodation: Bed and breakfast

Number of bedrooms: 5

Number of dogs accepted: 2 (1 in smallest room)

Enclosed garden: No

Local interest: Walks from the door, Exmoor National Park, North Devon beaches, Tiverton, Tiverton Canal, grounds of Knightshayes and Killerton National Trust properties

Best eats: The Red Lion, The Swans Neck Café at Halberton, cafés at Knightshayes and Killerton

HARRIS COTTAGE, NEWQUAY, CORNWALL

By Anne Dealtry

Near Newquay in Cornwall, Harris Cottage is a Duchy of Cornwall 5-star holiday property, which is close to the many beaches and attractions the area has to offer.

Harris Cottage was compact, yet stylish, with a reasonably-sized lounge and bedroom and a tiny kitchen. Despite its size, the kitchen had everything you'd expect and felt extremely homely, with white walls, chrome fittings and polished wood surfaces.

The adjoining property is also dog friendly and there's a secure garden behind each, with a table, chairs and barbecue, and both enjoy spectacular views of the surrounding countryside. The cottages are situated on a country lane but there's a main road within walking distance, from which you can catch a train or a bus into Newquay.

Newquay was quaint in places and the harbour is probably one of the most attractive parts. We were there during the Fish Festival in early September, so it was a hive of activity. The most popular beach is Fistral Beach, which attracts hundreds of surfers.

One of the highlights of our holiday was Watergate Bay, which is just a few minutes east of Newquay. Walking along the golden sand, we made the most of the sunshine. It's enormous, especially at low tide, and dog friendly all year round.

The Heritage Coast around St Agnes is amazing but dogs are prohibited from Chapel Porth during the summer. However, there's a beach café where you can sit and enjoy the views, whilst sampling one of its legendary 'hedgehog' ice creams.

FACT FILE

Location: Newquay, Cornwall, TR8 4BP

Website: duchyofcornwallholidaycottages.co.uk

Contact: 01579 346473

Type of accommodation: Cottage

Number of bedrooms: 1 (sleeps 2)

Number of dogs accepted: 2

Enclosed garden: Yes

Local interest: Newquay, dog friendly beaches, Bodmin & Wenford Railway, King Edward Mine Museum, Pencarrow House, Camel Trail, Sealife Safari boat trips

Best eats: The Cornish Crepe Company and takeaway from Stein's Fish & Chips at Newquay, Blue Tomato Café at Rock, Beach Hut Café at Watergate Bay, Chapel Porth Beach Café (for 'hedgehog' ice cream)

THE BEDFORD HOTEL, SIDMOUTH, DEVON

By Hilary Keens

Situated right on the seafront, The Bedford Hotel makes a good base from which to explore the town and adjacent sections of Jurassic coastline, or make a short hop across the border into neighbouring Dorset.

Planning a short holiday with Tess, I chose The Bedford Hotel in Sidmouth. The reviews were extremely complimentary and it was obviously dog friendly. I was particularly encouraged by the sound of the 'shed' - a designated doggy lounge off reception. And, location-wise, it was ideal because it's right on the seafront.

There are 3 types of room - premier sea view with balcony, superior sea view and inland-facing. The rooms are modern, tastefully decorated and boast ensuite facilities. Many enjoy panoramic views across Lyme Bay. I made maximum use of the lounge, as it was lovely being able to relax completely and have breakfast, dinner or even afternoon tea there, with Tess beside me. There aren't many restrictions at all because you can leave your dog in your room, if you'd rather eat in the dining room or trendy bar.

Sidmouth is charming. There's a wide variety of independent boutiques, shops and galleries and I found it surprisingly dog friendly, with Tess made welcome in several establishments. The beach is mainly pebbles but the western end, Jacob's Ladder Beach, is much sandier - dogs are prohibited from all but the eastern end between Easter and the end of September.

The Byes Riverside Park makes a wonderful walking destination and there are several paths through the park. One of the most iconic sights is The Clock Tower Café, which is housed in a converted 17th-century lime kiln within Connaught Gardens.

FACT FILE

Location: The Esplanade, Sidmouth, EX10 8NR
Website: bedfordhotelsidmouth.co.uk
Contact: 01395 513047
Type of accommodation: Hotel
Number of bedrooms: 40
Number of dogs accepted: 2
Enclosed garden: No
Local interest: The Byes Riverside Park, South West Coast Path, Salcombe Hill, The Donkey Sanctuary, Lyme Regis
Best eats: The Blue Ball Inn at Sidford, The Chattery, Selley's Coffee Shop, The Swan Inn, The Black Horse and Dukes Inn at Sidmouth, The Clock Tower Café in Connaught Gardens

YEOMADON FARM, HOLSWORTHY, DEVON

By Trevor Thomas

Set within 130 acres of organic farmland, 4 dog friendly holiday cottages of varying sizes offer comfortable holiday accommodation in a peaceful location, where guests are free to explore the lakes and 4-acre woodland and enjoy the beautiful views and wildlife.

The Cottage was converted from a barn in the early 90s and has subsequently been renovated. Set within a large garden, it's a detached property and enjoys picturesque views across the surrounding countryside. Inside, the living space comprises a lounge, dining area and contemporary kitchen, with electric oven, microwave, fridge, washing machine and dishwasher. Upstairs, there's a stylish master bedroom, with a double bed, and a further bedroom with bunk beds.

One of the main highlights is being able to walk your dog so easily - pathways lead around the farm's 130 acres of gently undulating grassland, lakes and woods. The nearest village, Holsworthy, is just 3 miles away. It has several shops, including a supermarket, a bank and a post office and a choice of pubs, restaurants and cafés.

Cornwall's north coast is an 8-mile drive away, with Bude the most popular resort. Also worth investigating is Bude Canal. One of the most unusual canals in the country, it comprises a mini network of waterways on the border of Cornwall and Devon. The canal has become a popular walking route and the 5-mile section between Burmsdon Bridge and Lake Tamar is worthy of investigation, as is the branch that leads across the aqueduct and the wildlife-rich marshes.

We've visited Yeomadon Farm many times and have found that its peaceful grounds and the proximity of such lovely beaches and countryside, mean we rarely venture further afield.

FACT FILE

Location: Yeomadon, Holsworthy, Devon, EX22 6SH

Website: yeomadon.com

Contact: 01409 253378

Type of accommodation: Cottage

Number of bedrooms: 2 (sleeps 4)

Number of dogs accepted: 2

Enclosed garden: Yes

Local interest: Dog friendly beaches, Bude, Bude Canal, coast walks, Dartmoor, Bodmin, Port Isaac, Boscastle, Padstow, Tintagel Castle and the National Trust properties of Carnewas, Llanhydrock and Bedruthan Steps

Best eats: Crooklets Inn at Bude

WALES

Anglesey

Bangor

TWYLL Y CAE - P.70

Porthmadog

SNOWDONIA
NATIONAL PARK

DOGS LOVE
HOLIDAYS - P.71

GWESTY'R MARINE
HOTEL - P.75

ENGLAND

Aberystwyth

STALLION
VALLEY - P.74

BRECON RETREAT -
P.78

THE
PIGGERY -
P.79

MBROKESHIRE COAST
NATIONAL PARK

. David's

THREE RIVERS
HOTEL - P.81

CALON Y
FFERI - P.82

BRECON BEACONS
NATIONAL PARK

HILL CREST
HUT - P.76

TINTERN ABBEY
COTTAGE - P.72

STOCKWOOD
COTTAGE - P.80

THE CAREW
INN - P.73

Swansea

Newport

WATERWYNCH
HOUSE - P.77

Cardiff

TWYLL Y CAE, CRICCIETH, WALES

By Kathryn Austin

A charming, traditional Welsh cottage, Twyll y Cae, meaning 'hollow in the fields', is situated in the village of Pentrefelin, between Porthmadog and the seaside town of Criccieth.

We arrived for a long weekend on a wet afternoon in early February. As we were pulling onto the drive, the sun came out, bathing the cottage in wintry, golden light and making it look very inviting.

The cottage is spacious and all on one level, with a traditional slate floor throughout - great for muddy paws! We appreciated some of the extra details that provide a sense of place, like the choice of Portmeirion crockery, local maps, books and photographs. The owners had also kindly left fresh flowers and a basket of goodies, and we particularly enjoyed the special treats left for our 2 beloved schnoodles, Winnie and George.

If you're interested in history, there's lots to discover directly from Twll y Cae. A number of footpaths and 2 ancient churches are both within a mile or so of the property. There are also documented Roman remains nearby and a standing stone with an interesting story attached. The cottage and gardens themselves also have a fascinating past, with a connection to the famous Italianate, fantasy village of Portmeirion (although sadly Portmeirion itself is not dog friendly, so struck off our itinerary).

We thoroughly enjoyed a wonderful break in Twll y Cae, a lovely cottage based in a fabulous dog friendly location.

FACT FILE

Location: Twll y Cae, Pentrefelin, Criccieth, LL52 0PU
Website: twll-y-cae.com
Contact: 07761 385294
Type of accommodation: Cottage
Number of bedrooms: 3 (sleeps 5)
Number of dogs accepted: 2
Enclosed garden: Yes
Local interest: Snowdonia National Park, Bodnant Gardens (dogs welcome every day October to end March and on special dog days - Fridays, Saturdays and Sundays - from April to end September), Coed y Brenin Visitor Centre and Café, Criccieth Castle, Ffestiniog Railway, Harlech Castle (grounds only), Parc Glynllifon, Zip World Penrhyn Quarry, Llyn Peninsular
Best eats: Dylan's at Criccieth, Golden Fleece at Porthmadog, Kin & Co at Abersoch, Tir A Mo at Criccieth, Ty Coch at Porthdinllaen.

DOGS LOVE HOLIDAYS, HAFREN FOREST, WALES

By Jo Southway

Dogs Love Holidays is the ultimate destination for dogs and their owners - a holiday cottage designed for dogs first and their humans second.

Situated in the Hafren Forest, Mid Wales, Dogs Love Holidays is advertised as 'the perfect sanctuary for all dogs to come and holiday but, most especially, those dogs that can find certain aspects of their world overwhelming and stressful', which made it an obvious choice as a dog friendly holiday destination.

Outside the cottage, there are multiple gates for security and 6 foot fencing for the dog garden. Your dog cannot put a paw wrong. It doesn't matter if they are reactive to other dogs or people, chase wildlife or even decide to jump in the pond. The whole location is designed for your dog to get enjoyment and express their natural behaviours, without any worries about needing to conform, for fear of others judging. And there is a secure paddock for dogs that don't often get to run off-lead.

Inside, there are 2 good-sized bedrooms, an open-plan kitchen/living area and 2 bathrooms, plus a dog room, where they can chill out and dry off after their adventures. When it comes to equipment for your dogs, they have thought of everything - beds, bowls, enrichment, towels, a whole outside cabin of doggy delights and even more drawers full inside.

From the cottage, the walking opportunities are endless. If you're looking for mountains, forest or water, you can have it all. Access into the forest is direct from your own gate and, if you avoid the main trails, you can walk for miles and not see a soul.

FACT FILE

Location: Staylittle Llanbrynmair, Powys, SY19 7DB

Website: dogsloveholidays.com

Contact: 01686 430615

Type of accommodation: Cottage

Number of bedrooms: 2 (sleeps 4)

Number of dogs accepted: Multiple

Enclosed garden: Yes

Local interest: Walks from the door, Clywedog Reservoir and Dam, Clywedog Gorge Trail, River Severn

Best eats: Pwdin at the Old Mill, Llanidloes, Caffi Clywedog

TINTERN ABBEY COTTAGE, WYE VALLEY, MONMOUTHSHIRE

By Claire Thomas

Enjoying a peaceful setting with a stunning view of the Abbey, Tintern Abbey Cottage offers comfortable accommodation with plenty of personal touches to make human and canine guests feel at home.

Before even arriving at Tintern Abbey Cottage, Buster and I had already been given some really good insights into the local area. This is something which is often useful when planning adventures with your furry family members, especially when it's an unexplored area. Owners Fiona and Malcolm are clearly very knowledgeable and passionate about providing a great stay for all.

FACT FILE

Location: Chapel Hill, Tintern, Monmouthshire, NP16 6SF
Website: monmouthshirecottages.co.uk
Contact: 01600 860341
Type of accommodation: Cottage
Number of bedrooms: 3 (sleeps 6)
Number of dogs accepted: 2
Enclosed garden: Yes
Local interest: Tintern Abbey, Fedw Woods
Best eats: The Wild Hare and Anchor Inn at Tintern

On arriving, Buster opted for doing a quick perimeter check and, once you've shut the gates, the whole of the back garden is secure for dogs. The cottage looks directly towards the Abbey, so you're spoilt for views.

We headed in. The cottage is beautifully laid out, with a relaxed country style. It was clean, tidy and smelt lovely. Everything felt warm and inviting and the added personal touches for Buster really made it feel special.

All the floors are slate and sofas leather, so super-easy to keep clean. There's a wood burner in the lounge area, which you can use on those chillier evenings. All the bedrooms are lovely, with one being downstairs.

The cottage is fully equipped with all you could possibly think of needing, should you wish to cook. But, other than making some eggs for breakfasts and enjoying lots of tea and coffee, I opted for eating out both nights during our stay.

The views and location are simply stunning and Tintern Abbey Cottage reflects the area's feeling of calm and peace.

THE CAREW INN, CAREW, PEMBROKESHIRE

By Jonathan O'Shea

For those who like a quiet holiday with plenty of beaches and castles, an ensuite room in the cottage at The Carew Inn could be just the thing - with the added advantage of a pub right next door.

On arrival at The Carew Inn, you are immediately taken aback by the beauty of the surrounding area. It is a quaint old pub, with a cottage attached and a castle not 400 yds from the door.

My dog friendly room featured a king-size bed and a comfy ensuite. It was the only dog friendly room in the cottage, which put our minds at ease, as Loki can be very anxious around other dogs.

The area at the front of the cottage and vast open space in front of the castle meant we were not at a loss when the time came for Loki to venture outside. It is a quiet location, the most noise being bicycles peddling past or Loki shouting as someone walked their dog anywhere near our room!

Entry to the castle is relatively inexpensive and it is also dog friendly. Next to the castle is a lovely walk that is very suitable for any size of dog.

We spent the majority of our time exploring all the natural beauty of the area. Castles are in abundance and there are beaches left, right and centre. A favourite for us had to be Freshwater West, a beach that is dog friendly all year round.

It is easy to fall in love with this gorgeous part of the world. With so many undiscovered walks and locations dotted around, we were left desperate to stay for one more night.

FACT FILE

Location: Carew, Nr Tenby, Pembrokeshire, SA70 8SL

Website: carewinn.co.uk

Contact: 01646 651267

Type of accommodation: Bed and breakfast

Number of bedrooms: 3 (only one room is dog friendly)

Number of dogs accepted: 1

Enclosed garden: No

Local interest: Pembroke and Tenby towns, Carew Castle & Tidal Mill, Pembroke Castle, Manorbier Castle, Freshwater West Beach

Best eats: Lots of dog friendly places in Pembroke

STALLION VALLEY, CEREDIGION, WALES

By Hannah Istead

Surrounded by fields and streams, without a road in sight, Stallion Valley offers a safe and quiet environment, where dogs can have fun and people can relax.

At the start of November, we headed to west Wales with our 2 larger-than-life chocolate Labradors, Bernie and Tilly, for a stay at Stallion Valley, a beautiful cottage surrounded by rolling Welsh hills.

The accommodation was easy to find and we parked right outside, which is brilliant when you have a car full of things - who knew dogs packed so much!

Situated on just over 3 acres of land,'The Byre' is a rustic, 2-bedroom cottage with no stairs. It was spotlessly clean and everything is wipeable, so we didn't spend the whole time worrying about our dogs making a mess.

Owners, Mick and Julie, have really thought about all of the dog friendly features which Bernie and Tilly loved, especially the heated stone floors. We also felt safe to let the dogs out into the fully-enclosed garden.

After we arrived we went for a short walk at the fenced-off lake, which was a great addition for us, with 2 dogs that love to swim and the fences meant we could have them both off-lead. Back at the house, there is a heated dog shower and towels to dry the dogs off.

There are plenty of walks and stunning beaches nearby and it would be easy to fill a whole week with activities.

The Byre at Stallion Valley is great for switching off from the world and relaxing with your dogs and we would definitely visit again in the summer.

FACT FILE

Location: Cwm March Farmhouse Cottages, Llandysul, Ceredigion, SA44 4LR
Website: stallionvalley.com
Contact: 01559 363444
Type of accommodation: Cottage
Number of bedrooms: 2 (sleeps 4)
Number of dogs accepted: Any
Enclosed garden: Yes
Local interest: Walks from the door, dog friendly beaches, Aberystwyth Cliff Railway, Cardigan Island Coastal Farm Park, Castell Henllys Iron Age Village
Best eats: The Gwarcefel Arms, The Daffodil Inn and The Lunch Box at Llandysul

GWESTY'R MARINE HOTEL & SPA, ABERYSTWYTH, WALES

By Jonathan O'Shea

Away from the hustle and bustle of the town, beautiful sunsets over Cardigan Bay can be enjoyed from the family-run Gwesty'r Marine Hotel, conveniently located on Aberystwyth's picturesque promenade.

Arriving at the Gwesty'r Marine Hotel in Aberystwyth, we headed up to our dog friendly room. The gorgeous room-cum-apartment was much larger than I'd imagined, with an unbelievable view out to sea. It was filled with 3 large beds, a kitchen area, very large screen TV and an immaculate bath/shower. There were no specific enclosed areas for us to take our dog, Loki, but, as we were so close to the beach and with large stretches of grass either side of the hotel, there were places we could head when the need arose.

We didn't try out the dining facilities for an evening meal but we visited for breakfast and were led to the bar area, where we could all sit together. A buffet-style breakfast was provided, and a sneaky sausage or two may have fallen Loki's way!

Aberystwyth is a lovely, quiet town with much in the area to see and do. Although welcoming for dogs, I would struggle to say there were lots of specific dog friendly locations and, in the winter, we may have found ourselves slightly lacking. Although lovely, the sea breeze can really make itself known and sitting outside would be a completely different experience!

We were welcomed with our dog at the hotel, but, as with any holiday, it is what you do while there. Aberystwyth, in its tiny bubble, has coastlines you will spend hours losing yourself in, quaint cafés, views for miles and everything you could hope for and more.

FACT FILE

Location: Marine Terrace, Aberystwyth, Ceredigion, SY23 2DA
Website: gwestymarinehotel.co.uk
Contact: 01970 612444
Type of accommodation: Hotel
Number of bedrooms: 60
Number of dogs accepted: Depending on size of room - up to 3
Enclosed garden: No
Local interest: Waterfalls at Devil's Bridge, Aberystwyth town, Aberystwyth Castle, Ynyslas Beach (dogs on leads permitted)
Best eats: Woodlands Tea Rooms and Two Hoots Tea Room at Devil's Bridge, Backyard BBQ at Aberystwyth

HILLCREST HUT, REYNALTON, PEMBROKESHIRE

By Jenny Jones

Set on a 12-acre smallholding with an abundance of wildlife, Hillcrest Hut offers a chance to get away from it all, but with all mod cons available.

Hillcrest Hut is located in the small, rural village of Reynalton and is surrounded by beautiful countryside.

The hut is equipped with everything you could want for a cosy stay - seating area, double bed that folds down over the latter, table, television, an extremely efficient stove-type fan heater, a kitchen area with gas hob, microwave, kitchen utensils including pots and pans, sink with hot and cold taps, kettle and fridge with a small freezer compartment. There's also a bathroom area, with flushing toilet, a small sink with hot and cold water, and a shower. As this was more of a working 'holiday', free WiFi and electricity sockets were definitely an added bonus. Double patio-style doors open onto wooden steps that lead down to a small patio set and barbecue area.

Hillcrest Hut is securely fenced and the owner said I could use the field the hut was in as our garden. There are apple trees just outside and a wildflower meadow towards the far end. A family of badgers live at the bottom of the field and, with luck, may be glimpsed at dawn or dusk.

There's no end of stunning walks along the Pembrokeshire Coast Path and an array of beaches to explore. Manorbier beach is a 23-minute drive away and is dog friendly all year round.

Even if I wasn't working in the area, I'd definitely return if I was looking for a few days of coastal walking and beach adventures.

FACT FILE

Location: Reynalton, Tenby, SA68 0PH

Website: pembrokeshirebarnfarm.co.uk

Contact: enquire@pembrokeshirebarn.farm (use discount code **DogFriendly** when booking)

Type of accommodation: Shepherd's hut

Number of bedrooms: 1 (sleeps 2)

Number of dogs accepted: No limit but size of hut would probably only suit 2 or 3

Enclosed garden: Yes

Local interest: Manorbier Beach, Swanlake Beach, Pembrokeshire Coast Path

Best eats: The Boars Head at Templeton

WATERWYNCH HOUSE, TENBY, PEMBROKESHIRE

By Leanne Robins

Whether it's a wedding or a large family gathering, Waterwynch House makes a stunning venue, set in 10 acres of gardens and woodland, with beautiful views and its very own beach.

Searching online for the right venue for our wedding, I was hoping to find somewhere surrounded by wonderful countryside, where dogs would be welcomed warmly. Our dog, Bailey, is one of the family and it was vital he could take an active role in the celebrations.

Nestling picturesquely within a secluded bay, a few miles north of Tenby, Waterwynch makes a spectacular holiday location. The house takes full advantage of the sea views and its 10-acre gardens include colourful herbaceous borders, a swathe of woodland and its own beach.

Dogs are prohibited from certain areas, particularly the bedrooms, but Bailey was happy sleeping in the Boot Room, where a dog flap links with an enclosed area (and dog loo) outside.

Waterwynch is ideal if you're going away as a group because it's incredibly spacious inside, with 5 reception rooms, including a

Great Hall. The Sky Room is easily the most luxurious, with an expansive glass roof, white carpets and a grand piano, and the kitchen has everything you might need to rustle up a feast.

There are 12 spacious bedrooms, the majority with a king-size bed, seating area and ensuite. Several have balconies with views across the garden and the master suite overlooks Waterwynch Bay. The Bunk Room is ideal for children and can sleep 6 people.

The property is ideally located if you enjoy walking because the Pembrokeshire National Coast Path runs close by.

FACT FILE

Location: Narberth Road, Pembrokeshire, SA70 8TJ
Website: waterwynch.com
Contact: 07703 484207
Type of accommodation: House
Number of bedrooms: 12 (sleeps up to 30)
Number of dogs accepted: 5
Enclosed garden: Yes
Local interest: Manorbier Castle, Pembroke Castle, Carew Castle, Castell Henllys Iron Age Fort, Caldey Island, Tenby, Llys-y-Frân Reservoir, Narberth
Best eats: The Dragon at Narberth

BRECON RETREAT, BRECON, WALES

By Emma Bearman

With all the splendour of the Brecon Beacons National Park right outside the door, a stay at Brecon Retreat offers stylish and luxurious accommodation, designed with families and dogs in mind.

Brecon Retreat is a small, independent business in the heart of the Brecon Beacons, offering 5-star accommodation which is the ultimate in luxury. All 4 properties are dog friendly, family-friendly and promote green tourism. What's not to love?

We stayed in Swn-Y-Nant, which means 'sound of the stream'. The gorgeous, oak-framed lodge is beautifully decorated throughout. The rustic interior has been designed to bring you closer to nature and is a true escape from the hustle and bustle of everyday life.

The kitchen, living room and dining room space is combined. When looking for dog friendly accommodation, I always lean towards an open-plan layout, as it means you can easily spend time together as a family, even if you all want to do your own separate thing.

Like us, Brecon Retreat believes dogs are part of the family. On our holidays, the dogs are our priority, so the Brecon Beacons were just what we needed. We had multiple dogs on this trip, so were keen to find places where we could let the dogs roam free and have fun. We spent most of our days exploring, before heading back home to the log burner, for a family meal.

I have always loved a trip to Wales - as a child, it was our go-to holiday destination. There is everything you could possibly want from a family holiday right on the doorstep - gorgeous sandy beaches, delicious dog friendly restaurants and, of course, the breathtaking Brecon Beacons.

FACT FILE

Location: Aberyscir, Brecon LD3 9NP
Website: breconretreat.co.uk
Contact: 01874 636263
Type of accommodation: Oak-framed lodge
Number of bedrooms: 2 (sleeps 4)
Number of dogs accepted: 2 (3 if small)
Enclosed garden: Yes (fence hip height)
Local interest: Walks from the door, 4 Waterfalls trail near Ystradfellte, Pen-Y- Fan, Sugar Loaf mountain, Brecon Mountain Railway, National Showcaves
Best eats: Comprehensive list provided by Brecon Retreat

THE PIGGERY, PENAALT, MONMOUTHSHIRE

By Sue Pells

Owned by Kate Humble and her husband, Ludo Graham, the farm is a wonderful holiday destination for anyone with an enthusiasm for all things rural.

The Piggery at Humble by Nature has become one of our favourite places. The first time we visited, we didn't have a dog and stayed in the Hayloft, while David attended a hedge-laying course.

The farm was once owned by the council but, when the last tenant retired, the authority decided it should be broken into lots and sold. Kate and Ludo felt it should remain whole and be run as a business, showcasing rural skills and, after extensive repairs, the farmhouse became a family home again.

The Piggery, The Humble Hideaway and The Hayloft welcome guests, often those testing their skills on one of the many courses held throughout the year.

The Piggery is charming and has been tastefully decorated throughout. We particularly enjoyed relaxing beside the fire every evening and the lovely views across the fields. The kitchen is modern and spacious, with everything you need. Outside, there's a secure garden with a seating area and an orchard.

The farm is ideally located if you enjoy walking, as you can head down the lane or through the fields or, if you're feeling more energetic, explore the spectacular countryside of the Wye Valley Area of Outstanding Natural Beauty.

We had such a wonderful time that we immediately booked our next holiday.

FACT FILE

Location: Humble By Nature,Upper Meend Farm, Penallt, Nr Monmouth, NP25 4RP

Website: humblebynature.com

Contact: 01600 714595

Type of accommodation: Cottage

Number of bedrooms: 2 (sleeps 4)

Number of dogs accepted: 2

Enclosed garden: Yes

Local interest: Rural courses on the farm, Wye Valley, Tintern Abbey

Best eats: The Anchor Inn and The Old Station at Tintern, The Pig & Apple

STOCKWOOD COTTAGE, COWBRIDGE, VALE OF GLAMORGAN

By Steve Bennet

Only 100 yds from the popular and dog friendly Bear Hotel in the bustling heart of Cowbridge, Stockwood Cottage makes a good base for exploring the beautiful Vale of Glamorgan.

Arriving in Cowbridge, I was struck by how attractive it is, with a varied selection of interesting shops on either side of a traditional, yet bustling, High Street.

We'd been asked to check in at the reception of The Bear Hotel, as this was where we could collect the keys to Stockwood Cottage. Inside, the hotel was lovely, with a friendly atmosphere that was matched by the warmth of the staff. We were guided out of the hotel and along a quiet road where, after 100 yds, we found the cottage.

We opened the door and walked into a living area that has clearly been designed with dog owners in mind. The floor is wood-effect laminate and there were throws over the leather sofas. A decent-sized TV and a log-effect electric fire helped make the room feel more inviting. There's a well-equipped kitchen, a small dining room and French windows leading to a securely enclosed garden.

Upstairs, there's a double bedroom, a single bedroom and a bathroom with a full-bodied shower. We found a doggy welcome pack containing biscuits, bowls and a handful of poo bags.

During our short stay in the Vale, we visited only a fraction of the region's many attractions. However, what we experienced only made us want to find out more and we will definitely return. It's high on our list of holiday destinations.

FACT FILE

Location: High Street, Cowbridge, Vale of Glamorgan
Website: townandcountrycollective.co.uk
Contact: 01446 774814
Type of accommodation: Cottage
Number of bedrooms: 2
Number of dogs accepted: 2
Enclosed garden: Yes
Local interest: St Illtud's Church at Llantwit Major, Vale Trails, Ogmore Beach, Dunraven Castle, Glamorgan Heritage Coast
Best eats: The Old Swan Inn at Llantwit Major, The Duke of Wellington at Cowbridge, Cobbles Kitchen & Deli at Ogmore-by-Sea

THREE RIVERS HOTEL & SPA, CARMARTHENSHIRE, WALES

By Jennie Godden

Three Rivers Hotel is a country inn with rooms, where both two-legged and four-legged guests are made very welcome.

Carmarthenshire is lovely walking country, with miles of pathways to explore. Its golden beaches are a major attraction, as are the Brecon Beacons and the many ancient castles that litter the landscape. It's a picturesque part of the world where you can escape the tribulations of modern life and relax completely.

Nestling within beautiful countryside near Ferryside, Three Rivers Hotel is a stylish and rather handsome Georgian property which enjoys wonderful views. I had one of the deluxe rooms, which meant I had a balcony with river views.

All the bedrooms are dog friendly, which makes a pleasant change. The hotel has a restaurant and a Welsh-themed brasserie. There's also a spa with swimming pool, Jacuzzi, steam room, sauna and gym and I made maximum use of these during my holiday. Although dogs aren't allowed in the restaurant, they're welcome in the bar and lounge. The hotel's owner, manager and staff made a real fuss of our dogs and

they enjoyed meeting the resident dog.

The hotel is just a short walk from the river and there's a large sandy beach at Ferryside. Although the village doesn't have many amenities, there's a pub, shop and a café. I also walked on the beaches at Bury Port and Pendine.

We had a wonderful holiday at Three Rivers Hotel. The staff couldn't have been more friendly or welcoming and even helped make my birthday special. The food was tasty and the hospitality exemplary, so I would highly recommend it. I can envisage visiting many times.

FACT FILE

Location: Undercliff, Ferryside, Carmarthenshire, SA17 5TU

Website: threerivershotel.co.uk

Contact: 01267 267270

Type of accommodation: Hotel

Number of bedrooms: 15

Number of dogs accepted: 2

Enclosed garden: No

Local interest: Beaches at Ferryside, Bury Port and Pendine

Best eats: Three Rivers Hotel, The Ferry Cabin at Ferryside

CALON Y FFERI, CARMARTHENSHIRE, WALES

By Kathryn Austin

If you value community, great food, thoughtfully designed rooms and a truly warm Welsh welcome then Calon y Fferi is the place for you - located within walking distance of Ferryside train station, the local beach and only a 15-minute drive from Carmarthen.

Translated, Calon y Fferi means the 'heart of Ferryside', and it is certainly that. The not-for-profit enterprise provides vital local support and opportunities for the entire community to come together to enjoy events, great food and a wide range of services. On-site there is a post office, a shop, a café, a superb fine dining restaurant and bar, art gallery, small business units, and a boutique hotel. The hotel has been created with 2 specific needs in mind - to provide a great place to stay for visitors with additional access needs and also to welcome guests travelling with dogs.

A number of seaside-themed rooms work brilliantly for both target audiences. The spacious dog friendly rooms all have direct access to the outside and are practical, with hard flooring throughout and wet rooms that are perfect for sorting out muddy paws. I would recommend planning your visit and booking both a room and dinner. The continental breakfast was also good with lots of choice, great service and, as with dinner, you can eat together with your dogs in the foyer.

We squeezed a lot into 2 days and can all happily recommend visiting this beautiful part of Carmarthenshire and staying at Calon y Fferi. We will definitely be back to visit the community hotel and the dogs are already demanding another trip to Parc y Bocs!

FACT FILE

Location: Carmarthen Rd, Ferryside, SA17 5TE

Website: calonyfferi.wales

Contact: 01267 874040

Type of accommodation: Hotel

Number of bedrooms: 5 (3 dog friendly)

Number of dogs accepted: 2 (negotiable)

Enclosed garden: Small enclosed patio and fenced park nearby

Local interest: Kidwelly (town, beach and castle), Llansteffan Castle, Laugharne (home of Dylan Thomas), The Grist walk, National Botanic Garden of Wales

Best eats: Pryd o fwyd on site café and restaurant, Parc y Bocs Farm Shop and Café, Arthur's at Laugharne, The Kings Arms at Llansaint, The Red Lion Inn at Llandyfaelog, Wrights Emporium at Llanarthne

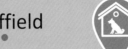

THE OLD
BRICK PITS - P.86

Sheffield

PEAK DISTRICT
NATIONAL PARK

THE CHEQUERS
INN - P.97

SHERWOOD
HIDEAWAYS - P.84

THE CASTLE
HOTEL - P.92

Stoke-on-Trent

Nottingham

PUDDLEDUCK
COTTAGES - P.87

Leicester

SHROPSHIRE
HILLS

Birmingham

TITCHBOURNE
COTTAGE - P.96

WALTON HALL
HOTEL - P.93

COLWELL PARK
HOTEL - P.94

THE POINTER - P.90

LUDLOW CASTLE
APARTMENTS - P.88

COTSWOLDS

Oxford

CHILTERN
HILLS

NORTH WESSEX
DOWNS

SHERWOOD HIDEAWAYS, THORESBY, NOTTINGHAMSHIRE

By Louise Furby

At Sherwood Hideaways, luxurious lodges and log cabins occupy a tranquil forest setting, with plenty of walks and places to visit nearby.

Sherwood Hideaways, where we spent a long, relaxing (and sometimes rainy) weekend in May, are situated deep within forest, on the Thoresby Estate. The area is on the outskirts of Nottingham, where there are long woodland walks and you are surrounded by stunning scenery. If there

was one word to describe it, 'tranquil' would fit the bill perfectly.

Arriving early on a Friday evening, we were thrilled to see the cabins were really well spaced out, giving complete privacy. Every plot is surrounded by plenty of grass - great for our mini Schnauzer, Laika, who can be very particular about where she chooses to toilet! The car parking space, near to the cabin, made it easy to unload and settle in quickly.

Our lodge was pretty spacious, with 2 bedrooms and 2 bathrooms, a well-equipped kitchen and a lounge area with 2 sofas for relaxing in front of the log burner. There is a hot tub, nestled in the corner of the decking area for maximum privacy, with a table and chairs opposite. There are robes and slippers provided for use with the hot tub, but you need to bring your own towels.

Laika was thrilled to find there were open woods at the back of the cabin for squirrel-watching and plenty of long grass to sniff and explore all around the plot.

You can walk to Thoresby Hall from Sherwood Hideaways. There are multiple

FACT FILE

Location: Blyth Road, Perlethorpe Newark, Notts, NG22 9EB

Website: sherwoodhideaway.com

Contact: 01623 824594

Type of accommodation: Forest lodge

Number of bedrooms: 2 (sleeps 4)

Number of dogs accepted: 2 (negotiable)

Enclosed garden: Fenced decking area

Local interest: Thoresby Park and Hall, St John's Church on the Thoresby Estate, Sherwood Forest and the Major Oak, guided forest walks

Best eats: The Dolphin Fish Bar at Ollerton, The Courtyard Coffee Shop and Café on the Thoresby Estate, The Rose Cottage at Rufford, The Old Plough Inn at Edmonton, The Dovecote Inn at Laxton, The Dog & Duck at Clipstone

routes to choose from and we followed the route through the trees and alongside fields. The walk was a joy. Winding through the Thoresby Estate, it was flat, well signposted, with dog litter bins along the way and we didn't meet a single person. Laika was in total heaven, with endless smells to investigate. We came across a couple of stiles with a nifty little opening for her to trot through.

We couldn't stay so near to the iconic Sherwood Forest without going to see the world-famous Major Oak. What's really great about visiting the forest is that you can choose to walk the grounds via the pathways, which are great for prams,

pushchairs, bikes and wheelchairs, or you can go off-path and take your own route through the woods, which is what we decided to do. The weather was just beautiful, with bright sunshine bringing the forest to life, as we trekked through trees and clearings with Laika off-lead.

Monday morning started early as you need to vacate the cabin by 10am, but we made certain we had enough time for one more hot tub dip with our morning coffee! Sherwood Hideaways offer peace and tranquillity. It's somewhere to relax and unwind, near to a wealth of places to walk and visit with your 4-legged friend.

THE OLD BRICK PITS, STURTON BY STOW, LINCOLNSHIRE

By Angie Aspinall

Once the site of clay pits, The Old Brick Pits is a great spot for appreciating nature, from the comfort of a thoughtfully-designed and well-equipped cabin, right on the water's edge.

Travelling south from Scotland to tour the charming and leafy villages around Lincoln, you notice several things the locals might take for granted. The landscape is gentle and the hills, such as they are, are low, yet afford amazing views across the flatlands of the county and just about any small rise will reveal Lincoln Cathedral in the distance.

Just 15 minutes from Lincoln, The Old Brick Pits is a newish venture. The owner has reworked the landscape of this former quarry to create a wonderful, small lake and added 3 beautiful, identical wooden cabins, each of which faces onto the water. You can sit with a drink on the built-in veranda or enjoy a barbecue at the cabin's outdoor area.

The cabins are wonderfully finished and each has an excellently-equipped kitchen, comfortable seating, a decent television and comfy beds. There are lots of hedges and trees, which give the cabins a great deal of privacy.

Henry had a fine time exploring. He's a dog who loves to stick his snout into the vegetation and have a good sniff. He can wander off, though, and, as the land around each cabin isn't entirely dog-proof, we kept an eye on him throughout.

For me, being interested in wildlife, the cabins were superb. We visited in early May, so the dawn and evening choruses were at their best.

FACT FILE

Location: Mill Lane, Sturton by Stow, Lincoln, Lincolnshire, LN1 2AS

Website: westpoolcabin.co.uk

Contact: 07985 229439

Type of accommodation: Wooden cabins

Number of bedrooms: 2

Number of dogs accepted: 2

Enclosed garden: No

Local interest: Lincoln Cathedral, Lincoln Arboretum, Stow Minster, Doddington Hall & Gardens (grounds only)

Best eats: The Inn on the Green at Ingham, Doddington Café

PUDDLE DUCK COTTAGES, TELFORD, SHROPSHIRE

By Emma Bearman

Beautiful, traffic-free walks, dog friendly eateries and tourist attractions are all accessible on foot from the award-winning, luxury Puddle Duck Cottages.

Duckling Cottage, the smaller of the 2 Puddle Duck Cottages, really did feel like home, from the moment we walked through the door. The lamps were on and it was warm. Downstairs, there is a very cosy open-plan living area, with a wonderful, fully-fitted kitchen. The little dining area is tucked away under the stairs and the rest of the room is the living room, with the lovely inglenook fireplace and log burner taking centre stage.

The beautifully-decorated bedrooms and family bathroom are upstairs. The master bedroom has a king-size bed, an ensuite bathroom and scenic views of the River Severn. What I loved most is that they are flexible - if your dog would rather be near you at night, they can sleep on the floor in the bedrooms. My older boy, Alfie, truly is a velcro Spaniel, so this made for a stress-free stay.

Each cottage has been designed with dogs in mind, with private, secure rear gardens with 6ft fencing. There is also access to a large, three-quarter-acre, stock-fenced garden, overlooking the River Severn.

Puddle Duck Cottages are perfectly located for visiting Ironbridge. You can park up on arrival and spend the rest of your stay exploring on foot.

When it comes to a holiday with the dogs, I always seem to head to the coast or the mountains. I hadn't considered staying so close to home, so I was keen to see just what the historic Ironbridge Gorge had to offer. I was blown away by just how beautiful the area is. What a gem!

FACT FILE

Location: The Tuckies, Ironbridge Gorge, Telford, Shropshire, TF8 7LT

Website: puddleduckcottages.co.uk

Contact: 07973 466243

Type of accommodation: Cottage

Number of bedrooms: 2 (sleeps 5)

Number of dogs accepted: 2 (more by arrangement)

Enclosed garden: Yes

Local interest: Walks from the door, Blists Hill Victorian Town, Enginuity, Jackfield Tile Museum, Tar Tunnel, Coalport Tile Museum, Wrekin Way

Best eats: Numerous dog friendly cafés and pubs within walking distance

LUDLOW CASTLE APARTMENTS, SHROPSHIRE

By Caroline Hodson

A Ludlow Castle apartment offers unique accommodation, right in the centre of town, and is very convenient for visiting the dog friendly castle.

When we tried to book a special hotel offer for a trip to Ludlow with friends, it was fully booked - and then I remembered hearing about Ludlow Castle Apartments.

The restoration of Castle House to create 3 apartments was completed in 2007 and they've done it rather nicely. Only one of the apartments, the Sir Henry Sidney,

allows dogs. It was available and the price, once split 4 ways, wasn't much different to the hotel we'd been looking at. What's more, it's brilliantly situated right in the middle of town.

The layout of the Sir Henry Sidney apartment is great. There is a small entrance hall and, to the right, is the impressive light lounge, with leather sofas and diamond pane windows overlooking the castle itself. There is a fireplace and small television, and the dining table was big enough to seat at least 8.

Through the lounge is the kitchen, which we found to be very well equipped, spacious and also overlooking the centre of the castle. There was a water/food bowl for the dogs and an impressive welcome pack for us, with wine, a small amount of butter, local cheeses, some small pots of jam and 2 freshly-baked loaves of bread, supplied by local makers. What a good way to showcase the area and give us some ideas for where to get our supplies.

Both bedrooms were to the left of the entrance hall. One was a double with ensuite bathroom, overlooking the centre

FACT FILE

Location: Castle Square, Ludlow, Shropshire, SY8 1AY

Website: ludlowcastle.com/accommodation-page
Contact: 01584 874465

Type of accommodation: Apartment (Sir Henry Sidney)

Number of bedrooms: 2 (sleeps 4)

Number of dogs accepted: 2 small

Enclosed garden: No

Local interest: Ludlow, Ludlow Castle

Best eats: The Clive Arms at Bromfield

of the castle. The second bedroom, a twin, also with an ensuite bathroom, had a tiny opaque window opening towards the town, behind a window seat.

We loved the layout of the apartment because the living areas were to one side of the hall, and the sleeping areas to the other. There was space to socialise, and space to retreat if quiet time was wanted and the view of the ruined parts of the castle through the windows was spectacular.

Our stay included tickets to visit the castle. The dogs were permitted on leads but some of the spiral staircases were a bit steep and bit tight for small dogs who, for some reason, insist on going headfirst down the narrowest part of the stair tread. So we took it in turns to go up, in some areas, or we carried them.

Ludlow is, on the whole, pretty dog friendly. When I visit places, I usually assume dogs are not allowed unless there's a sign to say they are welcome but, in Ludlow, the opposite is true.

There are also plenty of other places to visit nearby. Shropshire is a beautiful county with some spectacular hills and scenery.

THE POINTER, BRILL, BUCKINGHAMSHIRE

By Alex Frith

Gastro pub, The Pointer, demonstrates the perfect balance of country charm and contemporary style, with food very much part of the agenda.

The Pointer was named Pub of the Year in the 2018 Michelin Guide and Hotel of the Year by The Sunday Times. It's also dog friendly so, as writer of lifestyle blog, Barkarama, I thought I'd check it out.

We were shown to one of the dog friendly, ground floor rooms and what immediately grabbed our attention were the beds – we had a super-king-size Hypnos bed, with

countless plump pillows and crisp White Company bed linen. Basil wasn't neglected, as he had a little sofa-style bed with its own pillow.

The room could have graced the pages of an interior design magazine, with its country chic style of soft, muted French greys with distressed, country-style, vintage furniture, basket weave pendant lights, sheepskin throws and blackout Roman blinds.

Beyond the excitement of our sleeping arrangements, was the spacious and incredibly inviting bathroom. Double sinks, underfloor heating, a massive walk-in rain shower, soft robes, luxury toiletries and, best of all, a free-standing bath.

The foyer is also well equipped, with spare wellies, complimentary filtered water and fresh-from-the-udder whole milk.

The Pointer has its own farm nearby - it supplies the kitchen with the likes of grass-fed, English Longhorn beef, a highlight of the daily-changing 'Field to Fork' menu, which is dictated by the seasons and what's best on the day. The main restaurant has its own open kitchen, so dogs are only

FACT FILE

Location: 27 Church Street, Brill, Bucks, HP18 9RT

Website: thepointerbrill.co.uk

Contact: 01844 238339

Type of accommodation: Bed and breakfast

Number of bedrooms: 9

Number of dogs accepted: 2

Enclosed garden: No

Local interest: Brill village and windmill, Shotover Country Park, Bernwood Butterfly Trail, pre-booked farm tours, Bicester, Thame, Oxford, High Wycombe, Aylesbury, Blenheim Palace, Waddesdon Manor, Bicester Village designer outlet

Best eats: The Pointer

permitted to dine with their owners in the bar or, on warmer days, outside in the beer garden. We were drawn by the snug areas with their comfy armchairs, sofas and throws, and the roaring flames of an open fire. After our meal, we continued with our Malbec (the wine list is amazing), all cosied up on a sofa in front of the fire.

We'd already been impressed by dinner but we were blown away by breakfast. A table was groaning with everything from fresh yoghurts and fruit, to homemade jams and pastries. This was all just a precursor to hearty English breakfast of Pointer Farm bacon, eggs, homemade sausages and black pudding, which was accompanied by another bag of bread, fresh out of the oven.

Our stay at The Pointer was very much about having a relaxing, grown-up night away, with nice food and wine and Basil as company, so we didn't plan much else. There's a wide variety of attractions nearby, if you're so inclined, including the Bernwood Butterfly Trail and the windmill, which is open at certain times of the year.

So, if you enjoy great food, fine wine and stylish surroundings, I'd recommend The Pointer without any hesitation. I'm already planning our return, perhaps in summer, as I fancy sampling The Pointer's adventurous menu outside in the garden.

THE CASTLE HOTEL, BISHOPS CASTLE, SHROPSHIRE

By Caroline Hodson

Dogs are made very welcome at The Castle Hotel, a 4-star establishment offering stylish accommodation and quality food, in a charming south Shropshire market town.

Our room at The Castle Hotel was large, with enormous windows overlooking Market Square at the front and, from the bathroom, the distant hills. It was wonderfully spacious, with a large bed in the centre, a seating area with a table and chairs, drink-making facilities and a television. Although it was one of the first that other guests passed on the staircase, the room had 2 doors, with a lobby in between. This meant our dogs, Daisy and May, were insulated against any noise outside and there was less chance of anyone outside hearing them barking.

Of all the places we stayed on this holiday, this ticked the most boxes. It was very dog friendly and, although dogs are prohibited from the dining room, they're welcome in one of the bars and that's where we had breakfast in the morning. It was great, with an extensive menu of locally-produced ingredients.

The evening meals were just as worthy of praise and we enjoyed it so much, we thought we'd sample one of the hotel's specialities - Afternoon Tea, a rather indulgent treat of cakes, scones, sandwiches, biscuits and homemade treats.

The garden was a real highlight of our stay and we walked round it each evening with Daisy and May.

Despite the unusually high standards, we felt completely relaxed during our stay, and so did our dogs. This is a place that likes dogs, and there were plenty of them around, so we never felt as if we were inconveniencing anyone else.

FACT FILE

Location: Bishops Castle, Shropshire, SY9 5BN
Website: thecastlehotelbishopscastle.co.uk
Contact: 01588 638403
Type of accommodation: Hotel
Number of bedrooms: 13
Number of dogs accepted: 2 (negotiable)
Enclosed garden: No
Local interest: Stokesay Castle, Offa's Dyke, Stiperstones, Clun Castle, Ludlow
Best eats: The Bog Centre at Stiperstones, The Maltings Café and The White Horse Inn at Clun, The Cliffe at Dinham, The Clive Arms at Bromfield

WALTON HALL HOTEL, WELLESBOURNE, WARWICKSHIRE

By Emma Bearman

At the historic Walton Hall Hotel, you can enjoy luxurious accommodation, spa facilities and fine dining in an atmosphere redolent of a bygone era.

Standing on the site of several older houses and with cellars that date from the reign of Elizabeth I, Walton Hall dominates the landscape. It is now part of the Mercure Hotel Collection, a nationwide chain that includes a number of old, stately homes.

We approached slowly along the picturesque, tree-lined drive, with me imagining how it might have been in a horse-drawn carriage. Our Springer, Alfie, was more excited about the gently undulating parkland in which the hotel stands, the lake and the sight of other dogs playing in the grounds.

Our suite was delightfully large, with a gigantic bed, dressed invitingly with colourful throws. Light flooded through the windows, bouncing off the high ceilings and creating a reflection of the gardens outside in the ornamental mirror above the fireplace.

Walton Hall has always been dog friendly and Alfie was excited when he found a welcome pack containing a bed, treats and toys. We unpacked our things and headed outside. As Alfie was recovering from an operation, our explorations were quite limited, but we had a pleasant stroll around the gardens and learnt there are plenty of walking opportunities through the fields and woodland, and that a number of pathways connect the grounds with the surrounding countryside.

I would heartily recommend Walton Hall but suggest you save your pennies, so you can stay in one of main suites and pretend, even just momentarily, that you're enjoying the luxurious lifestyle of the Edwardian age.

FACT FILE

Location: Wellesbourne, CV35 9HG

Website: mercure.com

Contact: 01789 842424

Type of accommodation: Hotel

Number of bedrooms: 168

Number of dogs accepted: 2

Enclosed garden: No

Local interest: Walks in the grounds and surrounding countryside

Best eats: Walton Hall Hotel

COLWALL PARK HOTEL, MALVERN, WORCESTERSHIRE
By Courtney Hockey

For a luxury break which is truly dog friendly, the prestigious Colwall Park Hotel offers comfortable accommodation and delicious food, in an area which is great for walking and studded with charming villages.

Colwall Park prides itself on being dog friendly - and so it proved, when I stayed there with my Border Terriers, Elsa and Albie.

A prestigious hotel, bar and restaurant, Colwall Park was built around 1905 and is mock Tudor in style. A large, half-timbered building, its white plasterwork complements the red brickwork and stone mullioned windows.

There's quite a variety of rooms available, each individually designed. We were staying in one of the suites and found a high standard of decoration throughout. The suites are larger than the double rooms, so there was plenty of space, even when we used the dog beds provided. The bathroom was immaculate - clean and light, with shiny chrome fixtures and White Company toiletries.

The reception rooms are a real credit - smart, stylish and refined, with natural wood, tapestries and soft lighting creating a welcoming atmosphere. There's a well-established garden at the rear, which is ideal if your dogs need a quick walk and you can reach the garden easily, as there are various points of entry.

The Malverns attract countryside-lovers from around the country and the hotel has created a number of walking guides, which are available from reception. After checking in and leaving our bags upstairs, we chose one of the shorter routes and ventured out with the dogs. Leaving the grounds of the

FACT FILE

Location: Colwall, Malvern, WR13 6QG
Website: colwall.co.uk
Contact: 01684 540000
Type of accommodation: Hotel
Number of bedrooms: 22
Number of dogs accepted: 3
Enclosed garden: Yes
Local interest: The Malverns, Worcestershire Beacon, Iron Age remains at British Camp, parkland at Hanbury Hall and Croome Court, Witley Court & Gardens, The Black & White Trail, Great Malvern, Ledbury, Worcester, Hay-on-Wye
Best eats: Colwall Park Hotel, The Garden Tea Rooms at Witley Court

THE CHEQUERS INN, WOOLSTHORPE-BY-BELVOIR, LINCOLNSHIRE

By Tony Groom

The award-winning Chequers Inn is a quintessential English country pub, nestled in the unspoilt and stunning Vale of Belvoir.

We arrived at The Chequers Inn quite late in the afternoon and were shown to our room, which was one of 4 in a converted stable block. With no corridors and stairs, it felt quite cottage-like and we loved the cosy atmosphere. The dog friendly rooms are both on the ground floor and we were able to park right outside, which always makes things easier.

Inside, alongside a king-size bed, a desk and a compact, but well-appointed, shower room, we found tea and coffee-making facilities, bottled mineral water, a range of complimentary toiletries, a Freeview TV and a dog cushion, where Oscar could sleep. We loved the stable door as it meant we could let fresh air circulate around the room, without Oscar making an escape.

We had our evening meal in the bar with Oscar and were seated at a large, shared table. The food was absolutely delicious, the dishes were extremely well presented and the portions were generous.

After a relaxing night's sleep, I walked Oscar through the village, enjoying the solitude that the early morning provides. Back in the bar, we were served a delightful breakfast and both chose the full English but I did feel a tad envious when I noticed another guest's Eggs Benedict! We finished it all off with toast and marmalade, plus copious amounts of tea and declared ourselves ready to face the day.

'We set out on the 'King of Belvoir Castle' walk - a circular 5-mile route that leads around the village and along the Grantham Canal. Oscar decided against swimming and we were glad as it meant we didn't have a damp dog in the back of the car!

FACT FILE

Location: Main Street, Woolsthorpe-by-Belvoir, Lincolnshire, NG32 1LU

Website: chequersinn.net

Contact: 01476 870701

Type of accommodation: Bed and breakfast

Number of bedrooms: 4

Number of dogs accepted: Multiple

Enclosed garden: No

Local interest: King of Belvoir Castle walk, Grantham Canal, Viking Way

Best eats: The Chequers Inn

97

SCOTLAND

NORTH WEST

LANEFOOT FARM - P.115

THE SWAN - P.129

LOW NEST STUDIOS - P.99

Carlisle

NORTH LAKES HOTEL - P.124

FOXWOLD - P.103

WORDSWORTH HOTEL - P.118

THE OLD DUNGEON GHYLL HOTEL - P.100

NORTH PENNINES

LANCRIGG - P.120

SCALEBECK COTTAGES - P.123

THE BURGOYNE - P.131

HOLBECK GHYLL HOTEL - P.130

LAKE DISTRICT NATIONAL PARK

THE RYEBECK HOTEL - P.127

THE ELTERMERE INN - P.135

THE ROTHAY MANOR - P.128

YORKSHIRE DALES NATIONAL PARK

CRAGG COTTAGE - P.108

PELTON WHEEL - P.112

BOWLAND FELL PARK - P.109

THE DEVON FELL - P.137

THE OLD BAKEHOUSE - P.117

Morecambe

THE PLOUGH INN - P.113

CAR HO P.1

BEACH RISE - P.105

Blackpool

THE MIDLAND - P.132

HIPPING HALL - P.126

BECK HALL - P.134

Leeds

CANAL COTTAGE - P.102

THE DERBY ARMS - P.100

ROUGH TOP COTTAGE - P.106

Manchester

PEAK DISTRICT NATIONAL PARK

LAUREL COTTAGE - P.121

Liverpool

THE MOON INN - P.111

Sheffiel

BIRCH COTTAGE - P.119

17 THE LANES - P.1

WALES

LOW NEST STUDIOS, KESWICK, CUMBRIA

By Anna Ward Murphy

In the heart of the countryside but conveniently close to the town of Keswick, Low Nest Studios offer the perfect place to relax.

My fiancé, Steve, and I weren't intending to go on holiday. Pandemic chaos, reports of overcrowded destinations and inflated prices had put us off. However, when my sister let us know they were planning a trip to the Lake District, we thought we'd see what was available. After a bit of internet-surfing we discovered Low Nest Studios - a relaxed, dog friendly place to stay, off the beaten track but not too far from Keswick. We stayed in 'Dollywaggon', one of a number of studios on Low Nest Farm, a location particularly suitable for countryside-lovers and walkers. The Studios are extremely dog friendly and we were greeted with a welcome doggy basket which Pepper was very pleased about.

Our accommodation was just what we needed. It is a split-level studio, with a small kitchen, table, sofa and TV downstairs. Up a few steps are the bed and ensuite bathroom. Outside there is a small, fenced yard with table and chairs. There is also a laundry/drying room, which includes a doggy bath and some dog shampoo - a nice touch and a welcome way to make sure we were all clean before returning to our studio after a muddy walk.

The farm also has some exercise areas for dogs and several handy poo bins dotted around. There are footpaths direct from the farm, for a wealth of countryside walks.

The Lake District is truly a wonder and Keswick, in particular, really stole our hearts. We will, undoubtedly, be back to explore more of what this inspiring landscape has to offer.

FACT FILE

Location: Low Nest Farm, Keswick, Cumbria, CA12 4TF

Website: lowneststudios.co.uk

Contact: 01768 772378

Type of accommodation: Studio

Number of bedrooms: 1

Number of dogs accepted: Multiple

Enclosed garden: Fenced yard plus exercise areas

Local interest: Boat trips at Derwentwater, walks from the door and local walks, including Catbells, Latrigg and Helvellyn

Best eats: Jasper's Coffee House, The Round, Riverside Café and The Dog & Gun at Keswick, The Kings Head Inn at Thirlmere

THE BIG ROAD TRIP

By Kathryn Austin

Hitting the road with dogs can take a bit of planning but, luckily, there's no shortage of dog friendly accommodation available.

'Go big or go home', as the saying goes. We decided we would 'go big' with a 10-day road trip from our home in Wales to the Forest of Bowland, Oban, Isle of Coll and the Lake District, staying in various types of dog friendly accommodation, including a pub, a holiday cottage and a hotel.

After 6 hours of the dogs snoring gently to the radio, we arrived at our first stop, The Derby Arms, on the edge of the Forest of Bowland. Longridge Fell is a 5 minute drive from the pub. The light was already starting to fade, so we could not cover the entire 8-mile round trip but we did enough to admire the scenery and tire out schnoodles, Winnie and George.

The Derby Arms is well prepared for muddy dogs coming into the bar and has thoughtfully reserved a nice section of the restaurant for guests with pets.

In the morning, after a hearty breakfast and walk, we waved goodbye and got on the road for the long leg up to Scotland. After buying a picnic of locally produced snacks at Tebay Services on the M6, we carried on northwards, stopping briefly at Loch Lomond for a quick stretch before the final run to Seashell Cottage in Ellenabeich, about 35 minutes from Oban.

Seashell Cottage is just a few minutes' walk to a local dog friendly pub, The Oyster Bar, and generally well-placed for some spectacular hikes around the island. The cottage itself was immaculate, cosy and has practical wood and tile flooring, with a secure garden for the dogs.

FACT FILE

Location: Derby Arms, Chipping Rd, Longridge, PR3 2NB
Website: derbyarmslongridge.co.uk
Contact: 01772 782370

Location: Seashell Cottage, Ellenabeich, Oban, Argyll, PA34 4RQ (Scotland)
Website: tramwaycottages.com
Contact: 07468 193536

Location: Old Dungeon Ghyll, Great Langdale, Ambleside, LA22 9JY
Website: odg.co.uk
Contact: 015394 37272

During our stay, we enjoyed a day trip to Oban and visited Dunstaffnage Castle and Chapel, one of the few castles in the UK where you can take your dogs around the ramparts, as well as the extensive grounds. We popped into the Oban distillery - the gift shop is dog friendly - then on to Cuan Mor, a nice restaurant opposite Oban harbour.

With some sadness after 3 days of lovely walks, swims and good food we waved goodbye to Seashell Cottage and left very early for our ferry to the Isle of Coll.

Coll is a wonderful place to visit with dogs, with miles and miles of empty and achingly beautiful crystalline sandy beaches and turquoise water. We were visiting friends who live permanently on Coll but there are a number of dog friendly holiday cottages and alternative places to stay, including The Coll Bunkhouse, which is far more luxurious than its name would suggest and a great place to stop if you are island-hopping. The Coll Hotel also has a fabulous dog friendly bar and restaurant, with incredible waterside views.

The final stop on Winnie and George's Celtic Adventure was Great Langdale in the Lake District and **The Old Dungeon Ghyll Hotel (ODG)**. We seriously loved this place. The hotel itself is a time capsule to the early 19th century, with a huge gothic lounge, roaring fires and deep Edwardian sofas. The owner, Neil, should be proud of his dog friendly hospitality.

Reflecting back on our entire holiday, the main piece of advice we would give readers planning a road trip is to seriously consider travelling in low season. It makes it so much easier to find great places to stay and, particularly with dogs, not having to fight the crowds is pure joy. If you are travelling to Scotland and the islands, the ferry services are more flexible (and cheaper) and, in general, everyone just has more time to be friendly and helpful.

CANAL COTTAGE, FARNHILL, NORTH YORKSHIRE

By Nigel Kirby

With the canal right on the doorstep, towpath walks can be enjoyed directly from Canal Cottage, with places of interest and more walks nearby.

Even before the awful pandemic caused overseas travel issues, we had always looked to explore the UK, as we like to take our two Labradors, Yogi and Ella, along with us. I was born in Yorkshire but neither of us had ever visited this part of England's largest county.

Access to the cottage is via an outdoor public staircase that leads to the canal but there is an alternative option which makes the cottage accessible to all. On reaching the towpath, you are literally at the front door. The immediate first impressions were fabulous, with a lovely clean, open-plan kitchen and lounge. The cottage also has a wonderful bathroom and bedroom, with the option of a pull-out bed on the balcony that looks down into the main lounge. There was a personalised touch of a welcome pack for both humans and dogs and it was immediately noticeable that the owner, Geraldine, was a keen dog-lover herself.

Opening the front door makes you fully appreciate the proximity to the canal. One of the advantages of this is that the front door often opens to the sight of ducks or swans gliding past.

The cottage has everything and more for what you would want from a break with your dogs and the surrounding area, whether by foot or a short drive, has so much to offer. Both humans and hounds had a fabulous time.

FACT FILE

Location: 1A Kirkgate, Farnhill, Nr Skipton, Yorkshire, BD20 9BA

Website: airbnb.com/h/skiptoncanalcottage

Contact: 07427 857495 (enquiries only, please book through website and mention DogFriendly to receive 5% refund on overnight accommodation)

Type of accommodation: Cottage

Number of bedrooms: 1 (sleeps 3)

Number of dogs accepted: 2

Enclosed garden: No

Local interest: Canal walks, Skipton, Skipton Castle Woods Trail, Keighley & Worth Valley Steam Railway, Yorkshire Dales, Ilkley

Best eats: The Dog & Gun Inn at Sutton-in-Craven, Kibble Bakery Coffee House at Skipton, The Treehouse Bar & Kitchen at Haworth, Coffee & Crumbs and The White Lion at Kildwick

FOXWOLD, PENRITH, CUMBRIA

By Tracey Radnall

A shepherd's hut in the beautiful Eden Valley offers quirky accommodation, with the opportunity to dine (and shower!) al fresco.

Cumbria is Britain's best-loved national park, for many good reasons. The Eden Valley, away from the bigger fells and lakes, attracts far fewer folk and the area has little of the celebrity status of the Lakes. It offers the visitor a more peaceful alternative, as well as being adjacent to the Yorkshire Dales National Park. All in all, an ideal location or stop-off when traversing the length of the UK.

Kat Thomas and Andy Askins run 4 individual shepherd's huts among spacious fields on their farm, which is located on a quiet lane. From the gated parking area, there are walks in all directions. My travelling companion, Bertie, a working Cocker Spaniel, immediately took to the spacious field location, while his mum took in the peaceful surroundings.

My visit coincided with meeting up with a friend from the south, while I travelled from the opposing direction in the Scottish Borders. Kat had provided a complimentary basket full of local goodies, such as shortbread, chocolate and dog treats, as well as handy poo bags. The unique folding bed opened up to form a large double, big enough for our sleeping bags and a spaniel. The huts are off-grid, so lit by solar-operated wall and fairy lights, plenty bright enough for a little light reading before bedtime.

On-site, there is a unique open air shower and I quite honestly admit this was my favourite part of the entire weekend - so invigorating and liberating.

All in all, a relaxing break and ideal when travelling with your best pal, too.

FACT FILE

Location: Newby End, Newby, Penrith, Cumbria, CA10 3EX

Contact: 01931 714174

Type of accommodation: Shepherd's hut

Number of bedrooms: 1

Number of dogs accepted: 2 (negotiable)

Enclosed garden: Site securely fenced

Local interest: Lake District National Park, North Yorkshire Dales National Park, Eden Valley

17 THE LANES, WIRKSWORTH, DERBYSHIRE

By Louise Furby

A cosy cottage in the Peak District makes an ideal base for exploring the area - and access to the secure garden from the first floor has definite advantages in the wee small hours!

We are very lucky to have the Peak District on our doorstep, where our miniature Schnauzer, Laika, loves to explore. So in November, we headed to Wirksworth for a 2-night stay at 17 The Lanes.

The cottage sleeps 4 and is a warm and cosy holiday home, situated close to the centre of Wirksworth village, so pubs and shops are within easy walking distance.

The layout of the cottage is considerate to dog owners. The first thing that stood out was the stable door into the lounge - super-useful for keeping your pooch shut away while you empty the car, with the front door open. I loved the layout of the cottage. Whenever we stay away, our Schnauzer wakes up at the crack of dawn, guaranteed, so the stairs from the first floor to the garden meant there was no trekking downstairs, half-asleep at 6 o'clock on a cold autumn morning.

Wirksworth is an ideal location to access many points of interest in the Peak District, with Black Rocks very close by, featuring incredible views across the national park, and a number of towns and villages within a 30-minute drive.

We really liked 17 The Lanes - it's a fantastic cottage in a great location. For us, the real standout was the garden for its security, position and views across the village.

I doubt this will be our last visit to the Peak District and we will certainly check out Wirksworth again.

FACT FILE

Location: Bolehill, Wirksworth, Matlock, Derbyshire, DE4 4GJ

Website: 17thelaneswirksworth.co.uk

Contact: 07841 869108

Type of accommodation: Cottage

Number of bedrooms: 2 (sleeps 4)

Number of dogs accepted: 2

Enclosed garden: Yes

Local interest: Black Rocks, Carsington Water, the grounds at Chatsworth House, Ashbourne

Best eats: Mainsail Restaurant/Café at Carsington Water Visitor Centre, The Hope & Anchor at Wirksworth

104

BEACH RISE, SILVERDALE, MORECAMBE

By Louise Furby

From Beach Rise, you can head north all the way to the Scottish borders, south to Blackpool or visit the Lake District - or you can simply relax and enjoy a comfortable house with stunning views.

When you think of Morecambe, you don't immediately think of stunning sunsets or beautiful bay landscapes - or at least I didn't before we spent 3 nights at Beach Rise in Morecambe. But that is exactly what springs to mind, following our sunny stay in June. The one thing that gives me more pleasure than a warm day, overlooking a stunning bay, is seeing our miniature Schnauzer, Laika, excitedly dashing across the sand, splashing through rock pools and darting up and down rocks and grass verges. I don't think I have ever seen her look so happy. And this is only one of the reasons why we loved Silverdale so much.

The house has been beautifully designed to make the most of the breathtaking scenery. Large windows are featured in both double bedrooms, the lounge and the kitchen/diner. Location-wise, it's a perfect spot. There are countless beaches nearby in Carnforth and Morecambe Bay itself but, frankly, once you've seen your beach in Silverdale, nowhere else quite matches up.

The decor is beautiful and the owners have thought of everything, including the binoculars on the bedroom windowsill.

We watched incredible sunsets, enjoyed breathtaking views and walked miles along the beaches, without a single soul around. A few days just wasn't enough and I'm excited to explore the area more but, more than anything, I can't wait to see Laika pound down those steps onto the sand, to run and explore until her tired little legs can't carry her.

FACT FILE

Location: 31 Shore Road, Silverdale, Carnforth, LA5 0TP

Website: silverdaleseaviewholidays.co.uk

Contact: 01748 825525

Type of accommodation: House

Number of bedrooms: 4 (sleeps 7)

Number of dogs accepted: 2 (negotiable)

Enclosed garden: Yes

Local interest: Dog friendly beaches, Lune Aqueduct, Lake Windermere

Best eats: The Pheasant Inn at Grange-over-Sands, New Inn at Yealand, Longlands Inn & Restaurant, The Canal Turn, Waters Edge Restaurant & Bar and Arnside Chip Shop at Carnforth

ROUGH TOP COTTAGE, TODMORDEN, YORKSHIRE

By Lucinda Herbert

Once a 17th century farmer's cottage, Rough Top is situated in a quiet hilltop area with stunning views and plenty of walks from the door.

When travelling, my top priority is knowing my Springer Spaniel, Poppy, will be treated as one of the family, and that is definitely the case at Rough Top Cottage. There's a large storage box filled with bits and bobs you may need and a decent-sized garden, completely fenced off with a secure gate.

The cottage is spacious, with a traditional rustic interior. The log fire is a gorgeous statement piece in the lounge, and the furniture is both comfortable and homely. There is a small study area and WiFi is provided, at no extra charge. The double bedroom is spacious, with plenty of storage. There is also a twin room and, downstairs, a single. Dogs are not allowed in the bedrooms, without prior agreement.

The kitchen/diner is stylishly equipped. If you're lucky enough to visit when the weather is fine, you can open the patio doors and fire up the barbecue in the outdoor dining area.

The majestic towering rocks of Bridestones Moor are literally a stone's throw from the driveway and, if you have an appetite for adventure and a good pair of walking boots, the circular walk to Redmires Waterfall is a must. We arrived at Rough Top Cottage to unseasonable snow, hail and wind, and ended up having an unexpectedly lazy, relaxing break. Although we didn't have the action-packed adventure we'd planned, it was a very welcome change of pace.

I would absolutely recommend Rough Top Cottage for a dog friendly Yorkshire break - we've already put down a deposit for a 7-night stay!

FACT FILE

Location: Kebs Road, Todmorden, Yorks, OL14 8SB
Website: roughtopcottage.co.uk
Contact: 07973 676560 or 01706 812291
Type of accommodation: Cottage
Number of bedrooms: 3 (sleeps 5)
Number of dogs accepted: 2, more by arrangement
Enclosed garden: Yes
Local interest: Bridestones Moor, Hebden Bridge, Redmires Waterfall, fly fishing at Pennine Trout Fishery, Calder Holmes Park
Best eats: The Shoulder of Mutton Inn at Hebden Bridge

CARR HOUSE, HAREWOOD ESTATE, YORKSHIRE DALES

By Laura Fletcher

With walks on the Harewood Estate from the door and a plethora of dog friendly places to visit nearby, Carr House makes a great base for a holiday with dogs.

My fiancé, Liam, and I stayed for 2 nights at Carr House with our 2-year-old German Shepherd, Klaus. On the Harewood Estate, surrounded by stunning countryside and with a view of Harewood House, Carr House is the perfect place to stay for the weekend and explore the local area. It is one of 2 cottages, the adjoining Carr Cottage being slightly smaller.

Carr House is bright and welcoming. The interior is beautifully furnished and spacious. The rooms were clean and modern, while the wooden beams and log burner in the lounge gave a rustic feel, befitting the local area.

Felicity had asked in advance if we could meet her and her colleagues, with their dogs, to welcome us and they arrived shortly after us. The team (and the dogs!) were all very friendly and Felicity informed us we would receive complimentary tickets to Harewood House. Walking around the Harewood estate, using the

map provided, we discovered the film set used for Emmerdale was just above our accommodation! The path was very busy with walkers but, unfortunately, we did not meet any famous cast members.

Overall, we had a fantastic stay at Carr House. We were never short of ideas for what to do with Klaus and our accommodation proved to be an excellent base for the surrounding towns and villages. We would certainly recommend this accommodation for anybody looking to explore the area around Harewood House.

FACT FILE

Location: Harewood Estate, Leeds, Yorkshire Dales, LS17 9LF

Website: harewoodholidays.com

Contact: 01132 181228

Type of accommodation: Cottage

Number of bedrooms: 3 (sleeps 6)

Number of dogs accepted: 2

Enclosed garden: Yes

Local interest: Harewood House, Rievaulx Abbey, Helmsley Traditional Sweet Shop, Helmsley Castle, Helmsley Walled Garden, Fountains Abbey & Studley Royal Water Garden

Best eats: Hunters of Helmsley (deli), The Royal Oak Hotel and Cornercopia Café at Helmsley

CRAG COTTAGE, CONISTON, CUMBRIA

By Andy Craig

With its Lakeland stone walls and open fire, Crag Cottage makes a cosy base for exploring Coniston and the surrounding area.

Set within a row of traditional Lakeland cottages, Crag Cottage makes a charming holiday destination. Like its neighbours, which include a property once owned by Beatrix Potter and now managed by the National Trust, it served men who worked in the copper mines nearby.

The cottage is set on a very quiet road and enjoys fine views across Coniston to the hills beyond. There's a pathway immediately outside the back door which leads towards the village, through fields of grazing sheep (dogs on leads) or several miles through the woods. The front garden is small and gated and there's a yard at the rear.

A car isn't vital because you can walk easily from the property itself. Coniston Water is within easy reach and you'll find a network of tracks around the shore. The area has strong associations with Beatrix Potter and Coniston Water inspired Arthur Ransome's *Swallows* and *Amazons*. The lake was also the site of several water speed records between 1956 and 1959.

Coniston lies at the heart of the Lake District and you'll find walking routes to suit all abilities, whether you fancy a gentle lakeside ramble or something more adventurous in the fells. The Old Man of Coniston and Wetherlam can be reached from Crag Cottage and there's also a choice of waymarked trails through Grizedale Forest, if you fancy something less taxing.

We left Coniston with a fond farewell and a promise that we'd return for longer walks, and maybe a trip on the steamship.

FACT FILE

Location: Far End, Coniston, Cumbria
Website: airbnb.co.uk
Type of accommodation: Cottage
Number of bedrooms: 2 (sleeps 4)
Number of dogs accepted: 2
Enclosed garden: Yes (possibly not secure for smaller dogs)
Local interest: Walks from the door, the Ruskin Museum at Coniston, Grizedale Forest
Best eats: The Yewdale Inn and Sara's Indian Restaurant at Coniston

BOWLAND FELL PARK, SKIPTON, NORTH YORKSHIRE

By Evika Kiene

A stay in an airy apartment at Bowland Fell Park means there's no need to travel far to experience some of the North Yorkshire Dale's most dramatic scenery and spectacular natural features.

Allowing yourself time to recharge is absolutely essential for your wellbeing and we were extremely lucky to find a place like Bowland Fell Park, situated in an area of great natural beauty - the Yorkshire Dales.

It had been a few years since we last visited this stunning location, so we knew we wouldn't be leaving disappointed. Needless to say, there are lots of dog friendly things to do in the Yorkshire Dales and Bowland Fell Park is an excellent choice as a base for exploring some spectacular and unusual natural features, such as Malham Cove, Gordale Scar and the dramatic waterfalls hidden in deep, wooded ravines at Ingleton.

One of 4 splendid apartments at Bowland Fell Park, 'Rahmell' was situated on the second floor. As soon as we opened the doors, we were blown away by its impressive size. High ceilings gave us an immediate sense of air, space and light but it was surprisingly warm. A hallway with

glass walls was an excellent example of design, as we could clean up the dogs and leave our dirty boots, before we entered the apartment.

A fully-equipped kitchen, with every utensil I could imagine, helped us make some tasty meals to enjoy at the dinner table in the open space living/dining room. Even our dogs, Boo and Bella, were provided with water bowls and their own bed.

But what surprised me the most was how *(continued...)*

FACT FILE

Location: Tosside, Skipton, North Yorkshire, BD23 4SD

Website: parkholidays.com

Contact: 01729 811334

Type of accommodation: Apartment

Number of bedrooms: 2

Number of dogs accepted: 2

Enclosed garden: No

Local interest: Numerous walking trails, Malham Cove, Gordale Scar, waterfalls at Ingleton, Ribblehead Viaduct, Settle market town

Best eats: Crowtrees Inn on Bowland Fell Holiday Park is dog friendly

much effort had been put into helping us enjoy our stay. We have stayed in hundreds of hotels and holiday parks, but Bowland Fell had left printed walk descriptions with maps and details of all the surrounding dog friendly places and activities, so we wouldn't need to worry about anything.

Although the sights are spectacular, the weather did not want to co-operate, so we opted not to go for a long walk in the drenching rain. Instead we decided to explore the historic market town of Settle. The town is full of quality independent shops, dog friendly cafés, inns and restaurants, which meant some shelter from the rain, while waiting for clearer skies. We then headed to Ingleton and the 4½-mile Ingleton Waterfall trail.

Usually, we need to take a holiday after our holiday but, this time, we returned so relaxed and at ease that we could just carry on with work and our daily tasks. We'll certainly return when we will be ready to conquer the 3 highest peaks of Yorkshire in a 12-hour challenge, as the Bowland Fell Park offers great accommodation close to all of the starting points and, most important, you truly feel at home!

THE MOON INN, STONEY MIDDLETON, DERBYSHIRE

By Steve Bridgewater

Situated in a pretty village with a story to tell, The Moon Inn offers comfortable accommodation and great food in the heart of the Peak District.

Stoney Middleton lies within the Peak District National Park and is popular with rock climbers but, if your 4-legged friend is happier on more horizontal ground, there is a multitude of walks to choose from. That said, the village has some steep inclines, so is perhaps not best suited to those less able to get around.

We had stayed at The Moon Inn twice with our dogs, Howie and Franklin, and were so impressed, we were determined to return. The next time, we took our friends, Alexandra and Jeff, along with their Border Terriers, Bobby and Rupert.

Dogs are very welcome in the bar and restaurant areas, as well as the 7 luxurious suites built onto the rear of the pub. The Denman suite has a 4-poster, king-size bed and 2 singles, while the others have king or super-king beds. Outside, there's a pleasant, enclosed beer garden.

Many of the walking routes can be downloaded in advance from the pub's website, including the 4-mile walk from the pub to Eyam, where there are 2 village shops and a number of delightful tea rooms, many of which are dog friendly.

Howie and Franklin loved their time at the Moon Inn. They enjoyed showing Bobby and Rupert around and the 'grown-ups' enjoyed the bar, restaurant and walking.

We will certainly be returning, but what about Alex and Jeff? Well, they loved it so much they booked to return for their wedding anniversary, just 2 weeks later!

FACT FILE

Location: High Street, Stoney Middleton, Hope Valley, Derbyshire, S32 4TL

Website: themooninn.com

Contact: 01433 630203

Type of accommodation: Bed and breakfast

Number of bedrooms: 8

Number of dogs accepted: Mutliple

Enclosed garden: No

Local interest: Bakewell town, Chatsworth House (gardens and parkland), Riley Graves, Boundary Stone

Best eats: The Moon Inn, The Old Original Bakewell Pudding Shop at Bakewell, Eyam Tea Rooms, Village Green Café and The Coolstone at Eyam

PELTON WHEEL, CONISTON, CUMBRIA

By Andy Craig

Set in a mountain landscape of disused copper mines and ore processing works, 4 unique cottages are well placed for enjoying walks to suit all abilities, as well as the many attractions of the area.

Pelton Wheel is part of a group of 4 characterful cottages, set among disused copper mine workings. All have been sensitively converted from an 18th century waterwheel-powered sawmill.

Pelton Wheel is on 3 levels, with a twisty staircase adding to the charm. It sleeps 4 but the cottages can be interlinked to provide accommodation for up to 27 people and each has its own hot tub. Surrounded by hills, you can sit in the warmth of your hot tub, with mountainous landscape on 3 sides and a view down the valley towards Coniston Water on the other.

Easy dog walks are available directly from the cottage, following the old mining paths that criss-cross the landscape and it is simple to walk down the dirt track into Coniston village, where you will find dog friendly pubs.

Being in the heart of the Lake District, there are walks nearby of all grades, from easy lakeside rambles to strenuous fell walks. Not far from the village is Coniston Water, which offers a network of footpaths along the lakeside. Dog friendly passenger boats operate on the lake and these can be used to create an interesting day of circular boating and walking.

We had visited Coniston before, but to drive up the Coppermines access road is to enter a different world of mountainous scenery and industrial archaeology. It is most definitely a place to escape the hustle and bustle of modern life - like no other I've ever visited.

FACT FILE

Location: Mountain Cottages, Coniston, Cumbria
Website: coppermines.co.uk
Contact: 01539 441765
Type of accommodation: Cottage
Number of bedrooms: 2 (sleeps 4)
Number of dogs accepted: 3
Enclosed garden: No but securely-fenced field available in village
Local interest: Walks and boat rides at Coniston Water, walks from the door, Ruskin Museum at Coniston, Tarn Hows, Grizedale Forest
Best eats: The Yewdale Inn at Coniston

THE PLOUGH INN, LUPTON, CUMBRIA

By Tracey Radnall

Set in a limestone valley linking the Dales and Lakes and just minutes from the M6, The Plough Inn is a boutique-style inn, ideally located for a stopover or a longer stay.

Lupton was an ideal location for a stopover on my road trip from Warwickshire to Scotland and The Plough Inn was a welcome alternative to characterless motorway motels. The traditional roadside inn appears, from the outside at least, much like many others, with the addition of a huge, cast iron shire horse, adjacent to the entrance.

Inside is a blend of modern, rustic charm, very much of the popular hygge style, with woollen fleece-topped bar stools and neutral colours blending nicely with enormous oak beams. The space comprises an open-plan, dog friendly bar, dining and lounge areas, and a separate dining/function room, all with wood-burning stoves.

Upstairs has been converted into 6 luxury rooms, each individually designed. With my best pal, Bertie, in tow, it would also be a great base to explore both the Lake District and the Yorkshire Dales on foot, and a perfect retreat for a mid-week or a weekend escape.

Our room, Hutton, features views up to Hutton Roof and Farleton Fell and is actually more of a suite than a room. The door opens to reveal an entrance lobby with a minibar, leading into the comfortable bedroom, where there is a king-size bed, tea and coffee-making facilities, TV and WiFi. There is a separate, huge bathroom, complete with roll-top bath and enclosed shower room. I decided on a slow soak, taking in the views of the limestone crags beyond the window. *(continued...)*

FACT FILE

Location: Cow Brow, Lupton, Cumbria, LA6 1PJ
Website: theploughatlupton.co.uk
Contact: 01539 567700
Type of accommodation: Bed and breakfast
Number of bedrooms: 6
Number of dogs accepted: 2
Enclosed garden: No
Local interest: Ruskin's View, The Devil's Bridge, Hutton Roof Crags, the Radical Steps, River Lune
Best eats: The Plough Inn

All residents automatically have a table booked at 7pm in the bar - a nice touch, adding to the relaxed approach of this fine, old inn. The menu features many specials and tempting dishes. On a Monday evening the inn was busy, with both residents and locals, which is always a good indicator.

From 8.30 to 9.30, the kitchen provides cooked breakfast, comprising eggy brioche and an array of full English derivations.

The nearby town of Kirkby Lonsdale sits on the spot where Lancashire, Yorkshire and Westmorland meet, with a choice of walks within a 10-mile radius.

The Plough combines contemporary, earthy, hygge-style luxury with great food, cracking beer and exceptional value rooms. There is some road noise but the comfort more than makes up for it. Request a rear-facing room for the best views.

LANEFOOT FARM, THORNTHWAITE, CUMBRIA

By Alison Beever

There is a range of camping and glamping options at Lanefoot Farm, near Keswick in the Lake District, and it's a good place to find out what life is like in a motorhome.

We had always fancied the idea of life on the open road and, in anticipation of my partner, Julie's, retirement in June 2020, we decided to hire a luxury motorhome for a long weekend. The 'try before you buy' element of this break really appealed to us.

We collected our rented Escape 664 automatic motorhome from Swift Go's hire depot in Stockport and were shown around our luxury home for the weekend. All my questions were answered with patience, which was no mean feat with our excited Springer, Mac, wanting to explore his new home.

We were amazed by how much was packed into a small space. There was a large fridge, a cooker and hob, microwave, toaster, shower room with chemical toilet, TV and DVD player, a fixed bed, bedding and towels, lots of storage space and a really delightful welcome hamper.

So, with Mac safely clipped into the rear passenger seat, we were ready for the off. The motorhome was amazingly easy to drive - you just need to keep in mind the length and width when negotiating winding, country lanes.

After a few hours' driving, we pitched up at our campsite, Lanefoot Farm in Thornthwaite, between Keswick and Bassenthwaite Lake. After checking in, we *(continued...)*

FACT FILE

Location: Thornthwaite, Cumbria, CA12 5RZ

Website: stayinthornthwaite.co.uk

Contact: 01768 778097

Type of accommodation: Campsite

Number of dogs accepted: No strict rule, as long as dogs are well-behaved and on lead when on site

Local interest: Walks from the door, Bassenthwaite Lake, Derwentwater, Keswick

Best eats: Middle Ruddings and The Coledale Inn at Braithwaite

Motorhome: Swift Go Motorhome Hire, Pear Mill, Stockport Road West, Bredbury, Stockport, SK6 2BP

Website: swiftgo.co.uk

Contact: 0333 247 2222

Type of accommodation: Motorhome

Number of bedrooms: 1 (sleeps up to 4)

found it really easy to fill up the tank with fresh water and plug into the electric hook-up.

The campsite is in a beautiful location and we had a decent-sized pitch. Although it was fully booked and there were quite a few families in the next field, our pitch was very quiet and the whole place had a really laid-back feel.

The shop on the site also doubled as the reception. All of it was lovely and clean and there was a convenient bench located next to a stash of books and reading material which you could buy, in return for making a small donation to a local charity.

Julie said her shower was lovely, with constant hot water, but the one I chose had one of those buttons you continuously press (like at the swimming baths), so choose carefully before you commit to your shower!

We had mixed weather over the weekend, but it didn't dampen our spirits and we still ventured out on some lovely walks. We even had time to sit outside the motorhome, soaking up the sunshine, reading a book, and Mac was not at all perturbed by the visit of the resident sheep who wandered around the pitches, saying hello to the campers.

It was relatively easy to pack up, simply unplugging the electric hook-up and pressing the buttons to empty the waste/fresh water over the grid near reception. The chemical toilet was a little more challenging and heavy to lift over the Elsan point.

We had a fabulous weekend in the Lake District. Our introduction to motorhoming was enjoyed by all of us and Mac can't wait to go on our next adventure.

THE OLD BAKEHOUSE, CONISTON, CUMBRIA

By Emma Bearman

At The Old Bakehouse, you can enjoy cosy nights in or take a short stroll to nearby dog friendly pubs - both very appealing after a day exploring the beauty of the local area.

We decided to book a cottage through Coniston Cottages, a small, family-run business, with 10 great value, dog friendly cottages, set right in the heart of England's beautiful Lake District. For me, finding truly dog friendly accommodation is my priority and, right from the moment we arrived at The Old Bakehouse, the dogs were made to feel at home.

The cottage has an upside down layout. Downstairs, there's a master bedroom and a bathroom. The bedroom was lovely and cosy, which was very appealing after a long day of exploring, and there was plenty of room to sprawl out with the dogs and watch TV. The spacious living space is upstairs. The dining area, living room and well-equipped kitchen are combined, giving you a great open space. We spent most of our evenings in this room, with the fire on.

Outside, there is an enclosed garden and access to an enclosed 2-acre paddock. Training the dogs is my downtime - imagine my joy when I discovered it's possible to have an on-site dog training session with APDT member, Chris Mancini.

We were a short walk from some great, dog friendly pubs, which were a 10-minute stroll down the old railway walk and it would be a crime if I didn't mention the dog friendly Herdwicks Café, which we visited almost daily. My favourite walk was around Tarn Hows and the Tom Gill Waterfalls, which is just under 2 miles from the village of Coniston and one of the most beautiful places I have ever seen.

I am completely in love with the Lake District and Coniston especially. I highly recommend it for a dog friendly break.

FACT FILE

Location: Little Arrow, Coniston, Cumbria, LA21 8AU
Website: conistoncottages.co.uk
Contact: 01539 441114
Type of accommodation: Cottage
Number of bedrooms: 1 (sleeps 2 plus 1 on sofa bed in lounge)
Number of dogs accepted: 2 or 3
Enclosed garden: Yes
Local interest: Walks from the door, Tarn Hows and Tom Gill Waterfalls
Best eats: Herdwicks Café at Coniston

THE WORDSWORTH HOTEL & SPA, GRASMERE, CUMBRIA

By Angie Aspinall

Once the Earl of Cadogan's shooting lodge, The Wordsworth is a grand country mansion, offering fine views, relaxation and fine dining in the heart of Grasmere - probably Cumbria's most popular village.

Grasmere nestles below Helm Crag, just north of the lake which gives the village its name. There are independent shops, galleries and cafés in the village, most of which welcome dogs.

The Wordsworth Hotel is located in the heart of Grasmere. It has 2 acres of grounds, with views over the neighbouring mountains and vales. Our room was situated on the ground floor and the first thing I noticed was the array of goodies for our Westies, Tilly and Henry - brand new beds, two feeding bowls, treats and a tug/throw toy each. There was a door to the outside patio area, which meant no late-night dashes through the hotel, if one of the dogs needed to go out. On the second night, we dined in the Wordsworth's dog friendly Dove Bistro. Ours were the only 4-legged friends in the bistro and they were immediately welcomed with a bowl of water and dog biscuits from the bar. While on the subject of dining, I must mention the tremendous breakfasts at The Wordsworth Hotel. The full Cumbrian breakfast was superb, as were the pancakes and pastries.

From the village, it is a short walk to the lake. There is a walk around the lake but part of it is on the main A591. There are a number of other walks from the village, including the ascent of Helm Crag.

Despite the dismal weather during our stay, we had a wonderful time and look forward to returning to explore the area in more detail.

FACT FILE

Location: Grasmere, Lake District, Cumbria, LA22 9SW

Website: thewordsworthhotel.co.uk

Contact: 01539 435592

Type of accommodation: Hotel

Number of bedrooms: 38 (3 dog friendly)

Number of dogs accepted: 2

Enclosed garden: No

Local interest: Allan Bank, Rydal Mount, local walks including around the lake and Helm Crag

Best eats: The Wordsworth, Sarah Nelson's Gingerbread Shop, cafés and pubs in Grasmere

BIRCH COTTAGE, WARSLOW, STAFFORDSHIRE

By Jenny Green

Only 20 minutes from the extremely dog friendly town of Bakewell, Birch Cottage enjoys glorious views over the Manifold Valley.

Situated in the small village of Warslow, Birch Cottage is around 20 minutes from Bakewell, near the Staffordshire/Derbyshire border. The cottage, which dates back to the 1700s, has been lovingly restored by 2 sisters and one of them, Sue, checked us in.

As the owner of 4 dogs herself, she made a big fuss of my Westie cross, Ernie, who was keen to investigate the sunny, enclosed garden, with its views of the Manifold Valley. My partner, Chris, and I were more interested in the cottage, which has 2 spacious bedrooms, a cosy lounge with wood burner and a well-equipped kitchen, with a cool, tiled floor, which Ernie loved to lie on.

We also had a welcome pack waiting for us and Ernie had not been forgotten, either - a wicker basket contained dog towels, poo bags and a Mud Daddy, to hose off any dirt after wet walks. Sue provided us with lots of helpful information about the local area and her pick of dog friendly places to eat and drink.

We were really impressed with the market town of Bakewell, where we enjoyed a stroll along the riverside path and it would be rude to visit the Derbyshire town without sampling some of the famous Bakewell tarts and puddings. Several bakeries claim to serve the original, so we had to try them all.

A return visit to the Peak District is definitely on the cards, as there's still so much to see and do.

FACT FILE

Location: Back Lane, Warslow, Staffordshire, SK17 0JR

Website: airbnb.co.uk

Type of accommodation: Cottage

Number of bedrooms: 2 (sleeps 3)

Number of dogs accepted: 2 or 3

Enclosed garden: Yes

Local interest: Monsal Trail, Crich Tramway Village, Tissington Trail, Edward & Vintage sweet shop at Tissington, Wonder of the Peak Tram Tour at Buxton, The Buxton Tap Room, Chatsworth House garden & park, The Roaches, Goyt Valley

Best eats: The Manifold Inn at Hulme End, The Crispin at Great Longstone

LANCRIGG, GRASMERE, CUMBRIA
By Tracey Radnall

Despite being only a leafy valley walk from the village, Lancrigg, in its peaceful, wooded and secluded spot, could be several miles away from the bustle of Grasmere.

Walkers were an abundant sight as we approached the village of Grasmere, described by William Wordsworth as "the loveliest spot that man hath ever found".

Although classed as a 'hotel', Lancrigg has all the air of a large, family home. Inside, it has a refreshingly relaxed feel and the nicely proportioned rooms contain old fireplaces, sofas and scrubbed floorboards.

FACT FILE
Location: Easdale Road, Grasmere, Cumbria, LA22 9QN
Website: lancrigg.co.uk
Contact: 01539 435317
Type of accommodation: Hotel
Number of bedrooms: 10 (5 dog friendly)
Number of dogs accepted: 3
Enclosed garden: No
Local interest: Walks from the door, Aira Force (National Trust)
Best eats: The Lancrigg, dog friendly pubs and cafés in Grasmere

My room, Whittington, featured perfect views across the valley to Blea Crag, with the Langdale Fells away in the distance.

With rain forecast, Bertie and I were eager to head out of the hotel door and straight onto the valley path, which we followed to the west of the Gill, eventually reaching Easdale Tarn, where Bertie splashed away in a carefree way, like only a spaniel can.

After jumping into the shower and fresh clothes, we made for the new Poet's Bar, a delightful room with a lovely octagonal bay window. The menu featured a host of local ingredients.

Easdale, Lancrigg and the surrounding area is a perfect retreat for those desiring to get away from it all, with stunning walks direct from the front door and well away from the year-round Cumbrian throng.

The hotel offers free Wi-Fi, but my suggestion is to turn it off and read a book instead. Or, better still, write a poem. What better inspiration do you need to get started?

LAUREL COTTAGE, SANDBACH, CHESHIRE

By Steve Bennett

Use of the swimming pool and jacuzzi make for a relaxing stay at Laurel Cottage which, despite being only 5 minutes from the M6, is in a surprisingly rural setting.

With a 10-year-old son, Jack, and 2 whippets, Charlie and Angel, we wanted a summer holiday with something for Jack to do, walks close by for the dogs and an opportunity for Lin and me to relax - so quite a tall order!

We had left the search for a holiday rather late and there was not much availability but we found a cottage which, on the face of it, matched our criteria. The only issue was the location. It was in a village close to Sandbach, an area that I knew only for the services on the M6!

Exiting the M6 at junction 17, we were surprised and a little concerned that our sat nav announced we were only 5 minutes away from our destination. It felt far too suburban for a countryside holiday. But in that 5 minutes, we teleported from suburbia into beautiful countryside, where we turned off a country lane into the grounds of a farmhouse.

The cottages are behind the farmhouse, surrounding a courtyard. The owner, Jackie, made us feel very welcome and showed us into the cottage.

Downstairs has an open-plan kitchen, a bathroom with a fantastic shower, and living room with a dining table close to a stable door, which opened to an enclosed, gravel garden at the back of the property.

Upstairs, there are 2 double bedrooms. *(continued...)*

FACT FILE

Location: Brereton, Sandbach, Cheshire
Website: sykescottages.co.uk (property reference 971361)
Type of accommodation: Cottage
Number of bedrooms: 2 (sleeps 4)
Number of dogs accepted: 2 (more by arrangement)
Enclosed garden: Yes
Local interest: Anderton Boat Lift Canal & River Trust (canal walk but grounds not dog friendly), Freshfield Squirrel Reserve at Formby, Formby Beach, Leek & Rudyard Railway, Southport
Best eats: The Bear's Head at Brereton, Tegg's Nose Tea Room at Tegg's Nose, White Hart Tearoom & B&B, The Wizard Tearoom at Nether Alderley

They are both light and airy, and have views over the courtyard at the front and the gardens at back, including a lovely duck pond.

Next door to the cottages is the access to the swimming pool and jacuzzi. There's a wipe board inside the doorway where you can book the swimming pool between 10am and 7pm, in hour slots. This is a great idea, as we enjoyed having the facilities to ourselves.

We had a great time at Laurel Cottage. The owners could not have done more to make our stay special. The pool and jacuzzi are lovely and we were able to use the cottage as a base to travel to dog friendly places around the area. If we were asked to pick a fault, we would find it difficult to do so, but there are limited places to walk directly from the cottage. If you are happy to drive, then the world (well, Cheshire, Staffordshire and Derbyshire) is literally your oyster.

SCALEBECK HOLIDAY COTTAGES, GREAT ASBY, CUMBRIA

By Andy Craig

The Eden Valley makes a fantastic holiday destination - boasting glorious walking country and many sites of interest, it is also adjacent to both the Lake District National Park and the Yorkshire Dales National Park.

An ancient farmstead set on 5 acres, Scalebeck Holiday Cottages is located in the heart of the countryside, with fields on all sides. It comprises 3 cottages that have been thoughtfully constructed from what was a 17th century hay barn.

There are a couple of outside sitting areas, a barbecue for sunny days and there is even a fenced-off exercise area for dogs, which is a great bonus feature. There is also a games room, with ping-pong and jigsaws, and a laundry room.

Since 2016 this area of the Eden Valley has been part of the Yorkshire Dales National Park, but it is a quiet corner compared to busier parts of The Dales. One mile away is the village of Great Asby, which has a great dog friendly pub.

We decided to explore Great Asby Scar, a large expanse of environmentally important limestone pavement, only a few minutes from Great Asby village. It was a fascinating walk across a strange, rocky landscape and the views from the summit of the plateau were breathtaking, looking one way towards the Pennines, another to the Lake District fells and yet another to the Howgills by Sedbergh. Daisy managed to find some muddy puddles to cool her paws in, so everyone was happy.

Back at Scalebeck, Daisy really appreciated the doggy field where she was able to run off the lead and chase her ball to her heart's delight, while the local livestock looked on from a safe distance.

FACT FILE

Location: Great Asby, Appleby-in-Westmorland, CA16 6TH

Website: scalebeckholidaycottages.co.uk

Contact: 01768 351006

Type of accommodation: Cottage

Number of bedrooms: 1 (sleeps 2)

Number of dogs accepted: 1

Enclosed garden: Yes

Local interest: Great Asby Scar

Best eats: The Three Greyhounds Inn at Great Asby, The Royal Oak at Appleby

NORTH LAKES HOTEL, PENRITH, CUMBRIA

By Andy Craig

A modern hotel, close to both the Lake District National Park and the Eden Valley, The North Lakes Hotel offers comfort, spa facilities and a warm welcome for doggy guests.

Nestling within picturesque, landscaped grounds, just outside Penrith, The North Lakes Hotel is ideally placed if you fancy exploring the Lake District. It's only 10 minutes by car from Ullswater and 30 minutes from Keswick, which has earned a reputation as one of the most dog friendly places in the Lakes.

FACT FILE

Location: Ullswater Road, Penrith, CA11 8QT
Website: northlakeshotel.co.uk
Contact: 01768 868111
Type of accommodation: Hotel
Number of bedrooms: 84 (7 dog friendly)
Number of dogs accepted: 2
Enclosed garden: Yes
Local interest: Wetheriggs Country Park, Pooley Bridge, Penrith Castle, Brougham Castle, Lowther Castle & Gardens, Long Meg and Her Daughters (Bronze Age circle), Ullswater, Keswick
Best eats: North Lakes Hotel, numerous dog friendly cafés and pubs in Penrith and surrounding area

The hotel is a large, modern building and the grounds were immaculate. It's very stylish inside yet, with a fire blazing in the hearth, it was also cosy and welcoming. The staff, who were helpful, friendly and knowledgeable, were charming and Daisy was given a treat on arrival. She thought she'd test their dog-friendliness by putting her front paws on the desk, a trick she learned in our local pub, and they didn't blink.

We were shown to our suite, which was lovely. There's a designated dog friendly entrance, where canine guests enter because it leads to a space where you can dry them off, remove wet weather gear and clean any shoes. There's also a dedicated fenced-off area, with a bin.

I asked if Daisy could join us while we ate and a member of staff immediately reserved a table on the terrace, outside the main restaurant. They placed a water bowl and a dog bed beside the fire, so Daisy didn't have any complaints. She was soon snuggled in and, while she slept, we enjoyed a lovely meal. Dogs can also join their owners in the bar.

The next morning, after a comfy night's sleep, we had a leisurely breakfast with Daisy, eating our fill from the buffet.

Penrith lies just a few miles outside the Lake District National Park and the imposing ruins of Penrith Castle dominate the surroundings. The scenery is inspiring and the area's rich heritage makes every outing an adventure.

There are plenty of landmarks nearby, including several castles and the Eden Valley is a real highlight. It's picturesque and quiet, with fewer of the crowds that you find elsewhere in the Lakes. And there's a wide variety of walking opportunities.

We had a super time at the hotel and would recommend it, if you have a dog. However, although there's a mixture of standard rooms and suites, only 7 welcome dogs, so check when you make a reservation.

The hotel goes beyond what most guests expect and they can use the spa facilities or just relax beside the fire with a warming drink - ideal after a day enjoying the amazing landscape.

LUXURY IN THE LAKES, CUMBRIA

By Helen Steel

Do luxury hotels and dogs mix? A road trip involving overnight stays at 5 of Cumbria's finest reveals the truth...

The Lake District is well known for being a dog paradise, with fells, streams, caves and public footpath signs around every twist and turn.

It's also got its fair share of luxury hotels. But ... muddy pets and cosy, 5-star lounges don't normally mix. Meg, my Jack Russell cross, my husband, Ed, and I made it our mission to disprove this. Oh, and thrown into the mix was our 13-month-old baby,

just to really challenge hotel staff.

Hipping Hall at Cowan Bridge was our first stop - not really the Lakes but close enough. It marks the spot where Yorkshire, Lancashire and Cumbria converge, so you've technically visited 3 counties in just one stop.

The triple AA rosette hotel has an impressive reputation. It boasts a restaurant named the best in the UK's hotel industry. The dog friendly rooms in its converted stables area provide a thoughtful doggy haven, boasting oodles of room, with a living room and bedroom, and the world's most comfortable bed. Meg had a welcome pack of her own, a bed, and freedom to explore the 5 acres, which were well cordoned-off and accessible from the lovely French doors. While she wasn't allowed in the elegant lounge or the stately, Shakespearian-era restaurant, she was welcomed with open arms in the comfortable Orangery, where tea and coffee were served on demand.

There are plenty of walks in the area and, along a path from the hotel, you can judge

FACT FILE

Location: Hipping Hall, Cowan Bridge, Kirkby Lonsdale, Lancs, LA6 2JJ
Website: hippinghall.com
Contact: 01524 271187
Number of bedrooms: 15 (7 dog friendly)
Number of dogs accepted: Multiple, depends on size of dog(s) and size of room
Enclosed garden: Yes
Local interest: Forest of Bowland, Devil's Bridge

for yourself whether Ruskin's description of the view as 'one of the loveliest in England, and therefore the world' deserves the accolade.

Next stop was **The Ryebeck Hotel** at Bowness-on-Windermere, which is smaller and more down to earth, and didn't prompt quite such a 'dogs, really?' reaction from us, when we walked into reception. It's clean, cosy and welcoming. The rooms were slightly more modest, yet still very pleasant, with courtyard access. Meg was again made to feel important, with doggy B&B (Biscuit and Bed).

The major plus was the option to eat with your 4-legged friend in the lounge area, which could be set up to take dinner. We opted to allow Meg to enjoy the fine dining with us and, with views across Lake Windermere fit for a Wainwright front cover to one side and a roaring fire to the

other, it made for a very special meal. The food was the 'upmarket comfort food' end of the fine dining scale.

And did someone say walkies? Another great plus was the option to walk straight from the door, through the garden, right down to Lake Windermere. *(continued...)*

FACT FILE

Location: The Rybeck Hotel, Lyth Valley Road, Bowness-on-Windermere, LA23 3JP

Website: ryebeck.com

Contact: 01539 488195

Number of bedrooms: 6 dog friendly

Number of dogs accepted: 2

Enclosed garden: Yes

Local interest: Lake Windermere, Orrest Head

The **Rothay Manor** at Ambleside offered perhaps the warmest welcome. Dogs were very much at the centre and the resident dog makes this clear, with his personalised note. We were also struck by how staff, at every opportunity, wanted to fuss over Meg and ask her life story. Not every room allows 4 paws but, unlike so many places which allocate the smallest bedrooms in an annexe, ours was very spacious, with a separate living room... perfect if your dog likes to get away from you at night!

Dining was a pleasure rather than a stress. Meg hates being left in unusual places and the solution here was perfect. Drinks were served in the drawing room, which had an open fire and open doors leading into the dining room. So while Meg was allowed to happily sit under our table, away from the main action, we could still see her. Which is exactly how she likes it.

The local area has to be the diamond in the Lake District's studded collar. So many pubs welcome dogs with open arms. Our favourite for value was the White Lion.

FACT FILE

Location: Rothay Manor, Rothay Bridge, Ambleside, LA22 0EH

Website: rothaymanor.co.uk

Contact: 01539 433605

Number of bedrooms: 25 (8 dog friendly)

Number of dogs accepted: 1 or 2 (depending on size)

Enclosed garden: No

Local interest: Ambleside, Lake Windermere

I've only been to a couple of MacDonald hotels - imposing spa and golf venues - but **The Swan at Grasmere** isn't your average. At the 17th century coaching inn, everyone bent over backwards to make us all feel special - and every other human and hound checking in (there were plenty of friends for Meg here).

Free-roaming babies and curious dogs were gladly received and not reproached. A cosy and reasonably priced bar was the option for dogs, but we would have picked this over the restaurant anyway.

All classic rooms allow dogs, which is a great plus and, should Meg have wanted to swing a cat (she definitely would), she could have swung lots of them in the bedroom, which had plenty of character and a picturesque outlook over the Lion and the Lamb.

Straight out of the hotel, you can walk in the valley, taking a detour up the Lion and the Lamb, or simply take in the view from the bottom, as we did. *(continued...)*

FACT FILE

Location: The Swan Hotel, Keswick Road, Grasmere, Ambleside, LA22 9RF (closed for refurbishment until April 2023)

Website: inncollectiongroup.com/the-swan-grasmere/

Contact: 01915 803610

Number of bedrooms: TBC when re-opens in April 2023

Number of dogs accepted: 2

Enclosed garden: No

Local interest: Grasmere, Helm Crag (the Lion & the Lamb), Rydal Water

129

Our final stop was at the impressive **Holbeck Ghyll Hotel** at Windermere. It was with a slight sense of trepidation that we entered the lobby - oak-panelled with high ceilings, it's certainly imposing. But the staff couldn't have been friendlier, while the hotel couldn't have been more exclusive.

As expected, the lobby, with its inglenook fireplace, was as far as Meg could go in the hotel itself. But its pet-friendly rooms were less a consolation, more a preference, as far as we were concerned. The 6 rooms in the separate lodge all had a balcony or terrace and access to the awe-inspiring view.

A spiral staircase, treats for Meg and even a little book left in the cot for Frankie all added to the feeling of grandeur, yet warmth. Meg reigned supreme over our sofa and bed and a note (left by the resident dog, Eva) told her she was welcome to do so, as long as she used the throw provided!

As for walkies, while most of the hotel was out of bounds, there was plenty of room for bounding around outside. Even escape artist, Meg, couldn't have got into any trouble. For a quicker, yet still quite strenuous, walk, the hotel has its own gardens which lead down to the lake, and back up. Up being the most important word. For a serious trek though, the surrounding fells such as Wansfell Pike and Jenkin Crag are easily accessible from the hotel, with no road-walking necessary.

FACT FILE

Location: Holbeck Ghyll Hotel, Holbeck Lane, Windermere, LA23 1LU

Website: holbeckghyll.com

Contact: 01539 432375

Number of bedrooms: 22 (8 dog friendly)

Number of dogs accepted: 3

Enclosed garden: Yes

Local interest: Lake Windermere, Wansfell Pike, Jenkin Crag

130

THE BURGOYNE, SWALEDALE, NORTH YORKSHIRE

By Andy Craig

Situated in the breathtaking Swaledale Valley, The Burgoyne is perfectly placed for exploring the Yorkshire Dales National Park.

Georgian in style and easily the most imposing building in Reeth, The Burgoyne enjoys a central location, overlooking the green.

We were greeted warmly when we arrived, particularly Daisy, who made the most of the attention. Given a choice of rooms, we chose Thwaite, which is south-facing with views of the village, and has a private bathroom across the corridor. It was immaculate, if traditional in design, and quite compact but the window seat more than compensated, as it meant we could enjoy the views of Swaledale at our leisure.

Reeth, which nestles within a natural amphitheatre, stands where Swaledale meets its neighbour, Arkengarthdale. It's surrounded by picturesque countryside and the best way of learning more about the region, its walking routes and many attractions, is by visiting Reeth National Park Centre.

The dining room at The Burgoyne is incredibly elegant but we fancied a more relaxed approach, so we chose The Buck Hotel instead. After a tasty dinner and a few pints of great beer, we slept well - fresh air is always one of the best relaxants!

We may have only spent one night in Reeth but I can imagine returning because we barely scratched the surface. Swaledale flattens out as the river reaches Richmond and there are plenty of walking opportunities there, particularly around the castle, which is one of the region's most popular landmarks.

FACT FILE

Location: On The Green, Reeth, Swaledale, North Yorkshire, DL11 6SN

Website: theburgoyne.co.uk

Contact: 01748 884292

Type of accommodation: Hotel

Number of bedrooms: 11

Number of dogs accepted: 2

Enclosed garden: Yes

Local interest: Reeth National Park Centre, River Swale, Great Shunner Fell, Addlebrough, Lovely Seat, Fremington Edge

Best eats: The Buck Hotel at Reeth

THE MIDLAND HOTEL, MORECAMBE, LANCASHIRE

By David and Sarah Edwards

Combining the glamour of the 1930s with today's mod cons, the iconic Midland Hotel offers elegant accommodation, panoramic views and fine dining, right on the seafront.

Morecambe Bay may be picturesque in its own right but it's also within easy reach of the Lake District, which is one of the most inspiring landscapes in the country, the Yorkshire Dales, where the countryside is much gentler on the eye, the lively resort of Blackpool, the elegant façades of Southport, and the many charming villages that line the estuary.

FACT FILE

Location: Marine Road West, Morecambe, Lancashire, LA4 4BU

Website: englishlakes.co.uk/the-midland/

Contact: 03304 042365

Type of accommodation: Hotel

Number of bedrooms: 44 (42 dog friendly)

Number of dogs accepted: 2

Enclosed garden: No

Local interest: Blackpool, Carnforth, Sizergh Castle, Grange-over-Sands, Lake Windermere

Best eats: The Midland Hotel, The Hazelmere at Grange-over-Sands

An imposing presence at the south end of the seafront, the Midland Hotel dates from 1933, when the ever-expanding railways brought thousands of holidaymakers to the Lancashire coast and it's become one of the county's most iconic buildings. Location plays an important role and the Midland Hotel provides guests with a tempting cocktail of glamour, elegance and panoramic views.

Open the doors and you could be centre stage in an episode of Agatha Christie's Poirot. Marble, wood and glass abound in the main lobby, a tastefully tiled area with reception beyond. The carpets were designed by Marion Dorn (whose creations can also be found in The White House) but other highlights include an Eric Gill frieze and a staircase that wouldn't look out of place in a royal palace.

We chose a Classic Sea View Room and weren't disappointed. It had 3 large windows, all overlooking the bay and was both airy and light, with all the mod cons you'd expect, including a TV, a minibar and the usual tea and coffee-making facilities. We were staying with our daughter and she slept in a single bed in an alcove. Orinoco's crate sat happily in the corner and he bonded instantly with a cuddly toy we found on the bed.

The dining room makes the most of the spectacular views and you can also relax over a drink in the foyer and the Ravilious Rotunda Bar, which transports you to another age - the decadent days of the 1930s. The Midland may be nearly 90 years old but, after extensive renovation, the overall standards are high. There's plenty of parking, ramps and lifts, the WiFi is good and the service was wonderful. Although dogs are prohibited from the dining room, Orinoco was welcome everywhere else.

Morecambe is surrounded by picturesque countryside but you can also walk your dog locally - just the ticket first thing in the morning. Simply head downstairs out of the hotel and you're on the seafront.

The first evening, tired after our journey from London, we wandered along the promenade, enjoying all the fresh air. We ate with friends in the dining room, while Orinoco, having been walked, watered and fed, was asleep in our bedroom, secure in what had quickly become a familiar environment.

Over the next 3 days, we explored more of the local area, including Blackpool, Carnforth, Sizergh Castle, Grange-over-Sands and Lake Windermere.

Our long weekend was over very quickly but one treat remained. On the day of our departure, we were given a tour of the whole building, which I would heartily recommend.

BECK HALL, MALHAM, YORKSHIRE

By Deb Bridges

Beck Hall, in the picturesque Yorkshire Dales village of Malham, doesn't just offer good food and comfortable accommodation - it takes dog friendliness to the highest level, too!

Anyone who's enjoyed a walking holiday with their dog will know that a number of variables can make or break the experience. Not least of these is finding accommodation where the owners don't merely welcome dogs as they arrive, but remain sanguine when they return - wet, cold and muddy - at the end of the day.

I found Beck Hall in Malham to be just such a place. The stone slabs shrug off muddy paw prints and dogs can dry themselves beside a roaring fire in the Snug, while their owners put their feet up, having delved into the fridge and made a quick note of what they've taken from the 'honesty baa'.

All the rooms are dog friendly and the owner's policy is simple - wherever human guests can go, their dogs can go with them, including the Bistro, where breakfast, lunch and dinner are served. There's a pile of dog beds at the entrance to the Bistro - fail to take one, as I did, and you'll find yourself suitably shamed by a member of staff, who'll quickly provide one.

Our room certainly ticked all the boxes - a comfy bed, a powerful shower and plenty of space, so Ula could stretch out on her bed, without becoming a trip hazard. We also found tea and coffee-making facilities, homemade shortbread and a bedside lamp that was sufficiently bright to read by. Nearby is the iconic Malham Cove and a short walk takes you to the base of the massive, curved limestone cliff-face. It's an unusual habitat and some amazing birds, including peregrine falcons, have made it their home.

FACT FILE

Location: Cove Rd, Malham, BD23 4DJ
Website: beckhallmalham.com
Contact: 01729 830729
Type of accommodation: Hotel
Number of bedrooms: 21
Number of dogs accepted: 3
Enclosed garden: No
Local interest: Malham Cove, Malham Smithy (female blacksmith, Annabelle Bradley), Malham Tarn, Gordale Scar, Weets Top, Skipton Castle, Parcevall Hall Gardens, Bolton Abbey, The Embsay & Bolton Abbey Steam Railway
Best eats: Beck Hall and The Lister Arms at Malham

THE ELTERMERE INN, AMBLESIDE, CUMBRIA

By Imogen Man

Set in the heart of the breathtaking Langdale Valley, and only minutes from the delights of Windermere, Grasmere and Ambleside, a warm and friendly welcome awaits at The Eltermere Inn.

Taking a holiday has taken quite a different perspective, now I have a dog. I've always been tempted by the Lake District, as it has some of the most spectacular scenery in England. And now walks would be even more enjoyable, watching Norman explore new places.

Our destination was Elterwater, which lies to the north of Windermere in the picturesque Langdale Valley. The Eltermere Inn is a small country house hotel which is ideally placed, as it's within easy reach of several of the region's most popular attractions. It was just what we wanted - personal, intimate and friendly, with a relaxed atmosphere and wonderful staff. It felt like we were staying with members of our extended family.

A traditional, stone-built property, it nestles attractively amongst trees, a short walk from the water's edge, it's whitewashed walls contrasting with the verdant landscape beyond. The bedrooms have been decorated with great care and it's clear that each has its own character. We particularly liked the bar, which felt more like a pub, with a roaring open fire, rustic wooden furniture and brassware that glinted in the lamplight. We ate at one of the tables here, rather than in the dining room, because it meant Norman could join us. We sampled several of the local beers and also a few cocktails, which included a delightful rhubarb prosecco.

Outside, there are extensive gardens and we enjoyed ambling around the colourful borders. I imagine these are particularly lovely in the spring, when the *(continued...)*

FACT FILE

Location: Elterwater, Ambleside, Cumbria, LA22 9HY
Website: eltermere.co.uk
Contact: 01539 437207
Type of accommodation: Hotel
Number of bedrooms: 13 (4 dog friendly)
Number of dogs accepted: 2
Enclosed garden: No
Local interest: Elterwater, Windermere, Grasmere, Ambleside, Hawkshead
Best eats: The Eltermere Inn

rhododendrons are flowering. There's a private jetty, if you fancy fishing on the lake, and all guests can use the facilities at The Langdale, which is just a short walk up the road. There's a swimming pool with sauna, Jacuzzi and steam room, a beauty spa and tennis courts.

One of the receptionists lent us a local guidebook that contained a wide range of walks. Norman suffers from 'short leg syndrome' and, like most Pugs, can sometimes struggle with his breathing problems because of his flat face, but he loves his walks. We chose an 8-mile route

and he spent the whole time running ahead of us. It was wonderful! The route was varied with a mixture of fell, farm and woodland tracks. We passed several waterfalls and Norman, clearly embracing the natural world after spending so long in an urban environment, splashed around in the stream.

The weather was amazing during our stay and we have such wonderful memories of our first dog friendly holiday that we shall definitely return.

THE DEVONSHIRE FELL HOTEL, BURNSALL, NORTH YORKSHIRE

By Angie Aspinall

With access to acres of off-road walking directly from the door, The Devonshire Fell Hotel prides itself on being fully dog friendly.

I wanted to take my husband away as a treat for his birthday, but the date coincided with us dog-sitting our friend's dog and I wasn't sure I'd be able to find anywhere that would take us, a Westie, a Cockapoo and a Cavalier King Charles. I needn't have worried because the staff at the Devonshire Fell happily accepted the booking.

The 'Dev Fell', (as it's affectionately known by the team that works there) is located on the edge of the picturesque village of Burnsall, less than a mile from its big brother, The Devonshire Arms Hotel & Spa, which sits beside the picturesque remains of Bolton Abbey. It's a lovely part of the world and, if you've never visited with your dogs, one I'd heartily recommend.

Burnsall is picture-postcard-pretty, with its oft-photographed bridge, which is visible from the Devonshire Fell itself.

Our room enjoyed views of the garden which was a tapestry of colour. It was extremely comfortable and had been styled with great thought - an eclectic mix of tasteful antiques and inspirational modern art complementing the elegant furniture. We liked the super-king-size zip and link bed so much, we bought one a few days later.

The next day, after enjoying a hearty breakfast, we headed out on a walk. Guests at the hotels receive complimentary parking permits which they can use on the estate, and its great walking country.

It was a fabulously relaxing, entertaining and über dog friendly weekend in the heart of Yorkshire.

FACT FILE

Location: Burnsall, North Yorkshire, BD23 6BT
Website: devonshirefell.co.uk
Contact: 01756 729000
Type of accommodation: Hotel
Number of bedrooms: 16
Number of dogs accepted: Mutliple
Enclosed garden: No
Local interest: Paths on the estate, Strid Wood, River Wharfe, the Strid
Best eats: The Devonshire Fell Hotel, The Burlington Restaurant at the Devonshire Arms Hotel & Spa, The Cavendish Pavilion

137

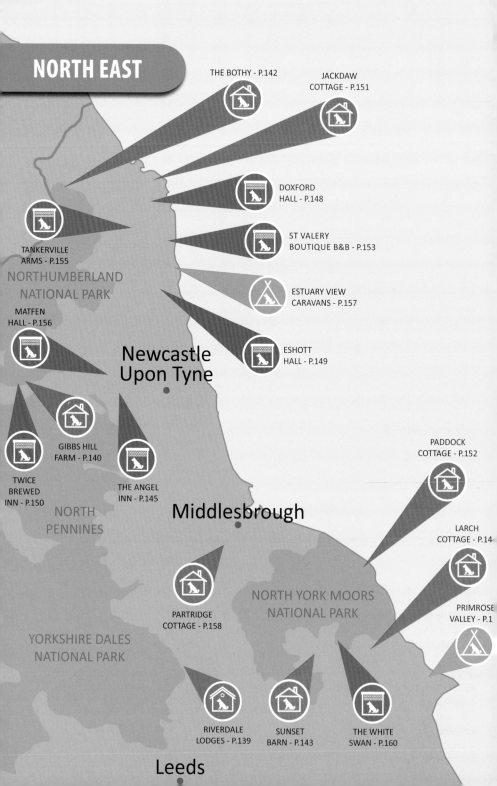

NORTH EAST

THE BOTHY - P.142

JACKDAW
COTTAGE - P.151

DOXFORD
HALL - P.148

ST VALERY
BOUTIQUE B&B - P.153

TANKERVILLE
ARMS - P.155

NORTHUMBERLAND
NATIONAL PARK

ESTUARY VIEW
CARAVANS - P.157

MATFEN
HALL - P.156

ESHOTT
HALL - P.149

Newcastle
Upon Tyne

GIBBS HILL
FARM - P.140

TWICE
BREWED
INN - P.150

THE ANGEL
INN - P.145

NORTH
PENNINES

Middlesbrough

PADDOCK
COTTAGE - P.152

LARCH
COTTAGE - P.14

PARTRIDGE
COTTAGE - P.158

NORTH YORK MOORS
NATIONAL PARK

PRIMROSE
VALLEY - P.1

YORKSHIRE DALES
NATIONAL PARK

RIVERDALE
LODGES - P.139

SUNSET
BARN - P.143

THE WHITE
SWAN - P.160

Leeds

RIVERDALE LODGES, WEST TANFIELD, YORKSHIRE

By Andy Craig

Located in the foothills of the Yorkshire Dales, Riverdale offers comfortable accommodation on a super-dog-friendly site which, says the management, 'is not just a word - it's what we do!'

'Curlew' is one of 4 luxurious wooden lodges at Riverdale (there are also 4 safari tents). The lodges have 3 bedrooms, sleeping 6 in comfort. They are extremely well equipped, with everything you could possibly need for a holiday, including WiFi, fridge and freezer, dishwasher, washing machine and nice touches, such as umbrellas and fans (depending on the weather). There is an outside firepit/barbecue area and the grounds are well maintained and attractive.

Riverdale sits within farmland and beside a beautiful, tree-lined river. Two walks lead from the park - one riverside and woodland walk to West Tanfield and a circular walk through woods and along field edges.

The lodges and tents are cleverly positioned to offer privacy and the reception block has a dog wash, with shampoo and a warm shower. Dog treats, bowls, towels and toys are all provided and dog beds are also available. The personalised dog treats were exceptional!

The attention to detail from the team at Riverdale is second to none. In advance of our stay, we received personalised directions from our home to the door of our lodge and we were welcomed, on arrival, with flowers and many suggestions for what the area has to offer.

Our springtime visit meant we walked through bluebells and wildflowers but the woodland and riverside are clearly beautiful all year round.

FACT FILE

Location: West Tanfield, Ripon,Yorkshire Dales, HG4 5JG

Website: riverdaleruralholidays.com

Contact: 01677 470532

Type of accommodation: Wooden lodge

Number of bedrooms: 3 (sleeps 6)

Number of dogs accepted: Mutliple

Enclosed garden: No

Local interest: Fountains Abbey & Studley Royal Water Garden, The Himalayan Garden & Sculpture Park, Hackfall Wood, Masham village

Best eats: The Bull Inn at West Tanfield, Bordar House Teas at Masham

139

GIBBS HILL FARM, BARDON MILL, NORTHUMBERLAND

By Scott Antcliffe

Cosy Felbridge Cottage is a good choice for visiting Hadrian's Wall and the many attractions of the local area, with limited signals offering the added bonus of a detox from WiFi and mobile phones!

Northumberland is, without a doubt, one of my favourite counties in the UK. Steeped in history, with the most castles per county (70) than anywhere else in the world, it really is a fascinating place, with so much to see and do. The Northumberland coast is also home to some stunning beaches - many of which are dog friendly all year round, too.

Our first impressions of Felbridge Cottage were great. It was small and cosy, but really inviting. It has an open-plan ground floor, with a living room and well-stocked kitchen. There was a nice little welcome booklet full of helpful information of things to do in the area and where the local amenities are. The upstairs consists of a large bedroom with a double bed and the bathroom has a shower/bath combo - the shower being surprisingly powerful, considering the remote location.

Once unpacked, we put on our walking boots and headed off for a local walk with Drift. With it being a working farm, dogs are encouraged to stay on a lead within the grounds, as farm machinery is often moving around. Also there are several friendly cats.

Within a 20-minute walk of the property, you will find Greenlee Lake, a lovely, quiet place for a stroll. Drift certainly approved of the water as, within a matter of seconds of seeing it, she had to go for a paddle!

FACT FILE

Location: Bardon Hill, Nr Hexham, Northumberland, NE47 7AP

Website: gibbshillfarm.co.uk

Contact: 01434 344030

Type of accommodation: Cottage

Number of bedrooms: 1 (sleeps 2)

Number of dogs accepted: 1

Enclosed garden: No

Local interest: Hadrian's Wall, Allen Banks & Staward Gorge, Hexham, Sele Park, Hexham Abbey, River Tyne, Greenlee Lake

Best eats: Spokes Kitchen at Corbridge, The Twice Brewed Inn and The Bowes Hotel at Bardon Mill, The Small World Café at Hexham, The Greenhead Hotel at Brampton

That evening we headed to Milecastle Inn, in the neighbouring village of Haltwhistle, just a 10-minute drive away. Although not dog friendly, it was a cosy, traditional pub with hearty, wholesome food. It had a good choice of real ales, which was great to see… and sample.

The next morning, we were up bright and early to walk along Hadrian's Wall. Luckily, just a short 7-minute drive away from the property is Steel Rigg, an access point to the Wall, with a payable car park. This particular part of the Wall is known for the Sycamore Gap, the famous tree that appears in the Kevin Costner 1991 blockbuster hit, Robin Hood Prince of Thieves. Along the Wall there are Milecastles, essentially a fort at every Roman mile, which were used to protect weaker areas from attackers.

Hexham is a lovely town with many dog friendly cafés, pubs and restaurants. What's even more impressive is that the car park, in the centre of town, is free. As a frugal Yorkshireman, this was a welcome surprise.

We'd certainly recommend Felbridge Cottage if you are looking to re-connect with your surroundings and absorb yourself in the rich, local history and stunning scenery. It was a thoroughly enjoyable stay.

THE BOTHY, REEDSFORD, NORTHUMBERLAND

By Steve Bridgewater

The Bothy lies in a sheltered spot in the remote and extremely picturesque Bowmont Valley, deep in the foothills of the Cheviot Hills.

The property is all on ground floor level and has a large open-plan lounge/dining/kitchen area, where there is a wood burner, HD Freeview TV, iPod dock, DVD player and a selection of board games.

The convivial dining area has bench-style seating for many guests and the 'country cottage' style kitchen is really well appointed, with everything you need to prepare a meal or even do some baking, although The Bothy's owner, Corinne, offers a homemade, ready-meal service.

There's a very plush bathroom and 2 large bedrooms. The master bedroom has an ensuite shower room and a king-size bed, while the second room has a 'zip and link' bed that can be set up as either a 6ft super-king or two 3ft twin beds. There's also a games room, with table tennis and pool tables, in an adjacent building. A deep freeze and tumble dryer can be found in the separate outhouse. Outside, there is a large, enclosed garden and a decked, south-facing patio.

The extensive folder of local information specifically details attractions, beaches, pubs and restaurants that are dog friendly and we found ourselves spoiled for choice.

The Bothy is an idyllic and luxurious rural hideaway and our break provided infinite pleasures - from beach walks to castles, walled towns and some of the nicest people you could hope to meet.

FACT FILE

Location: Reedsford, near Mindrum, TD12 4QQ
Website: crabtreeandcrabtree.com
Contact: 01573 226711
Type of accommodation: Cottage
Number of bedrooms: 2 (sleeps 4 plus up to 2 children)
Number of dogs accepted: 3
Enclosed garden: Yes
Local interest: The Lowry Trail at Berwick-upon-Tweed, Heatherslaw Corn Mill, Lindisfarne, Bamburgh Castle, Dunstanburgh Castle, Alnwick Castle
Best eats: Fantoosh at Berwick-upon-Tweed, Tack Room Café at Bamburgh Castle, The Terrace Café at Wooler

142

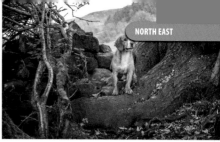

SUNSET BARN, NORMANBY, YORKSHIRE

By Andy Craig

Situated on a working farm, Sunset Barn provides bright and airy, dog friendly accommodation in an area steeped in history and surrounded by good walking country.

Sunset Barn is converted from an early 19th century farm building and retains many of the interior features, with bare brick walls, stone floor, quirky windows and a double-sided fireplace with a wood burning stove.

It is on the owners' farm, at the edge of the village of Normanby. The village has an excellent pub, selling well-kept local beers and good pub food. Their special nights are particularly good value.

The front door leads first to a boot room, which is great for storing outdoor things and for drying off wet dogs. The open-plan layout is clever, bright and spacious and the sense of space is enhanced by spectacular folding patio windows in both halves of the accommodation.

The generous king-size bedroom has a free-standing bath by the window, which is a very striking and welcome feature after a day walking the moors.

There are footpaths around the village and the owners suggest walking routes and fields where dogs can be safely exercised.

The dog friendly North Yorkshire Steam Railway, with miles of walking paths and bridleways, is just a few minutes' drive from the North Yorkshire Moors and the historic city of York is only a 40-minute drive away.

For me it was a perfect autumn break, combining relaxation, gorgeous walking, good photography opportunities and we learned some history too!

FACT FILE

Location: Westfield Barns, Normanby, Helmsley, North Yorkshire

Website: cottages.com

Contact: 07748 097486

Type of accommodation: Cottage

Number of bedrooms: 1 (sleeps 2)

Number of dogs accepted: 2

Enclosed garden: Yes

Local interest: Rievaulx Abbey, Helmsley Castle, the National Bird of Prey Centre, Castle Howard, North Yorkshire Steam Railway, York, Whitby, Robin Hood's Bay, Scarborough, Sutton Bank National Park Centre, Rosedale Abbey village

Best eats: The Sun Inn at Normanby

LARCH COTTAGE, RUSTON, NORTH YORKSHIRE MOORS

By Andy Craig

In a beautiful, rural setting, within easy reach of the North Yorkshire Moors, the self-contained Larch Cottage offers a peaceful getaway, with all mod cons.

Larch Cottage is a bright and immaculately maintained cottage, very tastefully converted from a 19th century barn. It is compact but very well equipped, with satellite TV and music on tap, as well as good broadband and USB ports for charging phones, etc. It has its own enclosed sitting out area and there is easy access to the owner's garden, for stretching legs and paws.

The village of Ruston is very picturesque and, because there is no through road, it is exceptionally quiet and peaceful. There are footpaths from the village, which make for excellent short dog walks. Once we had been welcomed warmly into Larch Cottage, Daisy and I explored some of the footpaths around Ruston and found our way through the woods to the Downe Arms Hotel for a drink and an excellent meal to end the day.

Next day, the North Yorkshire Moors Railway was an attraction not to be missed and I booked a compartment on a train pulled by a steam locomotive. Each compartment seats up to 6 and dogs are welcome on board.

The following day was misty but this part of the world always has options, so we headed back up onto the edge of the moors for a walk through Dalby Forest. There are literally miles of paths and a forest drive to explore. Ambling through the trees was delightful, with areas of conifer but also native British woodland to explore.

Would I return? Most certainly, I would.

FACT FILE

Location: Ruston, Scarborough, North Yorkshire
Website: larchcottageruston.co.uk
Contact: 07957 214161
Type of accommodation: Cottage
Number of bedrooms: 1 (sleeps 2)
Number of dogs accepted: Negotiable, depending on size
Enclosed garden: Yes
Local interest: North Yorkshire National Park, Flamingo Land theme park, dog friendly beaches, Dalby Forest, Whitby, Robin Hood's Bay, Goathland village, North Yorkshire Moors Railway
Best eats: Downe Arms Hotel at Wykeham, The Anvil Inn at Sawdon

THE ANGEL INN, CORBRIDGE, NORTHUMBERLAND

By Jeana Shippey

With Hadrian's Wall a short drive away, The Angel Inn makes a good base for exploring this historic area of the country.

The lovely village of Corbridge is like a fairy tale, with lots of toffee-coloured, stone houses and, as you drive over the magnificent old bridge, you can't miss The Angel Inn. Dating from 1569, it is one of the oldest inns in Northumberland.

What a lovely, warm welcome we received on arrival. We were promptly shown to our room, no 10, where a dog bed, jar of treats and 2 bowls were ready and waiting for our Wire Fox Terrier, Alfie. It was a nice thought, which put us immediately at our ease.

We had received an email from the hotel, detailing dog friendly walks and trails in and around the village, surrounding areas and further afield, which was a great help in planning our days ahead.

We could dine in the lounge with Alfie, which was good because, in other places, we have had to leave him in the room. The food was all locally sourced and they had a good choice on the menu.

In Corbridge, there are lots of dog friendly cafés and lovely independent shops, where Alfie was allowed inside.

The weather was changeable but nothing was going to stop us from seeing Hadrian's Wall, where we managed a walk, once the wind had died down, which Alfie loved. We enjoyed it, too, but I could imagine, on a better day, it would be great and we could walk further.

At The Angel Inn we had great food, a comfortable bed and a good shower. The best bits were the lounges, where we could take Alfie. They made us feel very relaxed.

FACT FILE

Location: Main Street, Corbridge, Northumberland, NE45 5LA

Website: theangelofcorbridge.com

Contact: 01434 632119

Type of accommodation: Bed and breakfast

Number of bedrooms: 10

Number of dogs accepted: 3

Enclosed garden: No

Local interest: Hexham town, Hadrian's Wall, The Pele Tower microbrewery at Corbridge

Best eats: The Angel Inn, The Heart of Northumberland at Hexham, Grant's Bakery at Corbridge

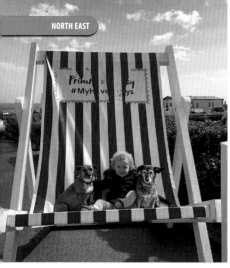

PRIMROSE VALLEY HOLIDAY PARK, FILEY, YORKSHIRE

By Helen Steel

With the beach and dog friendly town of Filey within walking distance, there's plenty to keep dogs and people of all ages happy at Primrose Valley, both on- and off-site.

We love the east coast and Haven's Primrose Valley website solemnly promised it thought of dogs as a 'big part of the family'. So, our toddler, Frankie, Cairn cross, Meg, my husband, Ed, and I packed our bags for a 3-night weekend break. And so did Grandma Jude and her rescue dog, Bella.

FACT FILE

Location: Primrose Valley, Filey, North Yorkshire, YO14 9RF

Website: haven.com

Contact: 01723 513771

Type of accommodation: Static caravan

Number of bedrooms: 2 or 3

Number of dogs accepted: 2

Enclosed garden: No

Local interest: Glen Gardens at Filey

Best eats: Mrs Bishops Doggy Deli at Filey, The Royal Oak

First impressions were that it was busy. But popular check-in times are Monday and Friday and it was half-term. The melee soon died down and we found our caravans. Dogs have recently gone up in the world at Haven - formerly only allowed in lower grade accommodation, they're now allowed in selected Deluxe and Prestige models, so we'd taken one of each (make sure you book the pet-friendly ones). Grandma the Bed Expert was most impressed by the size and comfort of her caravan and had a hard time keeping Bella in her own basket! Frankie and Meg thought there was plenty of room to play ball, which we quickly stopped.

Our first thought was to head to the beach, which is a 10-minute, well-signposted walk along the coast. For us there were the beautiful views and, for the dogs, there was an expanse of surprisingly deserted beach, if you turn right when you reach the bay. Frankie adored running in and out of the waves, and the dogs (and Grandma) delighted in following her.

When it rained, it was no problem. There were myriad cafés offering a resting place for pooches. In Filey, dogs aren't just allowed - it's assumed they'll be with you and we stopped off at one of the many cafés offering dog ice cream.

Every evening, we felt we couldn't retire without sampling the famous holiday camp-style entertainment. Our one worry was that dogs are the norm everywhere outside on-site, but nowhere inside and the caravans were fairly closely packed together. But we needn't have worried. The fact there was so much to do meant Meg and Bella were exhausted. And the soundproofing must have been good, because neither dog (both fairly needy rescues) gave a whimper when we left, and they were still silent during the mid-evening check.

The dogs weren't allowed inside the pubs and restaurants in the park but we opted to eat outside. Luckily the weather was good and there were covered areas. Opposite the park entrance, there's a lovely pub, the Royal Oak, which allows dogs.

All in all, it wasn't what I was expecting. What I thought would be a holiday juggling the needs of 3 generations and 2 dogs, turned out to be a break where everyone was catered for - a Haven for dogs, kids and grandmas, too.

DOXFORD HALL, ALNWICK, NORTHUMBERLAND

By Angie Aspinall

Set in 10 acres of private grounds, the timelessly elegant Doxford Hall is a great place to celebrate in style with your dogs.

Approaching a big birthday ending in '0', I opted for a quiet break with my husband at a dog friendly, luxury hotel. Doxford Hall had been recommended to us as the perfect place for a special celebration and we booked a 2-night break there.

With unseasonably sunny weather for December, we made the most of the first day of our mini-break by stopping off at Bamburgh Beach, where we breathed in the sea air while our Westies, Tilly and Henry, ran about like puppies.

The beaches in Northumberland are such a treat - unspoilt, quiet, and largely litter-free. They are also a beacon for dog walkers, so there are always interesting new friends for Tilly and Henry to meet.

Once inside Doxford Hall, the outside world seemed to fade to a dim and distant memory, as we were transported back in time to an altogether more elegant era.

Our room was on the ground floor - ideal for being able to let the dogs out with no fuss - and, what's more, it had a 4-poster bed.

We booked a table in the dog friendly lounge bar and sank into sumptuous leather chairs to enjoy our pre-dinner drinks. Everything was very friendly and relaxed, and the food was delicious.

For its elegance and relaxed atmosphere - and the warmth of the staff - Doxford Hall is hard to beat. I just hope I don't have to wait for another birthday that ends with '0' before I get to stay there again!

FACT FILE

Location: Chathill, Alnwick, Northumberland, NE67 5DN

Website: doxfordhall.com

Contact: 01665 589700

Type of accommodation: Hotel

Number of bedrooms: 42 (8 dog friendly)

Number of dogs accepted: 2 small or 1 large

Enclosed garden: Yes

Local interest: Bamburgh Beach, Bamburgh Castle (grounds only), Low Newton-by-the-Sea, Craster, Barter Books in Alnwick, The Fenwick Gallery in Warkworth

Best eats: The Saltwater Café at Beadnell, The Ship Inn at Low Newton-by-the-Sea, Shoreline Café at Craster, Bertram's at Warkworth

148

ESHOTT HALL, MORPETH, NORTHUMBERLAND

By Angie Aspinall

Nestled in the quiet village of Eshott, in the heart of rural Northumberland and surrounded by its own private estate, Eshott Hall offers luxurious accommodation and fine dining within easy reach of the Living Museum of the North at Beamish and the Northumbrian coast.

There are hotels that say they are dog friendly (when they merely tolerate dogs) and then there are hotels where the staff bend over backwards to make sure guests and their dogs have a great stay. Eshott Hall, a pretty Georgian manor house in the picturesque village of Eshott, is definitely one of the latter.

Our room, room 9, was on the first floor, overlooking the walled garden and tennis court. There was a super-king-size bed, a chaise longue and, my favourite of all features, a window seat! There was room for us, 2 dogs and all the paraphernalia that goes along with our travels. It was all so perfect - elegant, comfortable and welcoming. In the super-sized bathroom, there was a deep, free-standing bath, double sinks, a walk-in shower, Elemis toiletries and fluffy towels and bathrobes. Ahh, sheer luxury. I could see why the hotel was awarded 4 stars.

There was another couple staying at the hotel who had also brought their dog. To avoid any potential disruption, we were each offered separate dining areas. We dined in the drawing room, while the other guests dined in the library bar. It all worked out splendidly.

The dining at Eshott has been awarded 2 AA rosettes, and this is very well deserved. Home-grown and local produce feature on the menus throughout the seasons and there are plans to double the size of the herb garden to use 100% home-grown herbs.

FACT FILE

Location: Eshott, Morpeth, NE65 9EN
Website: eshotthall.co.uk
Contact: 01670 787454
Type of accommodation: Hotel
Number of bedrooms: 24 (11 dog friendly)
Number of dogs accepted: 2 small or 1 large
Enclosed garden: Walled garden
Local interest: Walks from the door, coast walks, Living Museum of the North at Beamish, Druridge Bay
Best eats: Eshott Hall

THE TWICE BREWED INN, HEXHAM, NORTHUMBERLAND

By Tracey Radnall

Set in breathtaking scenery beneath Hadrian's Wall, The Twice Brewed Inn provides comfortable ensuite bedrooms, while the bar features a roaring fire, craft ales brewed on the premises, an international wine selection and locally-sourced food in hearty portions.

The Twice Brewed Inn is nestled among both UNESCO World Heritage and Dark Sky designated sites. Home to some of the most breathtaking scenery in northern England, the inn lurks in the shadow of Steel Rigg, without doubt one of the most dramatic sections of Hadrian's Wall. It is close to all the main visitor attractions and Roman

sites and, perhaps more importantly, the inn has its own 'Brew House' on site.

I checked my bag into a comfy ensuite room, before walking with Bertie up to Steel Rigg, opposite the inn, and followed the wall east to Sycamore Gap, returning the same way. Despite visiting the area before, I am always stunned by the enduring order of the Roman army's craftwork. Back at the bar, there was a diverse group of visitors, many of whom were walking sections, or the entirety, of the Wall. My blackboard-special supper arrived, rivalling the size of a Roman army wall. The steak was exceptional and I declined the offer of pudding, due to lack of space, although they, too, looked delicious.

Retiring to my huge bed, complete with squidgy pillows, a sound night's sleep was had, without the need to count the endless gambolling of the lambs in the field opposite.

Whether you're simply passing through or aiming to walk coast to coast, Twice Brewed is a relaxing, cosy and friendly pub, set in the heart of beautiful Northumbrian countryside and a stone's throw from Hadrian's Wall - pun intended.

FACT FILE

Location: Twice Brewed, Bardon Mill, Hexham, NE47 7AN

Website: twicebrewedinn.co.uk

Contact: 01434 344534

Type of accommodation: Bed and breakfast

Number of bedrooms: 23 (7 dog friendly)

Number of dogs accepted: 2

Enclosed garden: No

Local interest: Hadrian's Wall, Sycamore Gap, Vindolanda Museum, Housesteads Fort, the Roman Army Museum

Best eats: The Twice Brewed Inn

JACKDAW COTTAGE, BUDLE BAY, NORTHUMBERLAND

By Rhian White

Situated on the Northumberland coastline, the comfortable, purpose-built holiday accommodation at Stablewood Cottages makes an ideal central hub to explore the wonders of this Area of Outstanding Natural Beauty.

We had a wonderful holiday in Budle Bay, staying in Stablewood Cottages. The facilities and design of the holiday home were superb.

Set 500 yds from the dunes of Budle Bay sands, Jackdaw Cottage is the perfect getaway. With a privately- owned sandy beach for all guests to enjoy, you can sit at peace, watch the day go by and not see another soul.

Part of the Heather House collection of purpose-built, self-catering properties, Jackdaw provides extremely comfortable living with fantastic panoramic views, ensuite bathrooms and an enclosed garden. There's a wash station for dogs, plus a separate hallway if they need somewhere to dry off. There is also a safely-fenced field for dogs to enjoy.

Budle Bay and Bamburgh are places that are very much undiscovered, it seems. They are so quiet and, quite often, we had the huge expanse of Budle Bay all to ourselves. At low tide, the beach really is enormous.

A highlight for us was taking a boat trip to the Farne Islands. We saw a wide variety of sea birds and hundreds of sunbathing seals, but the real treat was an unexpected 30-minute ride with dolphins, who swam alongside our boat - an experience I will never forget.

All in all, the perfect holiday, which I would recommend to anyone with a dog!

FACT FILE

Location: Lucker Steadings, Lucker Rd, Lucker, Northumberland, NE70 7JQ

Website: stablewoodcoastalcottages.com

Contact: 01668 219607 or 07501 470855

Type of accommodation: Cottage

Number of bedrooms: 3 (sleeps 6)

Number of dogs accepted: 2

Enclosed garden: Yes

Local interest: Budle Bay, Beau Monde spa (complimentary passes), Bamburgh Castle, Farne Islands

Best eats: The Apple Inn and The Apple Core at Lucker

151

PADDOCK COTTAGE, WHITBY, NORTH YORKSHIRE
By October Willis

Conveniently situated in the centre of Whitby, the beaches, harbour and historic town are all within strolling distance of cosy Paddock Cottage.

During what felt like a prolonged winter season, we were delighted to pack our bags and escape the gloom to the picturesque fishing port of Whitby. Located on the North Yorkshire coast, this bustling town is full of quaint shops, galleries, cafés, pubs and restaurants, with enough variety to keep you entertained for many days.

FACT FILE

Location: Whitby, North Yorkshire, YO21 3DD
Website: paddockcottagewhitby.co.uk
Contact: 07780 994545
Type of accommodation: Cottage
Number of bedrooms: 3 (sleeps 5)
Number of dogs accepted: Multiple, depending on size
Enclosed garden: Yes
Local interest: Whitby, Whitby Abbey, Whitby harbour and swing bridge, Whalebone Arch, beaches
Best eats: The Pier Inn, Rusty Shears, Sherlocks Coffee Shop and The Fuzzy Dog Bakery (handmade treats for dogs) at Whitby

From the moment we arrived at Paddock Cottage, all 3 of us were made to feel very welcome. The cottage boasts a fantastic location in the heart of Whitby, a short stroll from the quayside. It offers a modern, well-equipped kitchen and bathroom to contrast the period features throughout the living room and bedrooms. Ted, our 5-year-old Shih Tzu, felt immediately at home and very much enjoyed the pooch-safe garden.

After a walk around the town, in bracing temperatures, our first evening was spent in the cottage enjoying the famous Whitby fish and chips.

Up bright and early the next morning, we were greeted by sun and blue skies, so decided to head for the beach. Being out of season, the main beaches were relatively quiet but a long stretch of sand following the coast to the east of Whitby is likely to remain quiet throughout the year.

Our final day arrived too soon. After a last sprint around the beach, we took Ted to Rusty Shears, where we enjoyed quite possibly the best scrambled eggs on toast ever created and he was given a seemingly delicious Doggychino.

ST VALERY BOUTIQUE B&B, ALNMOUTH, NORTHUMBERLAND

By Caroline Pardy

With the emphasis on relaxation and luxury, St Valery offers superb, adults-only accommodation in an Area of Outstanding Natural Beauty.

September can be wonderful weather-wise, so we thought we'd escape somewhere special with our Springer Spaniels, Milo and Minty. They always join us on holiday but this was the first time they'd ever stayed in a guesthouse and we were a little nervous. We needn't have worried because the owner, Harvey, made us very welcome. He met us when we arrived and showed us personally to our room - and he wasn't alone because he was joined by his dog, Roxy.

There are only 3 rooms so, with a maximum of 6 guests at any one time, we were looked after extremely well. Every room has tea and coffee-making facilities and a jug of fresh milk was provided, without fail, every morning.

The bed is king-size and, with silk-blend pillows and duvet, we found it extremely comfy. The ensuite bathroom was immaculate, with a large shower, fluffy towels, bathrobes and slippers. We also found handmade dog treats and a dog bowl and could have requested a dog bed, but brought one with us.

It was cold outside so we relaxed by the fire, rather than using the seats in the garden. The atmosphere was wonderfully relaxing and breakfast was a leisurely affair - served between 9 and 10.30 am, so there wasn't any rush in the morning, which meant we could walk our dogs on the beach first.

The menu is extensive and our breakfasts at St Valery were superb, with everything cooked freshly once we'd ordered. I *(continued...)*

FACT FILE

Location: 27 Northumberland Street, Alnmouth, NE66 2RA

Website: stvaleryalnmouth.com

Contact: 01665 833123

Type of accommodation: Boutique bed and breakfast

Number of bedrooms: 3 (only 1 dog friendly)

Number of dogs accepted: 2

Enclosed garden: Secure decking area

Local interest: Alnmouth Beach, coast walks

Best eats: Numerous cafés and pubs in Alnmouth (recommendations available at St Valery) would suggest everyone tries the Marmite mushrooms - wonderful! There's a wide range of teas or you can have a Pilgrims coffee, which is local, as it's produced on the nearby island, Lindisfarne.

Alnmouth is a charming village, with gaily painted houses adding a splash of colour along the north shore of the river. But its main attraction is the beach, which is just a 5-minute walk from St Valery. An amazing expanse of sand with the estuary beyond, it's one of the most picturesque beaches on the Heritage Coast and welcomes dogs all year round.

There's a wide variety of cafés, pubs and restaurants in Alnmouth and the majority are dog friendly. Harvey is very knowledgeable and recommended several we could try. And, with St Valery so near the centre of the village, we found everything was within easy reach.

Northumberland is very dog friendly and Alnmouth, which lies within an Area of Outstanding Natural Beauty, makes a wonderful holiday destination.

We had a lovely time at St Valery and I would recommend it without hesitation. It's incredibly dog friendly, with canine guests made as welcome as their owners. Those who love dogs more than children may also appreciate the fact that it's an adults-only guesthouse, with no-one under the age of 16. It was the little extras that made the difference though, such as Harvey's special drawer, which contains an eclectic mix of dog-related essentials - ideal if you always leave something important back at home.

THE TANKERVILLE ARMS, EGLINGHAM, NORTHUMBERLAND

By Sarah Dodd

Only 7 miles from Alnwick, The Tankerville Arms is a traditional pub, offering outstanding food and stylish accommodation in a rural setting, which is ideally placed for exploring the Northumberland coast and the Cheviot Hills.

We've always found Northumberland really dog friendly, particularly the beaches, where the majority don't have any seasonal restrictions. For a relaxing few days there with our Border Terrier, Stanley, and Cocker Spaniel, Gilbert, we chose The Tankerville Arms because it was ideally located, being just a short drive from the coast, and clearly dog friendly.

In all respects, it's quite traditional but the food was outstanding and the atmosphere was extremely welcoming. The bedrooms were lovely. There are only 3 but they're wonderfully stylish, and each is uniquely designed with a host of little luxuries. We stayed in The Gold Room, but there's also The French Room and The Suite. Well-behaved dogs are welcome in the bedrooms and also in the bar.

The village of Eglingham lies within a conservation area and is surrounded by gently undulating countryside, a vibrant tapestry of woodland, farmland and moorland, with pathways galore. And it's just a few miles from the spectacular Cheviot Hills. We spent most of our time walking on the beaches and particularly enjoyed the golden sands of Bamburgh Beach. We also visited the National Trust property, Cragside, where we explored the grounds with our dogs.

Overall, it was a wonderful few days. I can't state how pleased we were that we found the Tankerville Arms and would highly recommend it if you've visiting the county.

FACT FILE

Location: 15 The Village, Eglingham, Alnwick, NE66 2TX

Website: tankervillearms.com

Contact: 01665 578444

Type of accommodation: Bed and breakfast

Number of bedrooms: 3

Number of dogs accepted: 2

Enclosed garden: Yes

Local interest: Bamburgh Beach, National Trust Cragside

Best eats: The Tankerville Arms

MATFEN HALL, MATFEN, NORTHUMBERLAND

By Angie Aspinall

Set in 300 acres of parkland, Matfen Hall oozes character and offers 5-star accommodation, along with fine dining, golf and spa facilities.

Already fans of the Northumbrian coast, we wanted to explore some of the county's inland treasures, so we booked an overnight stay at Matfen Hall, which is ideally situated for exploring Hadrian's Wall and Kielder.

Matfen Hall is a splendid, gothic house. Our room was huge and utterly gorgeous, with a super-king-size bed taking pride of place. Nevertheless, the first thing I noticed was the amazing view. Situated on the first floor and central to the house, our (enormous) windows overlooked the beautifully landscaped golf course. There was a VIP dog tray and a letter from Sybil, Sir Hugh and Lady Blackett's dog. Dog bowls were also provided and a mat, so we needn't worry about splashes on the carpet.

Tilly's welcome letter explained that dogs were welcome in the Conservatory Bar, so we changed our dinner reservation so she could remain with us. Tilly's normally very well behaved but I think the aroma of Richard's meaty sausages - with no titbits heading her way - was more than she could take. She didn't settle and yapped a few times so, for the sake of our fellow diners, we decided to resist dessert and finish our wine outside.

We took a leisurely stroll around the grounds and enjoyed the red sky (a good sign), whilst Tilly showed more than a passing interest in the rabbits that had clearly been snacking nearby.

After a good night's sleep, we popped Tilly in the car while we had breakfast. Our time at Matfen Hall was at an end and we left with great reluctance. But our spirits lifted when we remembered there was plenty to explore before we headed home again.

FACT FILE

Location: Matfen, Northumberland, NE20 0RH
Website: matfenhall.com
Contact: 01661 886500
Type of accommodation: Hotel
Number of bedrooms: 53 (3 dog friendly)
Number of dogs accepted: 2
Enclosed garden: No
Local interest: Hadrian's Wall, Chesters Roman Fort and Museum, Corbridge Roman Town, Kielder Forest, Leaplish Waterside Park
Best eats: Matfen Hall

ESTUARY VIEW CARAVANS, ALNMOUTH, NORTHUMBERLAND

By Gareth Salter

Situated on the south side of the estuary, the 3 caravans at Estuary View occupy a quiet and secluded position, just a short walk from the white sand and dunes of Alnmouth Beach and a stone's throw from the village.

Caravans may sometimes be the subject of derision but the accommodation they provide can be superb and has increased hugely in quality and spaciousness in recent years. They give an intimate sense of being in the outdoors - hearing the wind through the trees, the dawn chorus and the sound of rain when you're snuggled up inside. And many of the sites are in picturesque countryside, with a choice of walks directly from the door.

Some owners of static caravans have taken the plunge and created some really stylish retreats. One of the most welcoming is a site run by Simone Neri. What's even more surprising, considering how lovely the caravans are inside, is the fact that they're so dog friendly.

Northumberland has long been praised as one of the most dog friendly counties in England and Alnmouth, which boasts wonderful countryside, a rich heritage and sensational beaches, is a popular destination.

The 3 retro caravans, named Captain's Retreat, The Upper Deck and The Lower Deck, because of their waterside location, boast extensive areas of decking that enjoy views across the Aln Estuary. They are fully equipped and, for large groups, there's an 'At Home Dining' service.

The caravans are surrounded by fields and feel wonderfully secluded but are within easy reach of local amenities.

FACT FILE

Location: Waterside, Alnmouth, Alnwick, Northumberland, NE66 3QL

Website: estuaryviewcaravans.co.uk

Contact: 07801 447482

Type of accommodation: Caravan

Number of bedrooms: 2 or 3

Number of dogs accepted: Multiple

Enclosed garden: Enclosed decking area

Local interest: Alnwick Castle, The Alnwick Garden, Bamburgh Castle, Warkworth Castle, dog friendly beaches

Best eats: The Red Lion at Alnmouth

PARTRIDGE COTTAGE, CHOP GATE, NORTH YORKSHIRE

By Steve Bennett

For a cosy retreat, well off the beaten track, Partridge Cottage is a good choice - although, if visiting in winter, a 4-wheel-drive vehicle is advisable!

We'd been talking about the North Yorkshire Moors for such a long time that we decided we just had to show our 7-year-old son, Jack, why it was, in our opinion, a special area of the country. So, we booked Partridge Cottage, a dog friendly barn conversion in Chop Gate.

It was March and, as there had been heavy snow, the holiday company advised us we should be able to reach the cottage if we had a 4-wheel-drive, which we did.

Our journey was uneventful until we reached the moors where the landscape changes quite dramatically and, as we drove ever higher, we were surrounded by a thick layer of snow. The lane winds high into the moors and snow lay heavily everywhere - there was no way an ordinary car would have got through, but we soldiered on.

Opening the door to Partridge Cottage, we realised immediately our journey had been worthwhile - it was gorgeous! It may have looked like a barn from the outside, but the open-plan interior made the most of its period features. The conversion had been done with great sympathy, making a real feature of the sandstone brick wall at the end by placing a modern log-burner against it. We particularly liked the paved flagstone floor - ideal when you have dogs - and the fact that the underfloor heating keeps it warm, however icy the weather.

The lounge has comfy leather sofas, a decent-sized television and a dining

FACT FILE

Location: Chop Gate, Osmotherley, North Yorkshire, TS9 7JJ

Website: gorgeouscottages.com

Contact: 01237 426781

Type of accommodation: Cottage

Number of bedrooms: 2 (sleeps 4)

Number of dogs accepted: 2

Enclosed garden: No

Local interest: Whitby, Robin Hood's Bay, Saltburn, Stokesley, Helmsley, Northallerton, Helmsley Castle grounds, North Yorkshire Moors Railway

Best eats: Sherlocks Coffee Shop and The Pier Inn at Whitby, The Sitting Room in the station at Saltburn-by-the-Sea, Penny Bank Café at Kirkbymoorside

table and chairs. There's also a door that connects with the adjoining property. It was slightly unnerving at first but it was locked and, from a soundproofing point of view, we didn't hear our neighbours at all during our stay.

The kitchen is very well equipped and has everything you'd expect, including an enormous fridge, a microwave and a dishwasher.

Another door leads to the master bedroom, which boasts a large ensuite bathroom. Upstairs, via an open, wooden staircase (with a rather useful stair gate), there's another bedroom - again with a stylish ensuite bathroom.

One of the main highlights is the view. It doesn't matter which window you choose because the countryside beyond is wonderful, with the farm and the moors behind and the hills at the front. It really did feel like we were in the middle of nowhere.

There are plenty of hiking opportunities, with the Cleveland Way and Lyke Wake Walk nearby. Anyone who feels even more adventurous can try a section of Wainwright's Coast to Coast walk, which crosses the north of England. If you fancy really blowing the cobwebs away with a walk along the coast, then Whitby, Robin Hood's Bay and Saltburn are close by.

We had a wonderful time and are already investigating more of the company's properties, because so many are dog friendly. We've created a shortlist but any future visits will be during the summer. And the sun will shine!

THE WHITE SWAN, PICKERING, YORKSHIRE

By Marina Starke

Perfectly located in the beautiful North Yorkshire Moors, The White Swan bills itself as a family-run business which offers 5-star comfort at country inn prices.

We had a lovely time at The White Swan in Pickering and it's a great addition to our list of dog friendly hotels. Dogs are welcome in the Hideaway Rooms in the courtyard. These aren't the basic abodes that some establishments provide - they're large, cosy and luxurious. An offspring from the Vintage Rooms, they are tastefully decorated, with stylish fixtures, a flatscreen TV, DVD-player, minibar and underfloor heating. Each has an ensuite bathroom with a separate shower.

And you aren't confined to your room either. Dogs are welcome, and warmly so, in the bars (where you can eat off the restaurant menu) and the sumptuous residents-only bothy, which is about as far from a mountain bothy as you can get. Unless you know of a bothy with soft sofas, an open fire, magazines, free hot beverages and an honesty bar?

Originally built around 1530 as a worker's cottage, The White Swan was extended and eventually became a coaching inn on the York-Whitby road. It retains many period features, of which some of the most obvious are the joist stones that once supported an aerial walkway linking one of the bedrooms, via the alley, with the building next door. Legend suggests this was used by smugglers who moved salt across, whilst excise men searched the cellars below.

Pickering is a pretty little town with some interesting shops, a heritage railway and a castle. It is ideally placed, as it's just a few miles south of the North Yorkshire Moors National Park, with the walking opportunities it provides.

FACT FILE

Location: Market Place, Pickering, North Yorkshire, YO18 7AA

Website: white-swan.co.uk

Contact: 01751 472288

Type of accommodation: Hotel

Number of bedrooms: 21 (9 dog friendly)

Number of dogs accepted: 2

Enclosed garden: No

Local interest: North Yorkshire Moors National Park, North Yorkshire Moors Railway, Pickering Castle

Best eats: The White Swan

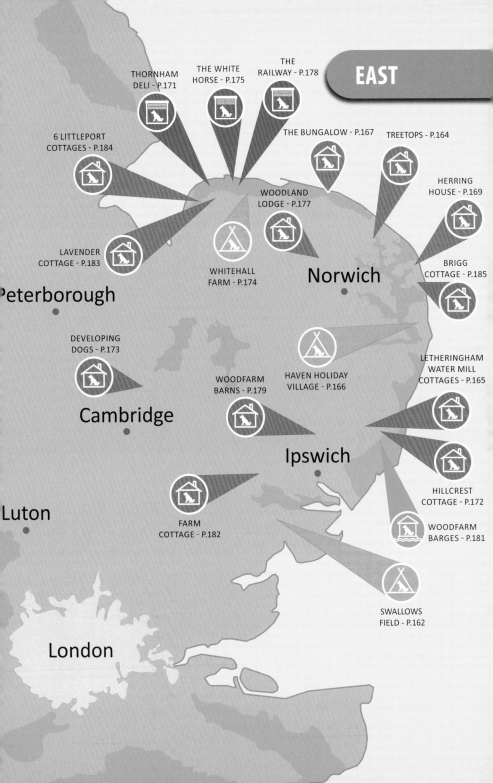

EAST

THORNHAM DELI - P.171

THE WHITE HORSE - P.175

THE RAILWAY - P.178

THE BUNGALOW - P.167

TREETOPS - P.164

6 LITTLEPORT COTTAGES - P.184

HERRING HOUSE - P.169

WOODLAND LODGE - P.177

LAVENDER COTTAGE - P.183

WHITEHALL FARM - P.174

Norwich

BRIGG COTTAGE - P.185

Peterborough

DEVELOPING DOGS - P.173

HAVEN HOLIDAY VILLAGE - P.166

LETHERINGHAM WATER MILL COTTAGES - P.165

Cambridge

WOODFARM BARNS - P.179

Ipswich

HILLCREST COTTAGE - P.172

Luton

FARM COTTAGE - P.182

WOODFARM BARGES - P.181

London

SWALLOWS FIELD - P.162

SWALLOWS FIELD GLAMPING PODS, FORDHAM HEATH, ESSEX

By Jenni Eley

Tucked away in the hamlet of Fordham Heath, Swallows Field Glamping Pods is an adult-only glamping experience, for those who prefer their camping with a bit of comfort.

The last time we went glamping we vowed it would be exactly that - the last time we went glamping. We realised we'd reached an age where we were no longer willing to sacrifice a comfortable night's sleep, a hot shower, or home comforts, in search of adventure. Then along came Swallows Field Glamping Pods to change our minds.

On their website, the pods look immaculate, with ensuite shower rooms, proper double beds, kitted out kitchens and heating. They actively welcome dogs and each of 3 available pods have fully enclosed gardens, as well as the option to hire your own private hot tub for your stay. This is glamping, but not as we had known it.

The owners, John and Liz, started to build the pods on a paddock by their house back in 2018. John designed and handmade them himself, and the craftsmanship is impressive. They launched in summer 2019 and, as lifelong dog owners themselves, they were determined to make the accommodation dog friendly.

We arrived on a wet and windy Friday evening and were greeted by Liz to show us to our pod 'Poppy', pass on some helpful local info and give us the all-important hot tub instructions.

The pod was larger than we imagined and, once inside, it felt surprisingly spacious. Unusually, it also looked just as good as the website photos. Poppy pod was warm,

FACT FILE

Location: 6 Heath Cottages, Heath Road, Fordham Heath, Colchester, Essex, CO3 9TN

Website: swallowsfieldglampingpods.co.uk

Contact: 01206 240626

Type of accommodation: Glamping pods

Number of bedrooms: 1 (sleeps up to 4)

Number of dogs accepted: 2

Enclosed garden: Yes

Local interest: Marks Hall Estate, Mersea Island, Cudmore Grove Country Park

Best eats: The Cricketers at Fordham Heath (will deliver), The Three Horseshoes at Fordham, The Artcafé at West Mersea

cosy and the perfect antidote to the weather outside. Woody settled in on the sofa immediately, which had been thoughtfully covered with a dog cover for us, and enjoyed a few treats from the welcome pack, before snuggling down for a snooze. We'd never seen him relax quite so quickly before - he clearly felt instantly at home.

The carefully considered layout and design maximises the use of space and includes everything you need for a comfortable stay away. There's no skimping on size of the important stuff either, with a double bed,

standard size shower, oven and fridge. The 3 pods are positioned at an angle so, although they are quite close to each other, you each have privacy.

Swallows Field is hard to put in a box and neatly categorise and that is exactly what makes it such a special place to stay. It's a mini escape from everyday life, with all the creature comforts of a luxury stay. We left relaxed, rejuvenated, and reconverted to glamping, or to glamping at Swallows Field at least!

TREETOPS, HONING, NORFOLK

By Jenni Eley

At any time of year, cosy Treetops makes the ideal base to return to, after exploring the many local walks.

We'd started 2022 on a mission to explore more, which is how we found ourselves setting off for Norfolk, on a weekend break in January. Our destination was Treetops, in the peaceful village of Honing.

We arrived late Friday afternoon. The cottage looked welcoming, with the owners leaving lamps on and turning the heating on, in advance of our arrival. It felt like we'd stepped into a cosy winter cocoon.

Stephen and Claire bought and renovated Treetops in 2019 and it's obvious they have spent a lot of care, time and energy on it. The overall effect is a home that feels effortlessly contemporary but classic. The fluffy bath towels and quality bed linen were an added luxury. Treetops has plenty of space for 6, so we were spoilt with just the 2 of us and Woody.

Talking of Woody, it is safe to say that he gave Treetops the paws up. The back garden is fully enclosed and perfect for exploring, the living room sofas had covers and throws, ready and waiting for snooze-time and there was even a plentiful basket of dog toys and balls to borrow. Dog crate, towels, bowls, poo bags, spare lead and dog tags are all provided so, all in all, everything you need for a hassle-free stay.

There are walking routes in every direction, all seemingly quiet and unspoilt, and the chance to explore and take on a new walking adventure each day. Arran did point out that my version of exploring was what most people would call getting lost, but I pretended not to hear.

FACT FILE

Location: 8 The Street, Honing, NR28 9AB
Website: packholidays.co.uk
Contact: 01692 535741
Type of accommodation: Cottage
Number of bedrooms: 3 (sleeps 6)
Number of dogs accepted: 3 (negotiable)
Enclosed garden: Yes
Local interest: Walks from the door, including Weavers Way, Cart Gap, Happisburgh
Best eats: Small Sticks Café at Cart Gap, Stalham Farm Shop, Doggie Diner at Cromer, The Ship Inn at Mundesley

LETHERINGHAM WATER MILL COTTAGES, WOODBRIDGE, SUFFOLK

By Jenni Eley

In an area of Suffolk which has so much to offer, a stay at Letheringham Water Mill makes an idyllic retreat for dogs (particularly those fond of water) and their humans.

The Woodshed is one of 4 supremely dog friendly cottages at the stunning Letheringham Water Mill, 8 miles from Woodbridge. There was a warm welcome from Jacqui, the owner, on arrival, along with greetings from the resident labradoodles, which made us all feel instantly right at home. It certainly looked like a big step up from your standard dog friendly cottage. A converted Grade II listed water mill, no less, set within 7 acres and surrounded, like a mini-island, by the river Deben and the mill water channels.

They've won lots of awards for their 5-star self-catering accommodation and it's easy to see why. The Woodshed is all about luxury and comfort. It is well designed and very well equipped, with all the kitchen kit you could ever need, plus extra touches like quirky dog-themed mugs and tasteful nods to our 4-legged companions at every turn. The doors from the living space and the bedroom open out onto the decked terrace, providing a great sense of light and space.

The owners have produced the most comprehensive information folders we have ever seen, with stacks of info about dog friendly places, bird spotting, ideas for days out and a whole folder brimming with favourite dog walks. There is so much to explore here that a weekend is not enough. It really is a special place.

FACT FILE

Location: Hall Road, Letheringham, Woodbridge, Suffolk, IP13 7RE

Website: letheringhammill.co.uk

Contact: 01728 747186

Type of accommodation: Cottage

Number of bedrooms: 1

Number of dogs accepted: Multiple

Enclosed garden: Yes (surrounded by water)

Local interest: Walks from the door, National Trust Dunwich Heath and Beach, Thorpeness, Aldeburgh (Scallop sculpture)

Best eats: Marlesford Farm Café and Shop at Marlesford, The Greyhound Inn in Pettistree

HAVEN HOLIDAY VILLAGE, HOPTON-ON-SEA

By Helen Steel

With the soft sand of a dog friendly beach only a short stroll away, a surprisingly spacious caravan makes the perfect base for a family holiday.

We were complete Norfolk newbies when we booked to stay at Haven Holiday Village in Hopton-on-Sea, with our band of 2 under-fives and the star of the show, Meg, the Cairn cross.

We arrived for a Monday to Friday stay, expecting huge queues to check in. But it took seconds and we were quickly unpacked and ready to discover that Norfolk has some of the best beaches in Britain. Crucially, dogs and their owners don't suddenly become pariahs, come May through to September. Yes, Hopton beach is the holy grail for dog owners - a restriction-free beach!

I was slightly dreading a tight squeeze inside the caravan, but I was pleasantly surprised at the space - plenty of room for a travel cot and a dog bed in the main bedroom and enough room to swing a cat (or, indeed, a Meg-sized dog) in the living area.

While 'value' caravan parks of my youth are remembered fondly, yet with a distinct smell of damp and mouldy windowsills, this was spick and span. Outside, the grass is kept lush and any wayward crisp packet is pounced upon by keen staff. There are none of the niceties like dog welcome packs/messages, but I'd waiver all that for easy access to beautiful beaches and lead-free walks, which is exactly what we got.

Finally, it must be said that Haven is brilliant value. Heaven for kids and an unexpected haven for dogs. We will be back!

FACT FILE

Location: Hopton-on-Sea, Great Yarmouth, NR31 9BW

Website: haven.com

Contact: 01502 730 214

Type of accommodation: Static caravan

Number of bedrooms: 3 (sleeps 8)

Number of dogs accepted: 2

Enclosed garden: Securely fenced dog park

Local interest: Direct access to a dog friendly beach, walks from the door, Pleasure Beach theme park at Great Yarmouth, Burgh Castle

Best eats: The Gorleston Doggy Diner at Gorleston-on-Sea, Munchies, Sara's Tearoom and The Lacon Arms at Great Yarmouth

THE BUNGALOW, CRABPOT COTTAGES, CROMER

By James Waters

Beaches, boats and The Doggie Diner - The Bungalow is a great base for enjoying all Cromer and the surrounding area has to offer.

The name *The Bungalow* gives away the general layout of the building, which is a pretty traditional plot. However, it has been greatly extended, giving a good amount of space for a visiting family of 5 or 6.

There are 3 good-sized bedrooms and a large diner-cum-living-room, as well as a delightful, large garden which wraps around the house, creating 3 little areas. The real treat of The Bungalow was the fresh décor.

Our dog, Stanley, was very taken with it all, but the garden was his absolute favourite thing, and he was quite happy sitting on the lawn, to while away the hours in the afternoon sun. It's enclosed with 3ft-plus fencing, but not especially good for larger dogs.

The property is in quite a good location. It's away from the busyness of the town/beach, but a walk of about half an hour takes you there, so quite suitable for the daily stroll. Most days we ambled into town with Stanley and stopped by the beach, had a drink or headed up towards the cliff and lighthouse.

The beach at Cromer is great, mostly sand with some pebbles. There are relatively small sections divided with groynes, which was good for Stanley as this prevented him running off too far. There are some beach restrictions, during peak season, but they are generally very relaxed.

Cromer itself is quite a traditional seaside *(continued...)*

FACT FILE

Location: 44 Hillside, Cromer, Norfolk, NR27 0HY

Website: crabpotcottages.co.uk

Contact: 01263 579435

Type of accommodation: Bungalow

Number of bedrooms: 3 (sleeps 6)

Number of dogs accepted: 2

Enclosed garden: Yes (possibly not suited to larger dogs)

Local interest: Cromer, Overstrand, Wells-next-the-Sea, Norwich Cathedral, Norwich Castle (grounds only), Martham Ferry Day Boat Hire, Horsey Mill

Best eats: The Doggie Diner at Cromer, Poppylands Tearoom near Horsey

resort, with some style to it. One great thing is the putting, but Stanley needed to be taken for a walk separately, as he got far too excited by balls moving towards holes!

As we were in Cromer, we thought it was only right that Stanley should visit The Doggie Diner, which was highly rated in the DogFriendly Awards in 2020. He loved his Afternoon Doggie Tea - a 2-tiered doggy snacks extravaganza and we had to take one of the items home, to make sure he didn't overdo it.

On one of the last days of our holiday, we hired a boat from Martham Ferry Boatyard. We rented a 6-seater, electric boat that launched from their base in Martham, on the east coast side of the Broads. To be honest, I didn't know electric boats existed, but it certainly is an easy way to travel, particularly with 3 kids and a dog.

Our holiday at Cromer was really good. Stanley definitely enjoyed his time there - the perfect garden, beach walks every day and not forgetting The Doggie Diner!

HERRING HOUSE, WINTERTON-ON-SEA, NORFOLK

By Jenni Eley

Herring House is extremely welcoming to dogs and a 10-minute stroll from the door takes you to the beach and dunes, which are the stuff of dog dreams.

Eight miles north of Great Yarmouth, Winterton-on-Sea is described as one of Norfolk's best-kept secrets, which normally translates as 'there's not much worth seeing here'. Happily, not this time. This isn't a seaside village with bright lights and amusement arcades - it's altogether more laid-back, with the natural beauty of miles of sandy beach and wild dunes rightfully stealing the limelight.

Our base for the weekend was Herring House, a few minutes from the centre of the village and a 10-minute stroll to the beach. It is part of a small collection of holiday lets, in tastefully converted barns.

Inside, Herring House definitely does not disappoint. The best compliment I can give is to say it instantly feels like a home from home. It's comfortable, well equipped and cosy.

The spacious upstairs living room, with exposed Norfolk brick walls, has enough seating so all 3 of us could lounge comfortably on our own sofa after a day exploring, Woody included. There's a pleasing lack of a doggy rulebook that makes relaxing on holiday so much easier. Dogs on the sofa - fine, throws provided. Muddy paws - no problem, there's an outside hose and plentiful towels. Forgotten your dog bowls, blankets, poo bags, lead? They're all here and even the most cunning escapologist wouldn't be able to scale the fence of the gated courtyard garden. *(continued...)*

FACT FILE

Location: Empsons Loke, Winterton-on-Sea, Norfolk
Website: packholidays.co.uk
Contact: 01692 535741
Type of accommodation: Cottage
Number of bedrooms: 2 (sleeps 4)
Number of dogs accepted: Multiple (depends on size)
Enclosed garden: Yes
Local interest: Dog friendly beach, Norfolk Coast Path, Great Yarmouth, Burgh Castle, Redwings Caldecott Horse & Donkey Sanctuary, the seals at Horsey (winter is breeding season)
Best eats: Dunes Café at Winterton Beach, Poppy's Tea Room and The Fishermans Return at Winterton-on-Sea

Out and about, everyone seems to have a dog and it's easy to see why. The coastal landscape is the stuff of dog dreams, a designated Area of Outstanding Natural Beauty and a National Nature Reserve. Woody enjoyed running up, down and around the dunes, onto the beach and generally behaving like he was having the best day of his life.

The vastness of the beach, the wild dunes backdrop and the fact that hardly anyone else was around made this place pretty spectacular. Winterton Beach is good for the soul, even on a distinctly unsunny March day. Dogs are allowed on the beach all year round although, at certain times of year, seal colonies are in residence, so extra care must be taken.

A few nights here isn't enough. Herring House, the village and beach gently lull you into a more relaxed state of mind. Granted, my sunglasses didn't get an outing but the many happy dogs we met this weekend want me to tell you all that Norfolk's best-kept secret is the real deal and well worth a visit.

THORNHAM DELI, HUNSTANTON, NORTH NORFOLK

By Helen Price

Ideally located on the North Norfolk coast, the Thornham Deli offers delicious meals, as well as comfortable, dog friendly accommodation.

Thornham Deli and its sister business, No. 33 Hunstanton, have selected B&B rooms available for guests with dogs. They also welcome dogs in their stunning Thornham Cottages, situated across the road from the Deli.

Our room was in the loft area, with its own private staircase for dogs to access the recreational areas. Tilly, our Jack Russell cross, bounded up the stairs, closely followed by Harry, our French Bulldog.

Tom, one of the many friendly faces of the Thornham Deli team, gave us a guided tour, and tea and homemade scones from the Deli were laid out, ready for our arrival.

Our room at Thornham Deli was the perfect cosy bolthole for a wet and windy evening. We cosied up with Harry and Tilly to watch a movie and opted to pop to the famous Eric's Fish & Chip Shop between films.

When you stay at Thornham Deli, breakfast is included. People travel from miles around for a Thornham Deli breakfast and both Ben and I could see why - it was incredible!

We had a couple of meals in the restaurant during our stay, including a light lunch and a Sunday roast and they were all fantastic. Dogs are welcome in the Greenhouse section of the restaurant.

This was a truly fantastic holiday, making memories with our little old hounds. Norfolk will now and forever have the biggest place in our hearts, full of fond memories of Harry and Tilly together.

FACT FILE

Location: Thornham, Hunstanton, PE36 6LX

Website: 33hunstanton.co.uk

Contact: 01485 524352

Type of accommodation: Bed and breakfast

Number of bedrooms: 4

Number of dogs accepted: 2 small or 1 medium size

Enclosed garden: No

Local interest: Old Hunstanton, Le Strange Old Barns, Holkham National Nature Reserve, Dalegate Market at Burnham Deepdale, Seahenge at Holme Beach

Best eats: The Ancient Mariner Inn at Old Hunstanton, Eric's Fish & Chips at Thornham, The Lookout at Holkham National Nature Reserve

HILLCREST COTTAGE, KELSALE, SUFFOLK

By Jenny Green

In the heart of the Suffolk Heritage Coast region, Hillcrest Cottage offers luxury accommodation with far-reaching views of the surrounding countryside.

Hillcrest Cottage is a lovely property, with a fully glazed gable end which takes in the ever-changing landscape. Ernie, my little Westie, certainly noticed the resident chickens but, fortunately, he couldn't get close enough to say hello. It is a truly stunning property, with underfloor heating throughout and floor-to-ceiling windows allowing light to flood into the double-height sitting area. A spiral staircase separates the lounge from the dining area and that flows into a stylish monochrome kitchen, with everything you need to cook up a feast.

The master bedroom upstairs is really rather special. A glass wall overlooks the sitting area, taking in even more of the beautiful views and it has a lovely ensuite, with freestanding bath.

The downstairs double bedroom has doors leading straight into the garden. The room, which wouldn't look out of place in a boutique hotel, also boasts a large ensuite shower room and comes complete with complimentary toiletries and fluffy white towels.

There is so much to see and do within a 20-mile radius that it's impossible to fit it all into one break. Whether you're keen to shop, walk for miles, explore the beautiful coastline or just chill out, Suffolk has it all. And with dogs guaranteed a warm welcome practically everywhere, one visit will never be enough. We'll be back!

FACT FILE

Location: Benstead, Main Road, Kelsale, Saxmundham, Suffolk

Website: kelsaleholidaycottages.co.uk

Contact: 07952 782101

Type of accommodation: Cottage

Number of bedrooms: 2 (sleeps 4)

Number of dogs accepted: Multiple

Enclosed garden: Yes

Local interest: Aldeburgh (statue of Snooks), Wag & Bone pet boutique at Aldeburgh, Dunwich, Southwold, Woodbridge, Sutton Hoo

Best eats: The Kings Head and The Griffin Inn at Yoxford, Munchies, Two Magpies Bakery and The White Hart Inn at Aldeburgh, The Ship at Dunwich, The Westleton Crown

DEVELOPING DOGS, ELY, CAMBRIDGESHIRE

By Jeff Porter

Set in 7 acres of securely-fenced paddocks, a well thought-out dog training facility offers the opportunity to combine a holiday with professional training sessions.

Developing Dogs was set up by Sian Ryan, the training and behaviour expert from BBC2's *Me and My Dog*. Its aim is to develop your relationship with your canine companion, give you the tools to understand each other and help your puppy or dog develop the life skills that make them part of the family.

Dotty is a loving dog, who's great to have around. She's great around other dogs, but not when on the lead. Unfortunately, on the lead is where she stays most of the time, unless we can find an enclosed field. Developing Dogs has such a field, backing onto their 3 cottages. You get your own private entrance, through 2 gates from your garden, and an allotted time, which means you never come face to face with another dog.

We stayed in Dragonfly, the middle of the 3 cottages. It has a large double bedroom, with a super-king-size bed, a wet room with a walk-in shower and bath, and a comfortable lounge/dining/kitchen space,

equipped with everything you could possibly need. There's a large throw for the couch, in case your dog should make himself at home, and an equally large one for the bed. There is also a hot tub.

We were acutely aware of just how well thought-out Developing Dogs have made their holiday homes. Each is completely detached, even the gardens, where there's a large area of astro turf, surrounded by pebbles, and 6-foot fences on all 3 sides, enough to contain any dog.

All in all, we figured our visit to Developing Dogs was a success, both for us and our dogs - despite the weather.

FACT FILE

Location: White Cross Farm, Whitecross Road, Wilburton, Ely CB6 3QB

Website: developingdogs.co.uk

Contact: 01353 885720

Type of accommodation: Cottage

Number of bedrooms: 1 (sleeps 2)

Number of dogs accepted: Multiple

Enclosed garden: Yes

Local interest: Holkham Beach, Ely and the cathedral

Best eats: The Lookout café at Holkham

173

WHITEHALL FARM, BURNHAM THORPE, NORFOLK
By Emma Bearman

A working farm, set within the breathtaking Holkham Estate, Whitehall Farm is only a 10-minute drive from North Norfolk's fantastic beaches.

For our first glamping experience, we arranged a weekend stay through 2Posh2Pitch, a small, family-run business on the North Norfolk coast.

Our bell tent was kitted out with everything we could possibly need for our stay. With soft, colourful rugs and coir matting, it is almost as if you are stepping into your own hotel room. There is a king-size bed, so you can rest up in the comfort of the fluffy king-size duvet, after a hard day exploring.

And it doesn't have to be just the 2 of you. Any extra guests (up to 4 in total) will be supplied with single airbeds with fitted sheets, duvets and pillows.

Kate really tries to think of everything you'll need to make the most of your glamping experience, but there are a few things you need to bring with you, such as toiletries, towels, wellies, a camping stove, kettle and some charcoal for the barbie.

North Norfolk is the perfect location for holidaying with a dog and it's probably one of the most dog friendly coastal locations in the UK. I have yet to find travelling there with dogs an issue, whether it's a run along the beach or finding a dog friendly restaurant.

When it comes to beaches, you're spoilt for choice and, if you're looking for the perfect beach to spend the day, then I'd definitely recommend Holkham Beach. If you want more of a seaside town, Wells-next-the-Sea is perfect.

Our first camping experience was a huge success - even our Springer, Alfie, loved it, and he is a complete princess!

FACT FILE
Location: Walsingham Road, Burnham Thorpe, PE31 8HN
Website: whitehallfarm-accommodation.com
Contact: 07879 773382
Type of accommodation: Bell tent
Number of bedrooms: 1
Number of dogs accepted: 2
Enclosed garden: No
Local interest: Brancaster, Holkham and Wells-next-the-Sea beaches
Best eats: The Lord Nelson at Burnham Thorpe

THE WHITE HORSE, BRANCASTER STAITHE, NORFOLK

By Rupert Paul

Set in an Area of Outstanding Natural Beauty on the marshland coastline of North Norfolk, a stay at the luxurious White Horse gastro pub in Brancaster Staithe offers a restorative antidote to modern life.

The White Horse in Brancaster Staithe isn't just an amazing place to stay with a dog, it's amazing by any standard. It has a mouth-watering reputation for seafood and the service, rooms and food are top drawer. But the location is even better - smack in the middle of an Area of Outstanding Natural Beauty, with a National Nature Reserve on either side and RSPB Titchwell, too. It's not cheap but for energetic dog-lovers with a taste for fine dining, it's a powerful antidote to the stress of work and city life.

You might think the building looks pretty ordinary from the A149, but the car park backs onto a huge salt marsh dotted with boats and teeming with birdlife. It's a constantly changing landscape, and just watching it does you good.

There are 8 luxurious rooms for dog owners, facing onto a well-kept garden. Twenty yards gets you to the Norfolk Coast Path which runs continuously off-road west to Brancaster harbour and east to Burnham Overy Staithe and the jewels of Holme, Holkham, Wells and Cley are all within easy reach.

Our room was ridiculously comfortable and, with floorboards on the first half, you can bring 4-legs back from the salt marsh without wrecking the carpet. It was as big as the ground floor of a small house, with a beautifully comfy bed, lavish bathroom, espresso machine and proper tea-making kit. Out of the back window, where so many *(continued...)*

FACT FILE

Location: Main Road, Brancaster Staithe, Norfolk, PE31 8BY

Website: whitehorsebrancaster.co.uk

Contact: 01485 210262

Type of accommodation: Bed and breakfast

Number of bedrooms: 15 (8 dog friendly)

Number of dogs accepted: Multiple

Enclosed garden: Yes

Local interest: Norfolk Coast Path, Brancaster Harbour, Burnham Overy Staithe, Holme, Holkham, Wells-next-the-Sea, Cley-next-the-Sea, Barrow Common

Best eats: The White Horse, The Jolly Sailors at Brancaster harbour

175

places would chuck the lawn clippings, are plants that can handle dry shade.

A White Horse breakfast features South African levels of lavishness, which is to say that if satisfying your hunger can be likened to squashing a pea, you are offered a sledgehammer. Cereals, muesli, fresh and dried fruit, yoghurt, pastries, plus a menu all the way up to full English. I had one of everything.

A meal like that needs walking off. Barrow Common, a local wildlife site which used to be a WWII radar station, is a heathy, wild area, with intriguing pathways between high walls of gorse. Benjy, our working Cocker, was in heaven, snuffling into the bracken and brambles, while we listened to the song of yellowhammer, chiffchaff, great spotted woodpecker, great tit and skylark.

It was a short stay, but all 3 of us were well fed, well exercised and well rested. This part of the world never disappoints. As more and more of the UK is eaten up by development, it gets easier and easier to appreciate the space and peace, which Norfolk still has in spades.

WOODLAND LODGE, HAVERINGLAND HALL, NORWICH

By Hilary Keens

A short drive from the coast, the Norfolk Broads and Norwich, Woodland Lodge is situated in a delightful park in over 150 acres of mature English woodland, with wonderful walks around the park and lakes just outside the door.

My dog, Tess, and I love Norfolk. It's one of the most dog friendly counties we've visited, with wonderful beaches, picturesque walking routes, prestigious stately homes, charming market towns and a wide variety of shops, pubs and cafés.

There are several developments at Haveringland Hall. Woodland Lodge is, like its neighbours, a smart, wooden structure with raised wooden deck. The lounge is spacious, with large leather sofas and a dining area. There are 2 bedrooms - a master with an ensuite shower room and a twin, plus a family bathroom. The kitchen has all mod cons and the lodge has double glazing. There's sensor-controlled lighting outside, which was handy when Tess had her last walk of the evening, and there are lights around the parkland roads.

It was extremely peaceful at night - the silence only broken by owls hooting or migrant geese honking as they flew overhead. There aren't any pubs within walking distance and the nearest village, Cawston, is a 5-minute drive away.

I was lucky with the weather and we spent the last day relaxing at the lodge, walking around the lake and enjoying a pub lunch. We chose The King's Arms in Reepham, where Tess snoozed with a black Labrador beside the fire.

I would heartily recommend Woodland Lodge because it has such an enviable location, and made a lovely retreat in the countryside.

FACT FILE

Location: Haveringland Hall Country Park, Norwich, NR10 4PN

Website: woodlandlodgenorfolk.co.uk

Contact: 01778 349512

Type of accommodation: Cottage

Number of bedrooms: 2

Number of dogs accepted: 2

Enclosed garden: Yes

Local interest: Winterton-on-Sea, Happisburgh, Felbrigg Estate, Holkham, Wells-next-the-Sea

Best eats: The Dunes Café at Winterton (outside only), The Stiffkey Red Lion, Deepdale Café at Burnham Deepdale, The Kings Arms at Reepham

THE RAILWAY, BURNHAM MARKET, NORFOLK

By October Willis

Situated in the picturesque, 17th century village of Burnham Market, The Railway is only a 10-minute drive from the golden sands of a number of North Norfolk's famous beaches.

Once the home of the stationmaster, The Railway retains many of its original features and is utterly charming. The line closed in the early '50s and it's this period that resonates in particular.

The bedrooms in The Railway are quite compact but the standard of decoration is incredibly high, with sumptuous fabrics, vibrant statement wallpaper and luxurious bed linens. Each has an ensuite shower - clean, modern and bright with chrome fixtures and plenty of towels.

Many people think Burnham Market is Norfolk's loveliest village and worthy of being a holiday destination in its own right. However, it's also ideally placed if you fancy exploring the coast. It has a wonderful atmosphere and shopping's a joy (though rarely cheap), with a wide variety of independent traders and none of the multiples that dominate most high streets.

One service I would particularly recommend is the Coast Hopper bus. Check the timetable and you can walk several miles in one direction and, if you're near the main coast road, catch it back again.

The Norfolk Coast has miles of golden beaches you can explore and most are dog friendly. We spent many hours playing on the beach at Thornham, making the most of the sunshine.

FACT FILE

Location: Creake Rd, Burnham Market, PE31 8EN
Website: barefootretreats.co.uk
Contact: 01485 512245
Type of accommodation: Bed and breakfast
Number of bedrooms: 8 (3 dog friendly)
Number of dogs accepted: 1
Enclosed garden: No
Local interest: Dog friendly beaches, Wells-next-the-Sea, Blakeney National Nature Reserve (restrictions between 1 April and 15 August), Norfolk Coast Path, Little Walsingham, Wells & Walsingham Light Railway (March to October)
Best eats: The Black Lion at Walsingham, Tuscan Farm Shop at Burnham Market

WOODFARM BARNS, STONHAM ASPAL, SUFFOLK

By Emma Bearman

Set in the glorious Suffolk countryside, Woodfarm Barns go that extra mile to ensure their selection of barns and thatched cottages is truly dog friendly.

I think Suffolk is an underrated holiday destination. I have no idea why - the gorgeous Suffolk countryside and heritage coastline combine to make the perfect dog friendly destination.

Towards the start of February my partner, James, and I headed to Suffolk with our Springer Spaniel, Alfie, to enjoy a week at Woodfarm Barns.

Woodfarm Barns is a collection of 7 Gold Award-winning, luxury, dog friendly holiday cottages, set in Stonham Aspal, in the heart of the Suffolk countryside. Whether you are looking for a week of relaxing on-site or exploring the local area, it makes a great dog friendly base.

We were staying in Gipping Barn. This cosy barn sleeps 2 people. You enter into a quaint, open living space, which is light and airy with bold oak beams and a log burner taking centre stage. It's something I look for when choosing our holiday destination as we don't have one at home, so it's a real treat.

Gipping Barn boasts a beautiful, farmhouse-styled kitchen, with some quirky antique pieces. The kitchen has everything you need for a home away from home, so if you don't want to dine out each night you can cook yourself some hearty home classics.

On arrival, we were welcomed to Gipping Barn with our very own breakfast basket - a hamper containing a whole selection of locally-sourced produce. This was a lovely personal touch. It also meant we could *(continued...)*

FACT FILE

Location: Woodfarm HQ, Woodfarm House, Stonham Aspal, Suffolk, IP6 9TH

Website: woodfarmbarns.com

Contact: 01449 710032 or 07810 371218

Type of accommodation: Cottage

Number of bedrooms: 1

Number of dogs accepted: 3

Enclosed garden: Yes

Local interest: Rendlesham Woods, Suffolk Heritage Coast

Best eats: The Magpie at Little Stonham

settle upon arrival, knowing our breakfast was sorted.

A winding staircase leads up into the mezzanine bedroom, with its gorgeous sleigh bed. There is a 'no dogs on the furniture' rule throughout all of the Woodfarm properties, so Alfie made do with his own bed.

From the kitchen you can head out into the garden. This is all enclosed so we could let Alfie out, without worrying that he would wander off. Now, the highlight! Gipping Barn has it's own private hot tub. It's all undercover so you can enjoy the bubbles, whatever the weather. Alfie is fascinated by a hot tub. He spends his time hovering,

hoping that someone will splash just a little bit, turning a relaxing experience into one big game.

As a dog owner, it's the little touches tailored to suit the dog that I really like. There was a selection of healthy, natural treats from their local pet shop waiting for us, and Alfie loved them. The thing I really loved was that there is an enclosed dog meadow, so dogs can play as they please. I can imagine it to be a great place for dogs to socialise, over the summer months. There is also a small corner fenced off - just in case you have a nervous dog, so they can still enjoy themselves without being disrupted by other dogs.

WOODFARM BARGES, SNAPE MALTINGS, SUFFOLK

By Emma Bearman

For a dog friendly holiday with a difference, Woodfarm Barges offers luxury accommodation aboard their award-winning, 100-year-old barges, moored in a picturesque spot on the River Orwell.

Woodfarm Barges has 2 Dutch sailing barges, lovingly converted into luxury accommodation. One is a small barge which is perfect for a romantic break, and then there is the magnificent Onderneming.

Moored at Pin Mill, a stunning hamlet, halfway between Ipswich and the beautiful Suffolk Heritage Coast, The Onderneming is 100 ft in length and 18 ft wide. No expense was spared in her conversion, creating the best of modern living but still keeping the original features, such as her portholes and panelling.

There are 2 large lounge and dining areas, or saloons as sailing people call them, both with ample seating, and fully-fitted kitchens. The lower saloon had a cosy log burner, perfect for the evenings.

I do like my home comfort and was a little worried I would have to compromise when it came to bathrooms, but I was pleasantly surprised. The Onderneming has an ensuite wet room and 2 additional bathrooms.

Staying aboard the Onderneming was a great experience and our Springer Spaniel, Alfie, took to it like a duck to water. Being moored at Pin Mill, the Heritage Coast was just a short drive away. We all love a trip to the beach and our favourite was Dunwich Bay. We started with a walk in Dunwich Forest before heading out to the bay to wash off Alfie's muddy paws.

If you are looking for some dog friendly beach inspiration, Aldeburgh, Southwold and Walberswick are great places to start.

FACT FILE

Location: Snape Maltings, Suffolk
Website: woodfarmbarges.com
Contact: 01449 710032 or 07810 371218
Type of accommodation: Barge
Number of bedrooms: 3
Number of dogs accepted: 3
Enclosed garden: No
Local interest: Suffolk Heritage Coast, Dunwich Bay, Dunwich Forest, Aldeburgh, Southwold, Walberswick
Best eats: The Crown Inn and The Golden Key Inn at Snape

FARM COTTAGE, GROVE FARM, PRIORY GREEN, SUFFOLK

By October Willis

The tastefully converted cottages at Grove Farm make a great base for exploring the glorious Suffolk countryside, beaches and villages.

Grove Farm enjoys a secluded position and is surrounded by a tempting network of paths, tracks and bridleways. It dates from the 1700s and each of the farm buildings has been converted individually, creating a wonderful collection of holiday properties, retaining many of their original features.

Entering Farm Cottage was like stepping back in time. With tiles or wooden floorboards, it's perfect if you have a dog. Downstairs, the layout is open-plan - it's compact and cosy but we found everything we could possibly need. I must mention the room under the stairs, where the ovens used to be, which makes an ideal storage space.

A door leads to the stairs and a small landing, with the master bedroom on the left. Although it had strong competition, it was easily my favourite room - light, spacious and beautifully decorated. The wrought iron bed was extremely comfy and, in the mornings, you can look out over the fields, from a well-positioned window.

A short hallway leads to a smaller bedroom, with a single bed, desk and chair - ideal if you have an older child.

The bathroom is compact, rustic and stylish, and we found there was always plenty of hot water.

The properties nestle within manicured gardens, complete with a dog exercise area. It's a short walk from the cottage but the route is lit by fairy lights draped through the trees and these look magical in the evening.

FACT FILE

Location: The Grove, Priory Green, Edwardstone, Suffolk, CO10 5PP

Website: grove-cottages.co.uk

Contact: 01787 211115

Type of accommodation: Cottage

Number of bedrooms: 2 (sleeps 3)

Number of dogs accepted: 3

Enclosed garden: Exercise area

Local interest: Lavenham, water meadows around Sudbury, Dunwich Heath, Dunwich Beach, Southwold

Best eats: White Horse Inn at Edwardstone, Hadleys Ice Cream Parlour and The Swan at Lavenham, The Black Lion at Long Melford

LAVENDER COTTAGE, DOCKING, NORFOLK

By Tracey Howells

A cosy retreat, Lavender Cottage is within easy reach of some of Norfolk's wonderful dog friendly beaches and even offers use of a beach hut.

Docking is just a few miles from one of Norfolk's main attractions, the Heritage Coast, which has a large number of dog friendly beaches. Tucked away down a quiet lane, Lavender Cottage is a charming holiday retreat and we knew immediately we'd made a wise choice.

Despite its size, it's very stylish inside and it's clear a great deal of thought has gone into creating a welcoming environment. It's a lovely property and felt surprisingly spacious.

The country-style kitchen is wonderful, open-plan and clearly bespoke with everything you need, including a choice of cafetières. It's the little things that make a difference and I loved the lavender theme.

Upstairs, there's a master bedroom and a twin, although the latter also has an extra bed. The beds were comfy and we slept peacefully each night, with the house remaining warm, despite the cold weather.

Outside, there's a shingled seating area with a table and chairs, where you can relax in the sun. The owner can also arrange the use of a beach hut at Wells-next-the-Sea, which stands on a dog friendly section of the beach.

It's often said that time flies when you're enjoying yourself and the weekend did, indeed, pass in a flash. We loved staying there and felt surprisingly sad when we left. Thank you very much, Lavender Cottage, we will definitely see you again.

FACT FILE

Location: Docking, King's Lynn, PE31 8NL
Website: naturally-norfolk.com/lavender-cottage
Contact: 01485 518779
Type of accommodation: Cottage
Number of bedrooms: 2 (sleeps up to 5)
Number of dogs accepted: 1
Enclosed garden: Yes
Local interest: Beaches at Old Hunstanton, Snettisham, Holme, Thornham, Heacham and Brancaster Staithe, Burnham Market, Burnham Thorpe, Burnham Deepdale (marsh walks), Sandringham, Oxburgh, Holkham, Houghton, Blickling, Castle Rising
Best eats: Old Town Beach Café at Old Hunstanton, The Orange Tree Inn at Thornham

6 LITTLEPORT COTTAGES, HUNSTANTON, NORFOLK

By Hilary Keens

In a peaceful location at the far end of Sedgeford village, 6 Littleport Cottages makes a comfortable and characterful base for exploring the many attractions of North Norfolk.

The cottage is one of a row in a gravelled lane, just off the road that runs through Sedgeford. It is achingly quaint and is full of knick-knacks which add to its character.

The front door opens immediately onto a tiled kitchen. It's compact but well enough equipped to eat in. There's also a lounge/diner and a shower room. I found it charming and the owner's attention to detail is evident throughout.

Upstairs, there's a small twin-bedded room and a master bedroom - a large room with lovely views of the garden. The property's best feature though is the lounge, with its elegant wood furniture, comfy sofas and log-burner.

The garden is enclosed but the fence only measures 3ft down one side and, with large sections hidden by shrubs, I wasn't confident it was completely secure. Nevertheless, it didn't cause any problems.

The cottage lies beside a long distance path, the Peddars Way. One of our favourite routes involved turning right and heading through the fields but we also bore left and joined the Peddars Way, continuing through the countryside to Ringstead.

I've had several wonderful holidays in North Norfolk and would heartily recommend 6 Littleport Cottages.

FACT FILE

Location: Sedgeford, Hunstanton, North Norfolk, PE36 5LP

Website: 6littleportcottages.co.uk

Contact: derri.shepherd@virgin.net

Type of accommodation: Cottage

Number of bedrooms: 2

Number of dogs accepted: 3

Enclosed garden: Yes (fence only 3ft in places)

Local interest: Dog friendly beaches, Peddars Way, Sandringham, Titchwell Marsh, Castle Riding, Blicking, Castle Acre, Cluniac Abbey, Burnham Market

Best eats: Gin Trap Inn at Ringstead, The Ostrich at Castle Acre, The Stiffkey Red Lion, The Orange Tree Inn at Thornham, The Lighthouse Café at Old Hunstanton

BRIG COTTAGE, SCRATBY, NORFOLK

By Jenny Green

Cosy Brig Cottage makes a great base for exploring an area of Norfolk which is well-known for its dog friendliness.

Brig Cottage is a lovely 2-bedroom property, close to Scratby beach. It had everything we needed for a relaxed, dog friendly stay, including a secure garden.

Downstairs, there was a compact yet well-equipped kitchen, a spacious lounge with large dining table and an airy conservatory. There was also a shower room and an alcove - quirkily called the games room - which was packed with board games, cards and books.

Upstairs were 2 spacious bedrooms (a double and a twin), an on-trend, grey bathroom and a large landing area. There were lots of nods to the seaside around the cottage too, in the cushions, ornaments and bedding.

As it had already started to get dark when we arrived, we promised the dogs we'd take them to the beach in the morning and headed out for dinner at The Smokehouse in Ormesby - a short drive away.

It's easy to get down on to the beach from

the California Tavern, which is where we headed early the next day. We spent the afternoon and evening relaxing back at Brig Cottage and planning our next adventure - to the Norfolk Broads. I was thrilled to discover you could still get out on the water in February.

To be honest, we found it really hard to tear ourselves away from Brig Cottage, as the boys were so comfortable there and we had everything we needed. We really hope to return to the area one day and sample more of its dog friendly delights.

FACT FILE

Location: Beach Road, Scratby NR29 3AJ

Website: eastrustoncottages.co.uk

Contact: 07766 665684

Type of accommodation: Cottage

Number of bedrooms: 2

Number of dogs accepted: 4 (negotiable)

Enclosed garden: Yes

Local interest: Beaches, Great Yarmouth, Britannia Pier, the Venetian Waterways, boating on the Norfolk Broads

Best eats: The Smokehouse at Ormesby, California Tavern on California Road, Great Yarmouth, Thatched Island Café at the Venetian Waterways, Gorleston-on-Sea Doggy Diner, The Lion at Thurne, Hirst's Farm Shop

185

SCOTLAND

ROSLYN - P.193

John o' Groats

FINDLAY COTTAGE P.219

TOGETHER TRAVEL - P.22

DEO NA MARA - P.192

KYLESKU HOTEL - P.191

ROSIE'S COTTAGE - P.201

TIGH MAIRI - P.189

LOCHOLLY LODGE - P.210

STABLE COTTAGE - P.217

HIGHLAND AUTO CAMPERS - P.196

Inverness

KIRKSTONE LODGE - P.197

Aberdeen

TRESHNISH & HAUNN COTTAGES - P.216

WHITEBRIDGE HOTEL - P.188

CAIRNGORMS NATIONAL PARK

Fort William

ATHOLL ARMS HOTEL - P.194

THIMBLEWYND - P.204

TIRLAGGAN STUDIO - P.187

ARDANAISEIG - P.221

Dundee

KEILL COTTAGE - P.208

LOCH LOMOND & THE TROSSACHS NATIONAL PARK

LITTLE BRIAR COTTAGE - P.206

EDNAM HOUSE HOTEL - P.198

THE WHEA P.21

SEASHELL COTTAGE - P.100

Edinburgh

THE GEORGE HOTEL - P.203

Glasgow

THE POTTING SHED - P.199

SADDELL CASTLE - P.190

CURLEW COTTAGE - P.207

THE COACH HOUSE - P.212

THE RED L HOTEL - P.2

GALLOWAY FOREST PARK

TIRLAGGAN STUDIO, ISLE OF LISMORE, SCOTLAND

By Scott Antcliffe

Just 10 miles long and 1 mile wide, with an abundance of wildlife, the Isle of Lismore in Scotland is the perfect place to take a walk on the wild side.

As a keen wildlife and landscape photographer, I always look for places off the beaten track. The island of Lismore certainly meets that criteria and has an abundance of wildlife as an added bonus.

From the ferry, we made the short, 1-mile journey to our accommodation, through single-track, winding roads with stunning panoramic views across the island.

Our first impressions of the accommodation were great. Floor to ceiling full-length, bi-folding windows allowed us 24-hour views of the sublime Scottish mountains. On a clear day, you can see 14 peaks, allowing you to immerse yourself in the natural scenery that Lismore has to offer. The studio is fully equipped and the garden is safe and secure.

We found places of interest and circular walks on an extremely helpful website, walklismore.co.uk and, driving the length of the island, we passed only 4 other cars on the way. Our favourite place was the 13th century Coeffin Castle. The bay has clear, pristine waters and Drift certainly needed no invitation to go in for a paddle. We could not think of a more perfect way to spend a day - beautiful views and time spent with our collie.

All in all, a truly memorable break on such a unique, special island. I, for one, will be back and I urge you all to visit.

FACT FILE

Location: Tirlaggan, Isle of Lismore, Oban, Argyll and Bute, PA34 5UG

Website: sykescottages.co.uk

Contact: 01244 356655

Type of accommodation: Apartment

Number of bedrooms: 1

Number of dogs accepted: 2

Enclosed garden: Yes

Local interest: Walks from the door, Lismore Gaelic Heritage Centre, Tirefuir Broch, Achanard village, Lismore Lighthouse, Glenfinnan Viaduct, the Sailean Project, Coeffin Castle

Best eats: Lismore Café (Lismore Gaelic Heritage Centre), The Pierhouse at Port Appin

WHITEBRIDGE HOTEL, LOCH NESS, SCOTLAND

By Tracey Radnall

With its quirky decor and relaxed atmosphere, Whitebridge Hotel is well situated for touring the local area or exploring from the door.

Whitebridge is a hamlet roughly midway along the south side of Loch Ness, where it crosses the River Fechlin, in the foothills of the Monadhliath Mountains.

Finding the prominent roadside hotel is straightforward and, on first impressions, it has all the air of a pleasantly old-fashioned highland lodge. Entering via the attractive vestibule, complete with dog towels and treats, it has a lovely relaxed feel about it. It is snug, mellow and welcoming, and there are fabulous views in every direction, too.

The hotel bar, with its attractive wooden pews, features in the CAMRA real ale guide. The staff are relaxed and friendly and, over dinner of local venison, resident waiter, Hamish, imparted some handy advice on dog walks from the hotel door.

Nearby is the village of Foyers, famous for the Falls of Foyers, where a well-maintained path descends to a viewing platform. The Falls are hugely high and perhaps not the best attraction for those who don't have a head for heights.

The road to Fort Augustus is well worth a visit, too. Do pause to take in the magnificent return view at the end of Loch Ness - tapering into infinity along its 22-mile length. Driving back to Whitebridge, the high road affords another stunning viewpoint.

Whitebridge Hotel is located in an area which is undoubtedly an outdoor enthusiast's dream. It's an ideal stay, too, if traversing the length of Scotland, or returning after rounding the North Coast 500.

FACT FILE

Location: Whitebridge, Stratherrick, Near Inverness, Inverness-shire, IV2 6UN
Website: whitebridgehotel.co.uk
Contact: 01456 486226
Type of accommodation: Hotel
Number of bedrooms: 12
Number of dogs accepted: 2 (up to 35kg)
Enclosed garden: No
Local interest: Walks from the door, Loch Ness, Falls of Foyers
Best eats: Whitebridge Hotel

TIGH MAIRI, ELGOL, ISLE OF SKYE

By Tracey Radnall

With stunning views that take in the Strathaird peninsula across to Glasnakille and beyond to Sleat and the wonderful Isle of Rum, Tigh Mairi is a traditional croft with all the comforts of home - apart from a mobile phone signal!

At the far south western end of Skye, the road concludes at the small fishing village of Elgol, with a backdrop of the Cuillin Ridge across Loch Scavaig.

Arriving at Elgol, you pass over a cattle grid and spot the unmistakable group of Mary's thatched cottages. Driving through the electric gates, you cross a stone bridge over the stream separating Tigh Mairi from the other cottages on the croft. It is an idyllic setting.

The cottage is made from solid local stone, with all the aesthetically pleasing characteristics of highland croft architecture, including tapered walls and rounded corners, topped off with a substantial thatch.

Inside, the open-plan format features a well-equipped kitchen, dining area and sitting room with an oil burning stove. It sleeps 4 people, with a traditional veiled,

boxed, king-size bed in the downstairs bedroom. A gallery room with 2 single beds upstairs (accessed via a foldaway ladder) is ideal for children and a separate shower room completes the cottage facilities.

Tigh Mairi has all the comforts you and your hound could possibly need, thanks to underfloor heating, double glazing and a terrific location. It makes the perfect base for exploring on foot, enjoying cosy evenings under dark skies, or simply a tranquil retreat to relax and recharge. Fantastic walks from the door guarantee your canine companion will love it, too.

FACT FILE

Location: Mary's Cottages, 26 Elgol, Skye, IV49 9BL
Website: skyecottages.co.uk/tigh-mairi/
Contact: 07985 585397
Type of accommodation: Traditional croft
Number of bedrooms: 2 (sleeps 4)
Number of dogs accepted: 2 by prior arrangement
Enclosed garden: The cottages are fenced off from the road and neighbouring properties, there is moorland behind the cottage, with sheep and red deer, so it is recommended you keep your dog under close control
Local interest: Coast path from Elgol, boat trips from Elgol Harbour
Best eats: The Coruisk House Hotel restaurant

189

SADDELL CASTLE, KINTYRE, SCOTLAND

By Tracey Radnall

Ever fancied a spell as sovereign of your own castle? Saddell Castle is a great place for families or groups of friends to get together in style.

On the shores of Kilbrannan Sound, Saddell Castle is located on the east coast of Kintyre, Scotland. Along with its neighbouring properties, it was renovated by The Landmark Trust and is now available for holiday weekends or mid-week breaks.

The castle is approached by a long, straight driveway, lined with vibrant green, lichen-covered trees. Its exterior has all the rustic grandeur and Scottishness I'd anticipated - appearing more than a little foreboding but

strangely compact and lofty, all at the same time. Our arrival was a bit of a muddle, thanks largely to 7 adults and 2 excited dogs all straining to get into the dry from the downpour.

The castle is beautifully proportioned for a house party and, even in moody weather, there are fine views of the bay from every window. A neat and compact kitchen is well equipped and the single spiral staircase leads to all rooms. With the keys to the castle, comes a key to a diminutive bothy, which houses basic furniture and a handy set of deck chairs.

There is much to do inside the castle, with board games, cards etc. Just keeping the enormous wood burner going takes a team effort. Best of all, on the 5th floor, among the roof space and adjacent to the walkable ramparts, is a ping-pong table - a word of advice, shut the door before playing, to avoid the ball descending 5 floors, via the spiral staircase!

All too soon, it was time for us to take our leave. It had been a fabulous early spring escape, chock-full of fun, frolics and historical interest.

FACT FILE

Location: Saddell Estate, Kintyre, PA28 6QS
Website: landmarktrust.org.uk
Contact: 01628 825925
Type of accommodation: Self-catering castle
Number of bedrooms: 5 (sleeps 8)
Number of dogs accepted: 2
Enclosed garden: No
Local interest: Saddell Abbey, Kintyre Way, Westport Bay, beaches
Best eats: Self-catering

190

KYLESKU HOTEL, SUTHERLAND, SCOTLAND

By Tracey Radnall

Ideally placed for exploring Sutherland's vast, rugged landscape and remote beaches, award-winning Kylesku Hotel bills itself as a small Highland hotel with a big heart and beautiful seafood.

The small hamlet of Kylesku features a slightly out-of-place, modern-looking bridge (conveniently replacing a mini ferry crossing), a small hotel and a handful of fishing craft.

The hotel, parts of which date from the 17th century, offers stylish accommodation with the emphasis on local fish and seafood, thanks to its handy location just metres from the slipway, where fishermen land their catches. No food miles here, merely food metres. Stepping into the recently refurbished hotel, we were greeted by owner and head chef Sonia. Immediately the place felt very laid-back and friendly, with its minimalist Scandinavian-style decor of painted cladding and wood burning stoves. The views from the glass-fronted hotel are reminiscent of Norway's fjords at Flåm, with which the place has a historical connection.

We were shown to our handy downstairs, ensuite, twin room, which was very cosy.

Behind the hotel a neat circular wooded path leads to the top of the hill, affording elevated views across the loch, a waterfall and a bothy away in the distance.

It's easy to see why GPs in Scotland are now prescribing the outdoors as an antidote to stress and depression. It was the most refreshing spring break, following a long Scottish winter, and the perfect base to reconnect with nature. Not bad for dogs either. During our time at Kylesku, we met 4 other dogs staying with their owners.

It is simply the most dog friendly hotel I have stayed in, to date. Dogs are not just welcomed here but positively encouraged.

FACT FILE

Location: Kylesku Bridge, Lairg, Sutherland, IV27 4HW

Website: kyleskuhotel.co.uk

Contact: 01971 502231

Type of accommodation: Hotel

Number of bedrooms: 11

Number of dogs accepted: 2

Enclosed garden: No

Local interest: Sandwood Bay, Cape Wrath Trail, Assynt and Sutherland

Best eats: Kylesku Hotel

DEO NA MARA, POOLEWE, NORTHERN HIGHLANDS

By Richard Aspinall

With its stunning views across Loch Ewe, Deo Na Mara is surrounded by spectacular hills and mountains, and is within a short drive of beautiful, deserted beaches.

Deo Na Mara - Gaelic for 'mist of the sea' - is a sizeable, 3-bedroomed family house. It is well equipped and warm, with a view of Loch Ewe.

It is situated in the small hamlet of Inverasdale, on the western edge of Loch Ewe. The geography is deeply complicated - a great number of lochs, freshwater and open to the sea, create an ever-so-confusing landscape that, to use simple terms, goes in and out a lot! The land goes up and down a lot, too and, if the air is clear, you can enjoy amazing views of hills and Munros.

Our Westies, Tilly and Henry, were immediately pleased with all the new sniffs, as we let them explore the secure, dog-proof garden for the first time. We didn't do much on the first day, other than take a walk to the seaweed-clad shore. Beaches are an important part of exploring the Scottish coast for us and much loved by the dogs, of course.

The weather in the north-west Highlands isn't always as we'd like. Atlantic storms can scupper your plans, but the warm, wet Gulf Stream air does have its benefits and, when it meets lochs and glens sheltered from the wind, little oases of warmth are created that are entirely unlike the rest of Scotland.

It was a special pleasure to see Tilly on her travels. She's getting on a bit and has a number of health conditions but, even so, she still managed a good few runs on the stunning beaches.

FACT FILE

Location: Inverasdale, Poolewe, Northern Highlands

Website: scottish-cottages.co.uk (Ref. CC511437)

Contact: 0345 268 1269

Type of accommodation: House

Number of bedrooms: 3 (sleeps 6)

Number of dogs accepted: 2

Enclosed garden: Yes

Local interest: Gairloch and Redpoint Beaches, Museum and Tourist Information at Gairloch, Inverewe Garden (estate trails, gardens not dog friendly), Attadale Gardens, Loch Carron, Plockton village

Best eats: The Old Inn and Badachro Inn at Gairloch, Café at Inverewe Gardens

ROSLYN, BETTYHILL, SCOTLAND
By Richard Aspinall

Exploring Scotland's northernmost coastline can be a rugged, wild and windswept experience but, if the sun happens to come out, it can be truly breathtaking.

Ask anyone who's toured the northernmost coast of Scotland and they'll tell you, "if you have the weather, there's nowhere better!".

Bettyhill is a crofting community, with a general store and café, but it remains unspoiled by tourism, which is commonplace along this coast. While there are many visitors, everything is quite low-key.

We stayed in Roslyn, a former family home situated above the narrow tidal valley of the River Naver. On our first morning, we watched the tide come in and, with a pair of good binoculars, spotted seabirds and a distant otter. The house is very well equipped, with a large dining room, cosy lounge, 3 bedrooms and a great kitchen, with everything you need. The lounge and dining room both have stunning views to the river and beyond to the sands of Torrisdale Bay in the distance.

The main road through Bettyhill makes up part of the North Coast 500. The route attracts many independently-minded travellers, so you'll meet lots of folk in camper vans and an awful lot of people travelling with their dogs. It can take ages to wander across even the quietest of beaches, as you share doggy stories and a tennis ball.

Sutherland and Caithness were kind to us and the weather, in particular, was wonderful. I found myself agreeing with all those people who had told us that there was nowhere better.

FACT FILE

Location: Bettyhill, near Thurso, Northern Highlands
Website: scottish-cottages.co.uk (Ref. UK5500)
Contact: 0345 268 1269
Type of accommodation: House
Number of bedrooms: 3 (sleeps 5)
Number of dogs accepted: 2
Enclosed garden: Fenced patio/decking area
Local interest: Farr Bay, Strathnaver Museum, 'Clach na Faraid' (the Farr Stone), Sango Bay, Smoo Cave, John o' Groats, Dunnet Bay
Best eats: Farr Bay Inn at Bettyhill, The Bettyhill Hotel, Windhaven café at Dunnet Bay

THE ATHOLL ARMS HOTEL, DUNKELD, SCOTLAND

By Natasha Balletta

A truly warm, Scottish welcome awaits dogs and their people at the award-winning Atholl Arms Hotel, where there are beautiful walks nearby and a visit to the superbly dog friendly Scone Palace is a must.

If you are visiting Dunkeld in Perthshire and looking for accommodation with your dog, The Atholl Arms Hotel is very dog friendly and has recently received an award for being the most pet-friendly hotel in Scotland.

FACT FILE

Location: Ridgehead, Tay Terrace, Dunkeld, Perthshire
Website: athollarmshotel.com
Contact: 01350 727219
Type of accommodation: Hotel
Number of bedrooms: 31
Number of dogs accepted: 2
Enclosed garden: No
Local interest: Scone Palace, local walks along the River Tay, Grandtully, the Knock of Crieff
Best eats: The Scottish Deli at Dunkeld

Overlooking the River Tay, this luxury, country hotel is in a stunning location, surrounded by rolling hills and panoramic lake views. All the rooms are dog friendly and every dog who stays receives a welcome pack. The staff are friendly, nothing is too much trouble for them and you are made to feel welcome straightaway.

The rooms are very comfortable, so it is like a home from home for you and your furry companion and dogs are allowed in the lounge, bar and meeting place. The hotel is also within walking distance of some lovely dog friendly pubs and cafés.

Staying in Dunkeld, there is a great choice of places to take your dog for walks and the hotel recommends a number of routes. Sadly, we didn't have time for all the walking trails but enjoyed a lovely walk by the River Tay, which features paddling spots, fields and stunning scenery.

If you would like to explore a different aspect of the River Tay with your dog, you can take part in kayaking. Outdoor Explore (outdoorexplore.co.uk) offers guided tours and outdoor activities.

Nearby Scone Palace hosts the annual, doggy event - Paws at the Palace, which was the purpose of our visit with rescue dog, Kratu, who had been invited as a VIP guest, having become famous when he represented Wood Green Animal Shelter in the Agility Class at Crufts. Scone Palace has been mentioned as one of the most pet-friendly places to visit in the world and came first in a voting contest with Trusted Housesitters (trustedhousesitters.com), for its beautiful location and dog friendly attitude.

Our favourite café was The Scottish Deli in Dunkeld. In the evening, you can enjoy their Scottish deli tapas, which was delicious and one of my favourite meals. They were excited to meet Kratu and made all dogs feel very welcome.

We wished we could have stayed longer. Kratu was sad to be leaving and looked very unhappy when he saw the suitcases all packed for departure.

If you are looking for a dog friendly break in Scotland, I can highly recommend Perthshire. There are many beautiful and historic places for you and your dog to enjoy that make you feel as if you are in the heart of the Highlands.

SCOTLAND BY CAMPER VAN

By Rhian White

A fully-equipped camper van is the ideal way to explore the Scottish Highlands and, with hundreds of places to explore, a week just isn't enough.

Highland Auto Campers was set up by Mark and Alicia, after many years of touring the UK and, in particular, the Scottish Highlands, in their own camper van.

They offer for hire the unique Marvin, the MRV camper van, which can be set up to suit your holiday requirements, whether that's taking your dog or your mountain bikes.

The van was a dream to drive and live in for a week and its diesel heater kept us warm and snug.

Everything was provided, including bedding, cooking equipment, gas and a barbecue (as well as the in-van hob). The dogs had secure floor harnesses, a comfy mat and there was also a shower-type attachment - useful when they were wet and muddy. The bed in the main area of the van was very comfortable, as was the one in the overhead extension.

After picking the van up in Inverness, we went up to Tain and then west across to Scourie and from there south towards Inverlochie, before heading east again to spend the last day on the Black Isle.

The sheer scale of the beauty of the Highlands has to be seen to be believed and I don't think I can really do it justice with words. If I were to do it again, I would take at least 2 weeks, preferably 4, as it's a long way from where I live and there is simply too much to see to cram into a week.

Boo and Betsy had a wonderful time. They visited a new beach every day, most of which were practically empty.

FACT FILE

Location: Highland Auto Campers Ltd, Brooklea, Oakleigh Road, North Kessock, Inverness, IV1 3XW

Website: highlandautocampers.co.uk

Contact: 01463 264050

Type of accommodation: Camper van

Number of bedrooms: 2 sleeping areas (sleeps 4)

Number of dogs accepted: 2 small or medium

Enclosed garden: No

Local interest: Ullapool, Lael Forest Garden, Corrieshalloch Gorge, Mellon Udrigle Beach, Loch Maree, Red Point Beach, Beinn Eighe Nature Reserve, views on the road from Torridon to Lower Diabaig, Rogie Falls, Rosemarkie Beach, Chanonry Point.

KIRKSTONE LODGE, INVERUGLAS, SCOTLAND

By Tracey Radnall

One of just 7 houses occupying an idyllic and peaceful spot in the foothills of the Cairngorm mountains, Kirkstone Lodge offers walks from the door and everything guests could need for a comfortable stay, whatever the weather.

From the exterior, the lodge has a whiff of 'arts and crafts' about it, although originally built in the 1980s. Inside, the unique styling comes into its own - open-plan, airy, modern and comfortable, and the west-facing picture window reveals a 180° uninterrupted view. Even the galleried kitchen looks out onto open countryside and the curvy Mondahliath Mountains beyond.

We were keen to stretch our legs following the drive from Edinburgh and the owner informed me I was unlikely to meet anyone along the trails. I followed the waymarked paths through a section of the ancient Caledonian Forest and we walked for an hour before turning back to the lodge.

I found our pad had all the mod cons you could need during a stay, punctuated with less decent weather, such as a full Sky TV package and a bookcase full of DVDs. Equally, it's geared up for sunny days, with

a sauna, hot tub and barbecue. The garden is enclosed, meaning your best pal is free to roam.

The following day we set off onto the Badenoch Way from the doorstep. It's a linear route of some 11 miles connecting Kingussie with Kincraig. The endless forest trails were lined with waves of fresh, luminescent green larch, beech and pine trees, and a plentiful supply of lichen pointed to the purity of the air.

It's worth mentioning the neighbouring property of Mountain View Lodge is also owned by the same people and, as the name suggests, the views are every bit as good from there too.

FACT FILE

Location: Invergulas, Insh, By Kincraig, Kingussie, PH21 1NY
Website: highlandlodgeescapes.co.uk
Contact: 07719 501964
Type of accommodation: House
Number of bedrooms: 3 (sleeps 8)
Number of dogs accepted: Multiple
Enclosed garden: Yes
Local interest: Highland Folk Museum at Newtonmore, the Badenoch Way, Ruthven & Glen Tromie Circuit

197

EDNAM HOUSE HOTEL, KELSO, SCOTLAND

By Genie Houlder

Ednam House is a spacious, stately mansion which sits on the banks of the River Tweed, surrounded by 3 acres of enchanting gardens, making it an ideal spot to relax, unwind and soak up the best of the Borders.

We arrived at Kelso and found the hotel easily in the centre of the bustling little town. We were immediately impressed by the grandeur of the entrance and excited to get inside.

The reception was large and hospitable, with thick tartan carpet, traditional furnishings and a fireplace fit for a king. The friendly receptionist greeted us for our 2-night 'Gourmet Getaway', with the emphasis on making my dog, Bobby, feel relaxed, with plenty of kisses and cuddles.

Dogs are allowed in all parts of the hotel, excluding the Riverside Restaurant, but can dine with you in the Lounge Bar.

Our room was number 42, a classic room with the most enchanting view overlooking the hotel's grounds and the River Tweed. There was enough room for us to spread out and not feel crowded, with a dog bed, other dog accessories and two suitcases. We refreshed ourselves in the large bathroom and dressed elegantly for our first evening meal in the Riverview Restaurant.

After finishing our wine, we took Bobby on a moonlit walk around Kelso. Quirky boutique shops line the cobbled streets and faint music from the dog friendly bars and pubs serenaded our stroll.

Our last evening at Ednam House was spent in the Lounge Bar, where Bobby could stay with us while we ate. The food in the bar is more relaxed but no less tasty than that in the restaurant.

FACT FILE

Location: Bridge Street, Kelso, Roxburghshire, TD5 7HT

Website: ednamhouse.com

Contact: 01573 224168

Type of accommodation: Hotel

Number of bedrooms: 33

Number of dogs accepted: 2

Enclosed garden: No

Local interest: Kelso, Abbotsford House

Best eats: Ednam House Restaurant and Lounge Bar

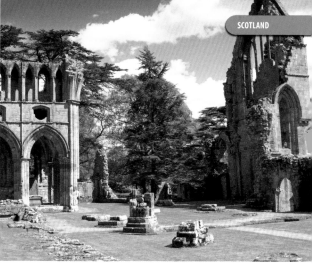

THE POTTING SHED, EARLSTON, BERWICKSHIRE

By Angie Aspinall

Surrounded by woods, wildlife and wonderful views, The Potting Shed is a quirky and cosy retreat in the heart of the Scottish Borders.

Hidden away, a mile down a bumpy woodland track, The Potting Shed is situated in a secluded walled garden on the private Cowdenknowes Estate. Formerly a derelict potting shed, it has been transformed into a cosy, romantic bolthole.

There's a parking space adjacent to 'The Shed' and storage for bikes, fishing gear and muddy boots. There's a fully enclosed garden with table and chairs for al fresco dining and there's more private outdoor space on a veranda, overlooking the River Leader.

As we got out of the car, I was struck by the sound of the babbling water mingling with the birdsong which filled the air. It was tranquillity personified.

For a former potting shed, the accommodation felt far roomier than we'd expected. The lovely, light-filled, open-plan living space provided ample room for us and our two Westies, Tilly and Henry.

We entered the bright, welcoming kitchen, which is very well equipped, complete with a stunning, deep blue range cooker. There was also an array of beautiful, brightly-coloured mugs on hooks, which matched the tiles on the wall behind.

At the far end is a large, comfy sofa and bookshelves filled with carefully-chosen guidebooks to the area and a few choice novels, and there's another small room, which we used to store our suitcases. There's a TV and a collection of DVDs, but we never switched on the TV. We turned the sofa round to face the gorgeous *(continued...)*

FACT FILE

Location: Cowdenknowes, Earlston, Berwickshire, TD4 6AA

Website: thepottingshedscotland.com

Contact: 01896 848124

Type of accommodation: Cottage

Number of bedrooms: 1 (sleeps 2)

Number of dogs accepted: 1 medium/large or 2 small

Enclosed garden: Yes

Local interest: Dryburgh Abbey, Smailholm Pottery, Born in the Borders, Hay Farm Heavy Horse Centre

Best eats: The Plough Inn at Lilliesleaf

stove and spent an evening watching the flames, chatting and enjoying a nice bottle of red wine, while Tilly snoozed in her bed and Henry stretched out on the floor.

Next to the kitchen, is a modern shower room which had been made up for us with thick, fluffy towels and a selection of organic toiletries. And, next to this, is the bedroom, with a very comfortable, king-size bed. Dogs aren't allowed in the bedroom and, as our two usually sleep in our bedroom at home, we left the bedroom door open, so they didn't feel abandoned.

Before we went out for the day, we met Kate, the owner. She greeted us warmly and checked if everything was OK. We assured her we were having a lovely time and explained we were heading off to Dryburgh Abbey to, hopefully, see the snowdrops. Kate recommended Smailholm Pottery and Born in the Borders (which has a micro-brewery and gin distillery).

We decided to eat out and followed the recommendation of a friend to book a table in the dog friendly bar area of The Plough Inn at Lilliesleaf, and were so glad we did. We couldn't have had a better meal or been greeted more warmly.

After another good night's sleep, we set off home, but not before crossing the border into England to visit the Hay Farm Heavy Horse Centre.

All in all, we had a wonderful weekend away and wouldn't hesitate in recommending it.

ROSIE'S COTTAGE, NEAR MELVICH, SUTHERLAND

By Tracey Radnall

Occupying a lofty position in the remote hamlet of Trantlemore in the northern Highlands, Rosie's Cottage offers comfortable accommodation, centred around a cosy, wood-burning stove.

Rosie's Cottage is an attractive new-build in a lofty position. We arrived as dusk was closing in and were soon cosy and warm, with the little wood-burning stove punching above its weight.

The next morning, we were keen to explore this most northerly stretch of Scottish A-road, east to west. Caithness is a wild and remote place, albeit with a curious proliferation of Pampas grass. The grasses have long since escaped their tidy garden plots and can be frequently spotted in wild clumps dotted around the vast landscape, accompanied by the more appropriate peat stacks. It's a remarkable sight and one I am pleased not to have missed.

Back at Rosie's Cottage - an ideal, comfortable location close to the main east to west road - we were soon feeling relaxed in this peaceful valley.

The next day, traversing Sutherland's

Mackay country, gable ends of abandoned stone crofts were further reminders of a once great habitation. I can only imagine, had the Clearances not occurred, the landscape may well look vastly different than it does today. Eventually, the plains give way to more country with cliff-tops punctuated by a string of pale, sandy inlets.

It's impossible to resist visiting the beaches along the way, especially when accompanied by an impatient spaniel. Each and every one is a gem. Strathy East is not to be missed, with many caves, including one linear cave you can enter from one end and emerge, several metres along the beach, at the other. *(continued...)*

FACT FILE

Location: Trantlemore near Melvich, Sutherland
Website: unique-cottages.co.uk
Contact: 01835 822277
Type of accommodation: Cottage
Number of bedrooms: 3 (sleeps 4-6)
Number of dogs accepted: 1
Enclosed garden: No
Local interest: Bettyhill, beach at Strathy East, Smoo Cave
Best eats: The Strathy Inn at Thurso

One of the best beaches on the north coast is to be found at the fairly new town of Bettyhill. The long valley of Strathnaver runs for 17 miles south from Bettyhill to Altnaharra and was once heavily populated. It formed part of the 1.5 million-acre estates of the Duke and Duchess of Sutherland, from which 15,000 people were cleared between 1811 and 1821. The Countess of Sutherland, in a move unusual for the time, had a replacement village built near the coast on the east side of the River Naver. This she named after herself, hence Bettyhill. Today, it's a vibrant holiday community - it's lofty location giving magnificent views across Torrisdale Bay.

Durness in the far north-west is home to a rather important cave, curiously known as Smoo Cave which is, apparently, a Norsk-derived name. I was warned by a chap further back along the road that this was an underwhelming place to visit, and I wasn't expecting too much, as we parked up adjacent to a block of pebble-dashed loos, with a steep staircase leading from them.

Bertie and I followed the steps down and round until we arrived at the opening of a cavernous aperture in the solid limestone. The cave is essentially a huge amphitheatre, carved out by centuries of pounding from tides of seawater, combining with further caves carved from above by freshwater falls. It is utterly awesome and jaw-dropping. The lesson... never heed the 'advice' of a fellow tourist.

When it was time for us to take our leave and head back to Edinburgh, we chose to traverse the road along the shores of Loch Shin - a peaceful cross-country route to the Kyle of Sutherland, the main routes south and home.

THE GEORGE HOTEL, INVERARAY, SCOTLAND

By Tracey Radnall

With a variety of individually styled options, The George Hotel offers comfortable accommodation and great food.

The George Hotel dates from 1860 and the Clark family, who ran it then, still does - 7 generations on.

The hotel has 17 bedrooms, each individually designed to complement the building's architectural heritage and there are 8 more bedrooms in an adjacent building, The First House. There's a wide variety of rooms available - doubles, Master rooms, Superior Master rooms, Deluxe Master rooms, The Library and Merchants, plus self-contained accommodation in The Wee Hoose and The Big Wee Hoose.

A friend had introduced me to The George the previous April, when driving to Argyll. We were starving when we reached Inveraray, well past lunchtime, and decided to pull in at The George and eat there. The bar was welcoming, with open fires warming the locals and their dogs. Our haddock & chips and smoked hake fillet with Mornay sauce were cooked simply, fresh and delicious, and we were reluctant to leave.

Having enjoyed our last visit, I thought I'd return with Bertie and found we were staying in The Barn, which boasts a spacious lounge (with a French-style chimney), 4 bedrooms and an open-plan kitchen with dining room attached. The lounge opens onto a private courtyard, with seating area, and is surrounded by a walled garden. One of the bedrooms has an ensuite but there's also a separate bathroom with jacuzzi.

I would heartily recommend The George Hotel if you're exploring this part of the world and hope I can visit again very shortly - it was lovely.

FACT FILE

Location: 1 Main Street East, Inveraray, PA32 8TT
Website: thegeorgehotel.co.uk
Contact: 01499 302111
Type of accommodation: Hotel
Number of bedrooms: 17 plus 8 rooms in The First House and self-contained accommodation options
Number of dogs accepted: Multiple
Enclosed garden: Yes
Local interest: Inveraray Jail
Best eats: The George Hotel (particularly fish)

THIMBLEWYND, PERTHSHIRE, SCOTLAND

By Emma Brown

Promoted as a luxury getaway, and with a Scotsman award as one of the 9 Best Airbnbs in Scotland with a hot tub, Thimblewynd offers comfortable accommodation with a variety of walks and places of interest nearby.

Daisy, our 4-year-old Labrador x Golden Retriever, was delighted to get into Thimblewynd and have a sniff around. She was even more enthusiastic when we went out to the garden, exploring her playground while my husband, Phil, and I eyed up the hammock and the brightly coloured, wood-fired hot tub.

As we unpacked, we discovered just how well equipped the cottage was. In the kitchen there were essentials such as teabags, ketchup and even a bottle of bubbly waiting in the fridge!

Both the cottage's website and welcome pack mentioned the local pub, The Kirkstyle Inn, which we pre-booked for dinner. The staff were immediately welcoming to Daisy, bringing a bowl of water and each waitress asking if they could give Daisy a biscuit. We were sitting at a large square table, so there was a perfect Labrador-sized space underneath.

After a restful night's sleep, we decided to tackle one of the walks recommended by the locals the night before - The Den. We followed the route of the Historic Dunning walk, which took us past some landmarks, such as the Thorn Tree which commemorates the burning of Dunning by Jacobite troops in 1716 (although the tree has been replaced a few times). The walk was more challenging in places than we expected but we were rewarded by the views - one over the hills and one looking down into Dunning, on the way home.

FACT FILE

Location: Bridgend, Dunning, Perthshire, PH2 0QW

Website: thimblewynd.co.uk

Contact: thimblewyndholidayrental@gmail.com

Type of accommodation: Cottage

Number of bedrooms: 1

Number of dogs accepted: No set limit

Enclosed garden: Yes

Local interest: The Den Walk, Maggie Wall's Monument, St Serf's Church

Best eats: The Kirkstyle Inn and Broadslap Fruit Farm at Dunning

Broadslap Fruit Farm is only a few minutes drive from the cottage. We browsed the gift shop and Daisy put on her best puppy-dog eyes for the staff member, who delighted her with a biscuit. We then had a lovely lunch in the snug. The farm was gearing up for pumpkin-picking season, at the time of our visit, which I'm sure would be a great day out (and dogs on leads are allowed).

On Sunday morning, Daisy and I were up early and I enjoyed some time relaxing on the hammock outside, in a covered area.

The benefit of the garden is there are so many different sections - 2 are covered, so we could enjoy the garden even in the rain, which there is definitely a high chance of getting in Scotland!

The local businesses we visited were so welcoming to dogs and, with lovely walks from the doorstep, I wouldn't hesitate to recommend Thimblewynd and Dunning to couples with dogs.

LITTLE BRIAR COTTAGE, STIRLING, SCOTLAND

By Angie Aspinall

There are fine views from the award-winning, dog friendly Little Briar Cottage, which makes a cosy base from which to explore all Loch Lomond & The Trossachs National Park has to offer.

It was a little misty when we arrived at Briar Cottages, so we were unable to enjoy the views, highly anticipated as they were, until the weather had improved. However, they were worth the wait, with Loch Earn below us and the Munro, Stuc a' Chroin, in the distance.

Little Briar is a 2-bedroomed cottage with an open-plan living area and it has everything you need on a self-catering holiday.

The grounds are extensive and Tilly enjoyed a good run in a sloping paddock above the property every morning. Just outside the kitchen door, there's a secluded dining area overlooking the loch. This decked area is fully enclosed, so you can leave your dogs outside quite safely. Down the hill and across the road is Briar Cottages' loch garden. There, guests are welcome to use the summer house, picnic tables, jetty, slipway, free trout fishing (during the season), 6-hole putting green, and petanque piste with boules.

The loch garden boasts a couple of sculptures, 'Blawn Wi The Wind' and 'Stan The Stag'. These lie on the BLiSS sculpture trail and we investigated a third, 'STILL', just a short drive along the lochside road towards St Fillans.

There are several dog friendly eateries around Loch Earn but we'd particularly recommend Mhor 84. We had breakfast there one morning, sitting opposite a display of mouth-watering cakes. How we didn't end up sampling their afternoon tea is a mystery.

FACT FILE

Location: Lochearnhead, Perthshire, Scotland, FK19 8PU

Website: stayatbriar.co.uk

Contact: 07917 416497

Type of accommodation: Cottage

Number of bedrooms: 2 (sleeps 3)

Number of dogs accepted: 2

Enclosed garden: Yes

Local interest: BLiSS sculpture trail, Rob Roy's grave at the church in Balquhidder, the Falls of Dochart, Loch Tay

Best eats: The Four Seasons Hotel at St Fillans, Mhor 84 at Balquhidder

CURLEW COTTAGE, GARTOCHARN, SCOTLAND

By Angie Aspinall

Perfect peace awaits at 2 eco-friendly holiday cottages which have been lovingly created from old farm buildings on a 5-acre smallholding, nestled in the heart of the Loch Lomond & the Trossachs National Park.

Curlew Cottage really has the 'wow' factor and I was blown away by the style and size. The kitchen was like something from a glossy magazine on stylish living - large, open-plan, with everything you could possibly need, plus added extras, including an upmarket coffee machine and a welcome pack containing freshly-baked bread and eggs from the hens we could see free-ranging outside.

The open-plan arrangement of the kitchen, dining area and lounge worked really well. On the ground floor, alongside the living space, there are 2 beautifully presented bedrooms (a double and a twin) and a shared bathroom. Upstairs, there's a huge master bedroom with ensuite, and a further twin, also with an ensuite shower room. We had exclusive use of a garden and terrace, where we dined al fresco and enjoyed sunbathing.

On our first night we headed to the dog friendly Loch Lomond Arms Hotel in the pretty village of Luss. After dinner, we wandered along the shoreline and enjoyed the sensational views.

Having learned from one of the rangers where he might see pine martens at 5 am, Richard thought he'd give it a try the following morning. An early start! At 6 am, I received a text saying, 'Pine martens spotted.' Success!

That evening, we enjoyed a picnic back at Curlew Cottage, making friends with the resident chickens and soaking up the evening sun. It was the perfect end to a perfect short break at a place I would heartily recommend.

FACT FILE

Location: East Cambusmoon Farm, Gartocharn, G83 8RZ

Website: lochlomondholidaycottage.com

Contact: 07905 093 997

Type of accommodation: Cottage

Number of bedrooms: 4 (sleeps 8)

Number of dogs accepted: 2

Enclosed garden: No

Local interest: Queen Elizabeth Forest Park, Loch Lomond, Loch Katrine (steamship cruises)

Best eats: Loch Lomond Arms Hotel at Luss

KEILLS COTTAGE, ARDTUN, ISLE OF MULL

By Lauren Fraser

Enjoying a secluded location, without any close neighbours, Keills Cottage makes an ideal holiday retreat on the beautiful Isle of Mull.

The cottage was once an old black house and retains many period features - the stained wooden cladding, slate and white render blend sympathetically with the countryside beyond. The garden is enclosed, with a gate across the drive and we made use of a seating area.

The property looks delightfully cosy from the outside and we weren't disappointed when we entered. The living space is open-plan, with a kitchen and dining area at one end and a lounge at the other. It was incredibly inviting, with cushion-laden sofas arranged around a large wood-burner. There were plenty of logs in a basket alongside and we found the burner surprisingly easy to light.

The kitchen may be compact but we found it very well equipped and the views across the island from its windows are spectacular. There's an abundance of wildlife in the countryside beyond. On our very first evening, we watched a curlew managing her chicks then, after catching a glimpse of red deer cantering through the undergrowth, we even caught sight of a hen harrier, hunting its prey.

Dogs are welcome everywhere, except the bedrooms, which is very much what we'd expect. We'd taken Peggy's bed with us but she found the sprawling rugs that kept our feet snug just as appealing!

One of our favourite walks was along the lane towards Ardtun. The panoramic views of Bunessan Bay that greet you as you round the corner make it incredibly

FACT FILE

Location: Ardtun, Isle of Mull, PA67 6DH

Website: isleofmullcottages.com

Contact: 01688 400682

Type of accommodation: Cottage

Number of bedrooms: 2

Number of dogs accepted: 2

Enclosed garden: Yes

Local interest: Ardalanish Weavers, Ardalanish Beach, Lip na Cloiche Gardens, Nursery & Crafts, guided island tours

Best eats: Arlene's Coffee Shop at Craignure, The Argyll Arms Hotel and The Blackbird Bistro at Bunessan (themed takeaway nights)

worthwhile. We often continued into the village and, feeling rather hungry one evening, enjoyed hearty haddock and chips at The Argyll Arms.

There's a wide variety of walking routes around the island. Those around Croggan and Loch Buie are quite level, if you're taking things easy. Large swathes of the island are managed by the Forestry Commission and you'll find a number of woodland pathways you can enjoy, many with car parks nearby. If you fancy more of a challenge, you can plan your own route using one of the OS maps in the cottage.

Mull is popular with wildlife enthusiasts and we booked an expert guide with Island Encounters. The weather was dreary but we saw otters, white-tailed sea eagles and even fallow deer, so don't let the rain deter you.

We couldn't have had a more enjoyable week on the Isle of Mull. Keills Cottage cosseted us during inclement weather and kept us warm in the evenings. It felt just like home, but with panoramic views to remind us that we were somewhere far more special.

LOCHOLLY LODGE, ACHILTIBUIE, SCOTLAND

By Tracey Radnall

Incredible 180° views can be enjoyed from the floor-to-ceiling windows of the first floor lounge, in this contemporary and luxurious holiday accommodation.

Nothing quite prepares you for the dramatic landscape of the north west Highlands when you first visit. It's almost as if each mountain - and, yes, I know in Scotland they're 'hills' - is competing with its neighbour. Each rises imperiously above the vast, glacial plain from which it was created - a humbling sight that's unlike any other in Britain.

On the Coigach peninsula, Stac Polly Lodge and Locholly Lodge stand in the shadow of Stac Polly - stylish and modern (and also identical), their clean lines, sleek wood cladding and large windows emphasise their contemporary design. First impressions count and, as a graphic designer myself, I couldn't help but admire the thought that had gone into their creation.

Locholly Lodge was designed to take maximum advantage of the views, by placing the lounge, with its blu-ray player, iPod dock and wood-burner, on the first floor. The large windows, which extend between floor and ceiling, frame the landscape, ensuring guests enjoy 180° views of the Summer Isles, an archipelago of islands at the mouth of Loch Broom, An Teallach and the Minch. It really is a room with a view - nautical types will particularly enjoy watching the CalMac ferry passing between Ullapool and Stornoway.

The property is minimalistic in style and, with sparkling white ceilings and walls, and a sensational wooden floor, it feels incredibly spacious inside. The main living space is open-plan, with a dining area, snug and kitchen. There's Sky TV in the lounge

FACT FILE

Location: 116 Polglass, Achiltibuie, Wester Ross, IV26 2YH

Website: highlandlodgeescapes.co.uk

Contact: 07719 501964

Type of accommodation: House

Number of bedrooms: 4 (sleeps 8)

Number of dogs accepted: Multiple

Enclosed garden: Yes

Local interest: Stac Pollaidh, Alchiltibuie Beach, Achnahaird Beach, Inverpolly

Best eats: Am Fuaran Bar at Altandhu

and every bedroom but the real highlights were the hot tub and sauna. I couldn't think of a more enjoyable way of relaxing after a day in the mountains.

What I found most pleasing though was that, despite the spectacular design and stylish fixtures, it was also extremely dog friendly, with a secure garden outside. You can walk straight from the house - the peninsula and beach being within easy reach, as is the nearest village, Achiltibuie.

Waking early on our first morning, we were greeted by the first murmurings of Storm Doris. Sheets of rain and wind-assisted gulls sped past the window, as if inspired by the jets of Top Gun. Red deer and sparrowhawks were clearly being propelled fast in the same direction - only a solitary sheep remained steadfast, grazing calmly as if it was just another day. Obviously, it takes a far bigger storm than this to halt the outgoing ferry. I suspect the locals consider it T-shirt weather!

Although Doris had promised us a visit, she headed south instead. It was a lucky escape but she made her presence felt by capping the peaks with snow. There was no wind at all but, strangely, the silence just heightened the senses. Whatever the weather, it's a spectacular place and one I can imagine visiting many times.

THE COACH HOUSE, CANONBIE, SCOTLAND

By Wendy Hopewell

People with several dogs will find a warm welcome from the resident Labradors (and their people) at The Coach House, in the small village of Canonbie.

Finding somewhere that welcomes more than one dog can be tricky, especially when they're Labrador-size, so it was lovely knowing The Coach House accepts 3. It is attached to the Old Manse and has been converted into a charming holiday retreat.

Decorated stylishly throughout, it is open-plan downstairs, with a kitchen and dining table at one end and a lounge, with fireplace and window overlooking the garden, at the other. The kitchen has everything you'd expect, plus a dishwasher, and we found a hamper of goodies awaiting us on the table. And if you can't miss your favourite programme, there's a TV and DVD-player. We slept in the master bedroom, which has an ensuite shower room, as does the spare room.

There's a secure garden, so we could let our dogs have a run around and, whilst they were exploring their surroundings, we flicked through the brochures describing the region's varied attractions.

Canonbie, a lovely village beside the River Esk, has a post office, shop and a dog friendly pub. Carlisle and Dumfries are within easy reach but we were more interested in Hermitage Castle, Sweetheart Abbey and the spectacular waterfall, Grey Mares Tail. And, if you enjoy shady woodland walks, Kielderhead National Nature Reserve is just a short drive across the border in Northumberland.

We really enjoyed staying at the Coach House. Trevor and Denise clearly know what dog owners need, which meant we relaxed completely. I would heartily recommend visiting this part Scotland.

FACT FILE

Location: Forgebraehead, Canonbie, DG14 0SZ
Website: 3dogsholidaylet.co.uk
Contact: 01387 371937
Type of accommodation: Cottage
Number of bedrooms: 2
Number of dogs accepted: 3
Enclosed garden: Yes
Local interest: The Fairie Loup on Byre Burn, River Ask, Powsfoot Estuary, Hermitage Castle, Sweetheart Abbey, Grey Mares Tail waterfall, Kielderhead National Nature Reserve
Best eats: The Cross Keys Hotel at Canonbie

THE RED LION HOTEL, EARLSTON, SCOTTISH BORDERS

By Angie Aspinall

The Red Lion is a former coaching inn, where today's guests can experience traditional hospitality and an authentic taste of the Scottish Borders.

A market town on the River Leader in Lauderdale, Earlston enjoys a wonderfully picturesque location. At the centre, overlooking the square, sits an impressive coaching inn, The Red Lion.

Our room had a super-king-size bed, a dressing table and a matching table with welcome tray. And there was a lovely, modern ensuite shower room. There was also a welcome pack for Tilly, with a note from Dave, the owner's dog.

There are plenty of walking opportunities nearby and copies of the Earlston Paths booklet were available to buy at the bar. One of Dave the Dog's favourite walks is a section of the Southern Upland Way, between Lauder and Melrose. The Red Lion makes an ideal starting point because you can catch a bus back.

Meals are served in the bar and in the lounge but the latter is a dog-free zone. Alongside traditional pub favourites,

including fish & chips and homemade burgers, there was also a mouthwatering selection of more unusual dishes.

Breakfasts are served in the dining room. However, if you'd rather keep your dog with you at all times, I'm sure they'd let you eat in the bar.

We had one last walk around the green, then headed home, reminiscing already about how much we had enjoyed exploring Roxburghshire.

FACT FILE

Location: The Square, Earlston, Scottish Borders, TD4 6DB

Website: redlionearlston.com

Contact: 01896 848994

Type of accommodation: Bed and breakfast

Number of bedrooms: 8

Number of dogs accepted: 2 or 3, depending on size of room

Enclosed garden: No but fenced park nearby

Local interest: Local walks, Melrose, Scott's View, Sir Walter Scott's house and estate at Abbotsford, Rhymer's Stone

Best eats: The Red Lion Hotel, Rhymers Fayre Café at Melrose

THE WHEATSHEAF, SWINTON, BERWICKSHIRE

By Angie Aspinall

Overlooking the village green in the quiet Berwickshire village of Swinton, The Wheatsheaf Hotel offers guests - human and canine - a very warm welcome indeed.

The Wheatsheaf attracted us immediately because it made clear on its website that dogs are welcome in the bar during dinner. Perfect, particularly as Tilly suffers from separation anxiety. With comfy armchairs, a roaring fire and dog friendly dining in the bar, we knew we'd found a winner.

The manager checked us in and helped us carry our things (and by our things, I mean mainly Tilly's things) upstairs to our room, Room 5. There was a lovely, king-size bed, a wardrobe, TV, and a gorgeous bathroom (which was much larger than ours at home).

The hotel has 10 rooms and the outside space is lovely, making it ideal if you're planning a summer wedding.

We'd reserved a table for 6.30 pm so, after changing quickly, headed downstairs to the bar. We were impressed by the choice of gins and, with a pre-dinner G&T, relaxed beside the fire.

While we dined, Tilly enjoyed extracting treats from her Kong. We apologised about the crumbs she left behind but the waitress assured us it wasn't a problem. She then asked if we'd rather have breakfast in the bar with Tilly or in the dining room. How nice to be given a choice! We were delighted that we could have breakfast in a dog friendly room.

After dinner, we walked Tilly around the village green. The Christmas lights were on in the trees and there was a definite frost in the air. It felt as though Christmas was on its way.

FACT FILE

Location: The Green, Swinton, Berwickshire, TD11 3JJ

Website: eatdrinkstaywheatsheaf.com

Contact: 01890 860257

Type of accommodation: Hotel

Number of bedrooms: 10 (2 dog friendly)

Number of dogs accepted: 2

Enclosed garden: No

Local interest: Walks around the village, Coldingham Bay, Kelso, Rutherford's micro pub in Kelso

Best eats: The Wheatsheaf, The New Inn on Bridge Street, The Cobbles at Kelso

After a good night's sleep, we had breakfast at a very civilised hour - 9 am. Having enquired about local walks we might enjoy with Tilly, we were recommended a few routes around the village, including a circular one that led from the hotel garden. Sadly, it was extremely foggy so we couldn't enjoy the views but I'm sure they're lovely. We headed to the coast, where the weather was better and the fog had lifted by the time we reached Coldingham Bay.

After our walk, during which Tilly exhausted herself running around, we only had one thing on our mind - fish & chips. Having driven past the New Inn on Bridge Street many times, we'd made a note of their 'Dogs Welcome' sign and thought now was as good a time as any. It was a quiet Monday and we were the only people there but the staff were friendly and made a fuss of Tilly. The chips were great and lunch really hit the spot.

After lunch, we headed into Kelso, which has been voted Most Dog Friendly Town in the Be Dog Friendly awards, which are organised yearly by DogFriendly and The Kennel Club. It certainly deserves this accolade. Dogs are welcome in so many of the businesses that I can't list them all here.

After dinner, we enjoyed a drink at another dog friendly watering hole in Kelso, Rutherford's. This micropub is the first of its kind in Scotland. It's very popular with holidaymakers and locals alike and wherever you've travelled from, you're made very welcome.

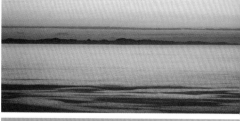

TRESHNISH & HAUNN COTTAGES, CALGARY, ISLE OF MULL

By Marina Starke

Near Calgary Beach on the Isle of Mull, Shieling Cottage is situated on the edge of a traditional farm square, with lovely views over the garden wall and out to sea.

Treshnish & Haunn Cottages are ideal if you fancy escaping the hustle and bustle of modern life, in a place where nature, if not always gentle, is always beautiful.

Sheiling Cottage is the smallest property, with just one bedroom. It's open-plan - compact, yet stylish - and retains many original features. It has an enclosed garden but we didn't let Bramble out unsupervised because there was a small flock of Herdwick sheep in the field next door.

The properties may be dog friendly but this hasn't reduced the standard of decoration. Each is individually designed, with eclectic furnishings that give them personality.

There's a shop in the nearby village of Dervaig and you can also buy meat produced on the farm. There's a strong environmental ethos and you're encouraged to walk, cycle and generally slow down and leave the clamour of modern life behind. And I can't think of anywhere lovelier.

Treshnish is near Calgary Bay, which is one of my favourite places. We had the beach to ourselves most of the time and Bramble even braved a paddle.

One of the highlights is the art centre, which boasts a gallery, workshop, woodland nature trail and café and, although this was closed because it was low season, there's a self-service facility so I could still enjoy one of the scrumptious cakes.

Mull is a beautiful island and Treshnish is a particularly spectacular corner. We were lucky enough to enjoy spectacular late autumn sunshine, which generated a number of glorious sunsets.

FACT FILE

Location: Treshnish Point, Calgary, Isle of Mull, PA75 6QX

Website: treshnish.co.uk

Contact: 01688 400249

Type of accommodation: Cottage

Number of bedrooms: 1

Number of dogs accepted: 2

Enclosed garden: Yes

Local interest: Calgary Bay, Art Centre

Best eats: Café at Art Centre

STABLE COTTAGE, MORAY, SCOTLAND

By Anne Dealtry

A cosy retreat in the north of Scotland, Stable Cottage makes a great base for walking and wildlife-watching, with the added advantage of a number of whisky distilleries nearby!

A winter holiday in Scotland may not be everyone's cup of tea but my partner, Chris, and I have visited several times at this time of the year, with our West Highland Terrier, Douglas. Obviously the weather can be temperamental but that just makes it more exciting.

We've stayed in a number of lovely dog friendly places in North Scotland, and several times at Moray Cottages. The properties stand in the grounds of a farmhouse near Dufftown and are the result of a stylish barn conversion. The area is rich in wildlife, with deer a regular sight in the woodland around the property.

Stable Cottage and Mill Cottage are decorated attractively, inside and out, and have everything you'd expect of a luxury holiday let. Stable Cottage, where we stayed, is charming, with an inviting lounge (with open fire), a cloakroom and a spacious kitchen with dining area. Upstairs,

there's a master bedroom with a king-size bed, a twin bedroom and a shower room.

Scotland gets cold in winter but we've always found the heating works well and logs are provided, if you fancy an open fire.

Each cottage has a large, private and enclosed garden and other dog friendly features include dog bowls, treats, poo bags (there's a bin in the barn) and stair gates, so doggy guests can't reach the bedrooms. *(continued...)*

FACT FILE

Location: Dufftown, Moray, Scotland, AB55 4DR
Website: moray-cottages.com
Contact: 07754 100823
Type of accommodation: Cottage
Number of bedrooms: 2
Number of dogs accepted: 2
Enclosed garden: Yes
Local interest: Local walks, distillery at Dufftown, Baxter's Highland Village, Spey Bay, Lossiemouth, Elgin, Torrieston and Culbin Forest, Glenlivet estate, Millbuies Country Park, Keith & Dufftown Railway, Loch Garten
Best eats: The Mash Tun and The Spey Larder at Aberlour

The properties stand in splendid isolation, about a mile from the nearest road. They can only be reached via a farm track and access can be tricky in snowy weather. However, there are 4-wheel drive vehicles, a digger and a tractor on the farm, if you get stuck.

Dufftown is only small but it has a rich heritage and plays an important role in the malt whisky industry of Speyside. It has a few shops and a choice of pubs and cafés.

The coast of Moray is relatively mild but the county extends south into the Cairngorms, where the weather can be more temperamental. The region attracts outdoor enthusiasts of all kinds but we particularly enjoy walking. Douglas can walk several miles easily so we spend our time observing the natural world around us. There are plenty of walking opportunities in Moray and these increase exponentially if you travel a little further.

We always visit a whisky distillery and investigated Glenfiddich (with Balvenie) quite early on, as it's just a mile away in Dufftown and boasts a café and restaurant. And if you enjoy a tipple, there are plenty of others nearby.

Although the weather during our holiday was extremely mild, it can vary quite widely and Douglas was delighted when it snowed. The scenery is always spectacular but becomes magical under a blanket of snow.

Luckily, the snow cleared and we received a visit from our friends and their baby, who live locally. Stable Cottage may be small but it coped admirably and we spent several hours catching up. I would highly recommend the cottages and will certainly return there again.

FINDLAY'S COTTAGE, ORPHIR, ORKNEY

By Andy Craig

A comfortably furnished, stone-built cottage on the north shore of Scapa Flow, Findlay's Cottage offers fine, unspoilt views south over the Flow and west to the hills of Hoy.

Few places have drawn us back as regularly as Findlay's Cottage on Orkney. It's one of our favourite holiday destinations. It's a long way from our home in Northumberland, and even further if you live in the south of England, but the journey's worth every minute.

Findlay's Cottage lies midway between Kirkwall and Stromness and about a mile from Orphir. It's surrounded by open meadows and only a short walk from the shore of Scapa Flow. The natural habitat attracts a wide variety of wildlife, particularly oyster catchers, curlews and lapwings.

Once a semi-derelict croft, it was converted in 1998 and has been a holiday let ever since. It's well decorated, clean and tidy, basic rather than luxurious, with solid fixtures and fittings that are built to last - ideal, if you have a dog. The living area, with its solid fuel stove, makes a comfy retreat in the evening and this links, via a dining area, with the kitchen.

The master bedroom is easily the best feature, as it enjoys picturesque views of Hoy, and a seating area has been created by the window so you can watch the sun set in the evening. There's a twin bedroom at the other end of the property and a pull-out sofa bed in the lounge.

Findlay's Cottage enjoys panoramic views *(continued...)*

FACT FILE

Location: Orphir, Orkney, KW17 2RB

Website: findlayscottage.co.uk

Contact: 01588 640941

Type of accommodation: Traditional croft

Number of bedrooms: 2 (sleeps up to 6)

Number of dogs accepted: 3

Enclosed garden: No

Local interest: The Ring of Brodgar, Wideford Hill, Marwick Head, Waulkmill Bay, Bay of Skaill, Mull Head, Yesnaby

Best eats: None in the area

across the island. Although it's part of a small crofting community, we've rarely met anyone else.

Orkney has a wealth of archaeological sites. Indeed, there are more visible remains on Orkney than anywhere else in the UK and, having visited the island several times, we can now incorporate several in one walk.

We spent most of our time walking the coast. We headed 5 miles east of Dounby and explored Marwick Head (where a crenellated structure celebrates the life of Lord Kitchener, who was lost when HMS Hampshire sank nearby in June 1916), the nature reserve at Mull Head and the red sandstone cliffs of Yesnaby, on the windswept west coast.

It's important to remember how far north Orkney is - and how flat, and thus how exposed to the elements. It can be warm, dry and sunny one minute and pouring with rain the next. The clouds roll in very quickly. Some view this as a negative but we love watching the weather fronts come and go and, if you take the right clothes, you'll have one of the best holidays of your life.

ARDANAISEIG, ARGYLL, SCOTLAND

By Andy Craig

Ardanaiseig offers luxurious accommodation, fine dining and spectacular scenery, and makes an excellent staging post for touring the Highlands and islands.

A listed building, Ardanaiseig remains virtually unchanged outside and, although some parts of the interior were altered when it became a hotel, these alterations have been carried out sympathetically.

Inside, Ardanaiseig retains the atmosphere of a private house and the rooms are stylishly decorated. There are 11 Master Suites that overlook either the garden or the loch and 5 Garden View rooms. Each has its own personality, having been designed individually and there's a strong colour theme throughout.

Our room, Inchrachan, boasted wonderful views across Loch Awe to the snow-capped mountains. After quickly unpacking our things, we headed outside so we could explore the gardens and let Daisy have a run at the water's edge. Ardanaiseig appears as one with its surroundings, its grounds merging imperceptibly with the landscape beyond, and we found this to be conducive to instant relaxation, as the stresses of a busy week faded away.

Ardanaiseig lies within easy reach of Ben Cruachan, the mountain that dominates the head of Loch Awe. It's popular with walkers but is quite a challenge, so should only be tackled if you're experienced. Those with an interest in engineering may prefer investigating the vast hydroelectric power station that's hidden underneath instead.

The manager of Ardanaiseig suggested a short walk around the nature reserve at Glen Nant, which is just a few miles up the road. Wandering along the tree-lined paths proved a memorable way of ending our Highland adventure. It's a place I would recommend wholeheartedly.

FACT FILE

Location: Kilchrenan by Taynuilt, Argyll, PA35 1HE
Website: ardanaiseig.com
Contact: 01866 0833 333
Type of accommodation: Hotel
Number of bedrooms: 16
Number of dogs accepted: 2
Enclosed garden: No
Local interest: Loch Awe, Inveraray Jail, Ben Cruachan
Best eats: Ardanaiseig restaurant

TOGETHER TRAVEL, JOHN O' GROATS, SCOTLAND

By Caroline Morgan

Benefiting from glass-fronted living areas, Together Travel's lodges make the most of the sea views and offer comfortable accommodation, in an area rich in heritage and wildlife.

There's a choice of holiday accommodation available. We stayed in one of the lodges but there are several apartments at the inn, although these aren't dog friendly.

The lodges are open-plan, with a spacious, glass-fronted living, dining and kitchen area, a family bathroom and 3 double bedrooms, one with its own ensuite.

There's also a walk-in utility room, which is ideal if you have a dog. A few of the lodges enjoy panoramic sea views but these are a little more expensive. Luxuries include free Wi-Fi, a complimentary hamper and a wood-burning fire. Although the lodges are dog friendly, there aren't any gardens, so that means walking your dog on a lead around the grounds.

We were lucky with the weather, so ate al fresco in the lodge garden several times. We didn't find any dog friendly restaurants, so cooked meals in the lodge's kitchen most nights. Since visiting, a pet friendly restaurant, The Northern Point, has opened up and offers meals and drinks with your dog.

The area has an amazingly rich heritage and we explored many interesting sites. One of the most obvious walks is between John O'Groats and The Stacks of Duncansby. There are a number of spectacular coves near John O'Groats and Bramble particularly enjoyed running off-lead along Dunnet Bay. There's a small harbour and, walking there in the evening, we could see fishing boats heading out.

FACT FILE

Location: John O'Groats, Wick, KW1 4YR
Website: togethertravel.co.uk
Contact: 01625 416430
Type of accommodation: Glass-fronted lodge
Number of bedrooms: 3
Number of dogs accepted: 2 (3 if small)
Enclosed garden: No
Local interest: Mary Ann's Cottage at Dunnet, Dunnet Bay, Sannick Bay, Orkney
Best eats: The Northern Point

Orkney makes a great day out and is within easy reach, using the John O'Groats Ferry. Sadly, only small dogs are welcome and we went by car instead, using the Pentland Ferries service between Gills Bay and St Margaret's Hope.

We saw a wide variety of wildlife, especially seabirds, plus hundreds of rabbits and several seals. On the last day of our holiday, after walking around Duncansby

Head, we paused a while at Sannick Bay - a spectacular stretch of sand, where seals are often present. Bramble played in the waves and, as I paddled, a seal appeared. We watched each other, as he or she dived and resurfaced.

Our visit was a bit of a taster and we left John O'Groats wanting more.